# Concord: Climate for Freedom

Concord Center on April 19, 1775, from a painting by Ralph Earle. This painting is now in the Concord Antiquarian Society Museum, a gift from the estate of Mary Brooks Buttrick.

# Concord: Climate for Freedom

## BY RUTH R. WHEELER

*If the heavens of America appear infinitely higher
and the stars brighter, I trust that these facts
are symbolical—for I believe that climate does
thus react on men. I trust that we shall be more
imaginative, that our thoughts will be clearer, as
our sky, else to what end was America discovered?*

*Henry Thoreau:* Essay on Walking

THE CONCORD ANTIQUARIAN SOCIETY
*Concord, Massachusetts*

*1967*

*Second Printing 1970*

© *Copyright 1967 by The Concord Antiquarian Society*
*Library of Congress Catalog Card Number 67-31527*

*Designed and Produced by*
*Printing and Publishing Production Associates*

*Yarmouthport, Massachusetts*

*Printed in the United States of America*

*To the Concord Town Meeting, for 330 Years an
Example of Democracy and a School of Freedom*

# Contents

# Illustrations

# Introduction

When Lewis Mumford wrote in *The Conduct of Life* that nineteenth-century Concord was the only cultural center in the world of its century and the only center on this continent up to the present day, he seemed to be making a challenge. Why was Concord so singled out?

The present study has tried to describe the Concord background with its imperfections as well as its advantages. So far as I know, no previous historian has described the perfect democracy of our earliest town meetings and their insistence on maintaining charter rights. None since Samuel Sewell has described the attempt to deal out even-handed justice to Indians and Whites alike which resulted so tragically for the Gobles, and none has described Concord's friendly treatment of the Acadian family. The larger field of Colony affairs has obscured the fact that the strongest support for independence came from the town meetings. Recent mapping of the terrain at the north bridge and study of British documents printed in French's *General Gage's Informers* make some changes necessary in the story of the day as understood in 1925. Too little is known about the effect of the emigration to new towns. These are some of the reasons why a new study is needed.

What was constant throughout Concord history was the love of Freedom, the trust in education, and the acceptance of the necessity of sacrifice for the causes our forebears believed in. To bear arms was a basic obligation, never questioned even when, in the act of incorporation, they asked for immunity from taxes. Many sacrificed their English property and risked their lives on the Atlantic crossing. They risked lives and estates at the time of the Revolution and in settling northern New England and the West. Debate was constant.

I am sure that Concord is only one of many towns of which the same could be said, but any town is worthy of close study if one is to understand the whole, of which the towns are the component parts. This book is the fruit of a lifetime of study helped by the work of many predecessors.

Shattuck's *History of Concord*, Walcott's *Concord in the Colonial Period* and Townsend Scudder's *Concord: American Town* are the best printed sources. The latter has a full account of events of the last hundred years, which I could not attempt to improve upon. The privately printed *Social Circle Memoirs* supplied many stories of nineteenth-century worthies. I have found much information in the Middlesex County Registries of Deeds and Probate. I hope that future historians will find the town records printed and indexed. I have used the copies made in longhand as a W.P.A. project, with occasional comparison with the originals. Here the Town Clerk, Mrs. Maxwell Lawrence, has been most helpful.

In earlier years, Judge Prescott Keyes gave me manuscripts by Charles H. Walcott, Dr. Edward Jarvis, and by his father, the "Old Judge" John S. Keyes, so that I had the material at hand for reference. Judge Keyes "Concord" in the *History of Middlesex County*, vol. II, pp. 570–612, is useful. Mrs. Harriette Forbes of Worcester shared with me her notes on seventeenth-century houses and old gravestones. Members of the Goble family in Chicago gave me photostats of the pertinent documents in the Goble case.

The daughters of Allen French gave me the notes he had begun to collect for a projected history of Concord and for the pageant which he wrote in 1935. His *Charles I and the Puritan Upheaval* as well as his books about the Revolution are models of careful research.

Mrs. Herbert B. Hosmer gathered facts about Rev. John Jones in England and also shared the research she had done for the Radcliffe Women's Archives concerning Concord girls in South Carolina during the Civil War. Mrs. Walter Upham of Fairfield, Connecticut sent me the list of Concord Planters in Fairfield.

I am especially indebted to Mr. Laurence Richardson for reading my manuscript and making suggestions, and to Mr. Robert D. Ronsheim, historian of the Minuteman National Historical Park, for reading and commenting on the chapters dealing with the Revolution. There are so many conflicting accounts of the events of that day that no two modern historians have yet found themselves in complete agreement.

Mr. Herbert Cahoon of the J. Pierpont Morgan Library brought the Earl of Suffolk's letter to my attention and allowed me to quote from it. The Henry E. Huntington Library in San Marino, California, allowed me to use a photostat of the letter from Richard Griffin and the other selectmen in 1645 about Symons' featherbed.

The Concord Free Public Library has been generous with its treasured material and their reference librarian, Mrs. Marcia Moss, has been most helpful. Mr. Samuel G. Kent, for many years my employer on the *Concord Journal,* has always encouraged my research. Mr. Keith Martin has generously lent his skill as a photographer.

The Concord Antiquarian Society, in publishing this book, is continuing its long record of assistance to studies of local history. Of course, it is not responsible for any errors or mistaken conclusions.

To my many helpers, named and unnamed, go my grateful thanks.

R.R.W.

A view of Concord River from the North Bridge. (Photograph by Keith Martin.)

# Chapter I    Beginnings

*Beneath low hills, in the broad interval*
*Through which at will our Indian rivulet*
*Winds mindful still of sannup and of squaw*
*Whose pipe and arrow oft the plough unburies*
*Here in pine houses built of new-fallen trees*
*Supplanters of the tribe, the farmers dwell.*
        Ralph Waldo Emerson: Musketaquid

For thousands of years the six miles square that was to become Concord had changed but little. The two branches of the Musketaquid, meeting here to flow northward to the Merrimack, had risen with the spring rains and the thawing snow and fallen in the summer droughts, sometimes flooding the meadows for long enough to kill any trees which had grown since the last high water, sometimes laying bare the sand bars which built up below the confluences of the many brooks. The river current normally dropped only two feet in twenty winding miles and made an easy highway for the dugout canoe and a smooth path for the winter hunter. The name Musketaquid or marsh-grass river has the same root as the mosquito or marsh insect. The Assabet, as the narrower branch was called, meant clear or drinking-water stream, for it was swifter than the other branch, scouring its bottom and at times of sudden flood even reversing the flow of the slow branch for a mile or two. Into it emptied the Nashoba or middle brook. Another brook which we know as the millbrook, draining a large area of fertile ground, joined the Musketaquid from the east below its meeting with the Assabet. On this brook the Indians had a fish weir to catch the alewives which ran in countless abundance upriver every spring.

Glacial action had left hills and ponds all through the area—the highest hill under four hundred feet, the deepest pond a hundred feet, and a gravel ridge a mile long above the fish weir. The hill between the rivers—Nashawtuc in the Indian tongue—was the most desirable camp site because the approaches to it were easily watched. However, any hill with a spring of good water close by was used at one time or another—Fairhaven, whose Indian name is forgotten; Annursnack or secure hill; and Punkatasset or broad-topped hill.

The Indians occasionally burned over sandy hills to improve the crops of blueberries and keep the land clear for corn planting. They ate the cranberries which grew in the river meadows. They had another camp site on the Mystic where they went for oysters, clams or salt water fish. They found fish so plentiful in the Musketaquid that they used them for fertilizer in their patches of corn, where they also raised pumpkins and beans. Game was abundant, although deer were also hunted down by the lynx, and grouse were the prey of foxes. Wolves and bear were found here, and beaver, otter, and muskrats supplied furs for warmth and for trade with other tribes. The larger skins were used to cover the wigwams, which were rounded frames of saplings. Woven mats were also used for this purpose and were easily packed up whenever the tribe moved. Theirs was a stone-age culture.

Earlier men, the aborigines, who lacked skill to make good bows and arrows, left heaps of shells of fresh water mussels mixed with a few bones of small animals and birds, but by 1635, the Massachusetts tribe of Algonquins had good arrow flints and a simple agriculture giving them a varied diet. However, a low birth-rate, disease, and war kept their numbers low. A particularly severe epidemic in 1617 and small-pox in 1633 had reduced the tribe to a mere remnant. These were the men who still made Concord their hunting ground. Of land ownership in the European sense they had no conception. If another tribe wanted their hunting grounds, they must fight them off or move elsewhere themselves to fight for a new range.

To the north of the Massachusetts Indians were the Pennacooks in southern New Hampshire and the Tarrantines or Abnakis ranging through Maine; to the west the Nipmucks and the Pocumtucks with the Mohawks beyond in the Hudson Valley. In the Plymouth Colony were the Wampanoags with the Nausets in the Cape Cod area. The Narragansetts were near Narragansett Bay and to their west the Pequots and the Mohegans in the western Connecticut area.

*What sought they thus afar?*
  *Bright jewels of the mine,*
*The wealth of seas, the spoils of war?*
  *They sought a faith's pure shrine.*
    *Felicia Hemans:* Landing of the Pilgrims

Historians put different amounts of emphasis on the causes of the great migration from England to Massachusetts in the decade after 1630. Was it an economic depression? Was it to find religious freedom? Was it because the nobles were enclosing common land? Was it a love of adventure? Was it the glowing, and misleading, reports sent home by explorers? Doubtless it was a mixture of all these causes in different proportion within the heart of each migrant. To me it appears that the desire to own land was the basic motive for the layman. Freedom to practice their own religion as their own consciences dictated was undoubtedly the over-riding reason why the ministers came.

To the philosophic historian it seems one of the most fateful migrations in all history, for it gave a selected group of independent men a chance to develop a new form of government different from any that had gone before. This government put its reliance on the consent of the governed rather than on unquestioning obedience to a ruler who claimed to have divine sanction, and discarded the caste system which even today mars the English ideal of fairness and justice.

Between 1533 and 1553, Henry VIII had suppressed the monasteries and distributed church lands among the nobles. He had been succeeded in 1553 by Bloody Mary, who left to her sister Elizabeth in 1558 an England which had learned through her intolerance to hate the name of Catholicism. Faith in religious certainties was shaken. In 1605, discovery of the gunpowder plot against James I was the excuse for numerous arrests and hangings until the popularity of the sovereign, so great under Elizabeth, was undermined. When Charles I succeeded in 1625, he inherited a mountain of debt and tried all sorts of expedients, not sanctioned by English law, to raise money. He also inherited a favorite, the Duke of Buckingham, whose advice was both expensive and bad, leading him into futile wars on the Continent. He had a Catholic Queen, which made him suspect. He had a religious advisor, Archbishop Laud, who took more and more power into his own hands and tried to restore some high church doctrine and practices, not only in his London area but throughout the country. If a local bishop had been lenient in enforcing conformity, clergymen in his area had not been bothered. Now Laud sent out agents, called pursuivants, through-out England, to seek out nonconformists and summon them to London for trial. Here the court, conducted in Latin, prejudged them guilty and had no ear for argument, although it sometimes accepted humble submission and allowed the penitent to return to his parish under close scrutiny. It might order him up for a second trial at any time.

*The best friend the Massachusetts Colony had, though much against his will, was Archbishop Laud . . . . His severity brought some of the best men in England to overcome their natural repugnance to emigration.*

    *Emerson:* Historical Discourse

One such hapless cleric was the Reverend John Jones of Abbots Ripton, Hants. Born in Northhamptonshire about 1593, he matriculated at Cambridge University as a sizar of Queen's College in the Michaelmas term 1608. That is to say, he was on a working scholarship at a college which was a center of non-conformity. The overwhelming majority of Puritan clergy were educated there. He received his B.A. in 1612 and his M.A. in 1616 and was ordained a deacon (Peterborough) on the nineteenth of December 1613, becoming the minister of Abbots Ripton in 1619, settling there with his wife Sarah who was seven years his junior. During the next fifteen years they had many children, six of whom were living when they emigrated: Sarah, 15; John, 11; Ruth, 7; Theophilus, 3; Rebecca, 2; and Elizabeth, the baby.

Jones had come to the attention of the High Court of Ecclesiastical Causes on December 20, 1623, when he was first warned to conform, and his final trial ended in June, 1630. In the decree, signed by Laud, Bishop of London, Abbott, Archbishop of Canterbury and three bishops more, three Knights and two Doctors of Law, he was deprived of his living, forbidden to preach anywhere in the kingdom, and heavily fined. The sentence read (as translated from the original Latin by the Concord historian, Allen French):

Jones had been both proven and confessed to have been uncontrollable, pug-nacious, refractory, disobedient, stubborn and incorrigible to the ecclesiastical ordinances and constitutions . . . concerning the form and manner of celebra-tion of the Divine Services of the Church. Nor had he, though warned fre-quently, earnestly, and lawfully to take his corporal oath to answer faithfully the articles against him, been willing to do so.

Thus we are sure that Jones was a man of tenaciously held convictions. His life during the next five years must have been difficult. With no means of support except what was given him by sympathetic parishioners or by known non-conformists among the gentry, he must have traveled from place to place, preaching where he could and waiting to hear of a chance to get to America. A sympathetic shipmaster must be found to take him aboard at the last minute under an assumed name. At last he sailed on the *Defense*, Edward Bostock, master, on August 10, 1635, to arrive in Boston, October 3, 1635.

A prominent layman, Roger Harlakenden of Earle's Colne, Essex, whose family had befriended Reverend Thomas Shepard for many years, was on board and doubtless assisted five distinguished stowaways. They were: Reverend Thomas Shepard, who became minister in Cambridge in 1636; Reverend John Wilson, returning to Boston; Reverend Hugh Peter, who settled in Salem for a time; Reverend John Norton who went to Ipswich; and John Jones with his wife and six children, who came to Concord. Shepard's diary gives some account of the voyage:

In coming we were refreshed by the society of Mr. Wilson and Mr. Jones and by their faith and prayers and preaching. The ship was very rotten and unfit for such a voyage and therefore the first storm, we had a very great leak, which did much appall and affect us, yet the Lord discovered it unto us when we were thinking of returning back again. We had many storms, by the shaking of the ship, my wife was pitched against an iron bolt but the Lord miraculously preserved the child in her arms and recovered my wife.[1]

*Riches and honors Bulkeley lays aside*
*To please his Christ, for whom he now doth war.*
  *Edward Johnson:* Wonder-working Providence

Reverend Peter Bulkeley was not so hard pressed. He was not suspended until 1634. He was minister in the parish church in Odell, Bedfordshire, assistant to his father in 1610 and succeeded his father, Reverend Edward Bulkeley, on his death in 1620. He lived in the handsome parsonage where he had been born in 1583. He had nine sons and two daughters by his first wife Jane Alleyn. Her nephew

---

[1] The spelling has been modernized in all the quotations used to make them more easily understood.

Odell Church.

Peter Bulkeley's
English Church
and his
English Rectory.

The Rectory. Odell.

Reverend Peter Bulkeley before emigration to the
New World. (Used by permission of the owner
Peter Bulkeley Brainard, Hartford, Conn.)

Oliver St. John was at one time Lord Mayor of London. His second
wife, Grace Chetwood, was twenty years younger than he. She married
him a month before sailing, in April, 1635, and came to Massachusetts
with him and three stepchildren in the *Susan and Ellen* sailing in May
1635. She suffered a mysterious coma on the voyage. Both wives were
daughters of baronets. Peter Bulkeley was a graduate of St. John's
College, Cambridge, in 1605. Afterwards he was a fellow and University
preacher and was a canon of Lichfield for one year in 1609. His
oldest son Edward had come to Boston in 1634. Edward probably prepared the way for his father who went immediately to live in an empty
house in Cambridge and made friends with Thomas Shepard. When
Thomas Shepard was chosen minister of the Cambridge church,
Bulkeley lent him the money to buy a parsonage. Young Edward became minister of the church in Marshfield. (Mrs. Bulkeley's "miraculous"
recovery is now explained as an incident of pregnancy.)

His wealth and connections with the landed gentry doubtless made Peter Bulkeley's path easier under Laud's persecution. When he was suspended in 1634, he confessed that he did not use the surplice nor cross, accounting them superstitions, but his case was allowed to drag while he liquidated his holdings. He was able to take £6000 capital with him to the new world. The authorities did not appoint a successor in Odell until a month after his departure. Cotton Mather expressly states in *Magnalia Christi* that the good Bishop of Lincoln connived at his non-conformity. In spite of the restrictions about emigration, Bulkeley left under his own name, while his wife and children joined him at the last minute on the *Susan and Ellen* after first signing to sail on another ship. With them they brought a carpenter, Thomas Dane, who was to work out his passage by building a house and mill for Peter Bulkeley in Concord.

Little is known about Simon Willard's life in England. He was born in Horsmonden, a small town in Kent, in 1605. His father died before Simon was of age and provided in his will that his son should be apprenticed. He was probably apprenticed to a London merchant for we find him referred to as a merchant. He arrived in the colony in May, 1634, after a short passage in one of nine ships, bringing, says Winthrop's *Journal*, a store of cattle and passengers. He settled in Cambridge where he had a house lot. With him were his wife Mary and his daughter Mary, first of seventeen children.

Simon Willard must have used the remaining months of 1634 and the first eight months of 1635 to explore the unsettled country beyond the Cambridge and Watertown settlements and to become acquainted with the few Indians left in that area. He then must have approached a few people with money to invest and with them petitioned the General Court for a new town. It is said that 200 acres of land were promised for every fifty pounds invested.

The order for the new town was passed by the General Court on September 3, 1635.

It is ordered that there shall be a plantation at Musketaquid, and that there shall be six miles of land square belonging to it and that the inhabitants thereof shall have three years immunities from all public charges except trainings. Further, when any that shall plant there shall have occasion of carrying their goods thither, they shall repair to two of the next magistrates where the teams are, who shall have power for a year to press draughts at reasonable rates to be paid by the owners of the goods, to transport their goods thither at seasonable times. And the name of the place is changed and henceforth to be called Concord.

*They ought, in these matters of difference of opinion in things not fundamental nor scandalous etc., to bear each with the other.*

John Winthrop: Journal, April 1636

John Jones and Peter Bulkeley found a controversy raging in Massachusetts Bay. Should each church be an independent self-governing congregation such as the Plymouth congregation or should it be governed by groups of ministers, as in Presbyterianism? John Jones was to favor congregationalism while Peter was inclined to the more rigid rule. He later worked on a joint statement of doctrine adopted in 1651 called "A platform of Church Discipline," to which all Massachusetts churches were supposed to subscribe. There were also doctrinal questions hotly disputed, including one between the covenant of Grace and the covenant of works. It was in the severe winter of 1635–36 that Roger Williams was banished and departed for Providence.

Jones and Bulkeley came late to these controversies, and could not have considered them as important as they seemed to those who had been involved in them from the start. They expected to live in concord and named the town for that reason.

Remaining in the Massachusetts jurisdiction, they expected to be apart from the controversies of the seacoast. This did not prove to be the case. The debates were fanned by a battle of pamphlets which examined many small points of doctrine and followed the Concord settlers up into the woods. The points of disagreement were argued in every household even after the extreme dissidents went off to Fairfield beyond the New Haven colony. Argument kept the citizens alert and was a sort of intellectual training for the discussions of forms of secular government which preceded the Revolution.

After securing the act of incorporation, the next months were spent in getting settlers. Although many settlers had moved off to Hartford, the towns around Boston Bay were overflowing with the thousands of new settlers who were now pouring in. Some of the earlier arrivals could sell out to newcomers and go west to Concord. Others could go directly to the new town from the ships.

Reverend John Jones with his large family and without capital was, we know, in Concord in 1636. Mr. Bulkeley had no reason to hurry. Since the colony records report him as presiding at the trial of Ann

Hutchinson, we can assume that he did not move permanently to Concord until after 1637 when Thomas Dane would have had time to build him a house in the center of town.

The next step came when the prospective settlers called a church gathering in the meetinghouse in Cambridge on July 5, 1636 (like the Cambridge church gathering which had been held the previous January, to replace the Cambridge church which had departed to Connecticut). Mr. John Jones and Mr. Peter Bulkeley, who, it was understood, would be the ministers of the new town, planned the gathering without consulting John Haynes, the former Governor of the colony, nor Sir Henry Vane, chosen Governor on May 25 that year. They invited these dignitaries to attend but only three days before. "They took it in ill part," says Winthrop, then deputy governor, "and thought not fit to go, because they had not come to them before, (as they ought to have done and as others had done before)." Thus the first official act of the new town was one of independence. The ministers were formally installed on April 6, 1637, in Cambridge. After the religious service, those who wished to become settlers signed the church covenant. This document is missing, but we know that many more than twelve first division house lots were granted, probably at least forty. Winthrop attended these meetings as did the ministers Shepard and Wilson who had crossed the ocean with John Jones.


*Now bold Massachusetts clear*
*Cuts the rounding of the sphere*
*Out the anchor, sail no more*
*Freedom lives, and right shall stand*
*Blood of faith is in the land.*
    Sidney Lanier: Psalm of the West


The new settlement of Massachusetts Bay, five years earlier, had survived the scurvy that followed the weeks on shipboard and endured the cold of that first winter with inadequate shelter and food. Later ships took along lemons as an antiscorbutic. Using the experience of Plymouth, they had brought their charter with them and they had a man of ability in John Winthrop to serve as their governor. He was an aristocrat but he soon saw that concessions would have to be made to the independent spirit of the new settlers. Before 1635 the number of freemen, or legal voters in colony affairs, had been increased. Separate governments in the several towns were to choose representatives to the General Court so that no tax could be levied without their consent and the distribution of land in the separate towns was placed in the hands of selected townsmen or selectmen as they were soon called.

The Governor and the Assistants could not be allowed to make laws to suit each case as it arose. A body of laws resembling a *Magna Carta* was demanded by the freemen in 1635, and committees went to work on it until, after it had been tried and amended, it was finally passed and printed in 1648 so that no man would be tried ". . . except by the virtue or equity of some express law." They knew this body of laws would need to be changed by succeeding General Courts, but as they said in the preamble, "it was no disparagement to that high court of Parliament in England that in four hundred years they could not so compile their laws but that they still had new work to do almost every Parliament, so they could not blame a poor colony unfurnished with lawyers and statesmen that in eighteen years they had not produced more nor better rules." The ministers had tried to include many of the laws of Moses. Laymen had regulated the size of a loaf of bread in relation to the cost of a bushel of wheat. These Englishmen were consciously improving on the state of justice in England, and insisting that they, too, should have a *Magna Carta.*

New towns had been set up in the first five years in Salem, Charlestown, Dorchester, Watertown, Medford, Boston, Cambridge, Roxbury, Saugus, Marblehead, Agawam, and the day before Concord, in Hingham and Weymouth. But with thousands pouring in, soon there was not enough free land available. Large numbers went off to the Connecticut River valley to settle Wethersfield and Hartford, encouraged by reports of its fertility brought back by the explorer and Indian trader John Oldham. Governor Winthrop's son, John, was one of those attracted. To keep his colony strong, the Governor knew he must find new land within the jurisdiction of Massachusetts Bay. He went on exploring trips himself. A book by William Wood, published in England in 1633, showed a river valley, the Musketaquid, which they hoped would rival the Connecticut in fertility. Simon Willard's petition fitted in with Winthrop's plans. The General Court was happy to grant it. Dedham followed in 1636 and Sudbury in 1638.

The name Walden was given to the pond very early, perhaps by Willard in honor of the Minot family of Dorchester who came from Saffron Walden, England, or in honor of Major Waldren, a contemporary of Willard who was also a trader with the Indians. Some doubt has been cast on the derivation of the name from Saffron Walden be-

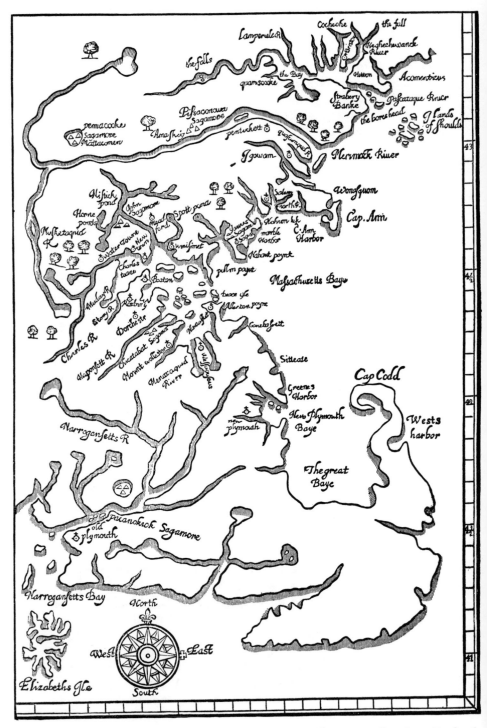

Map drawn by William Wood. Reproduced from William Wood's *New England Prospect*, 1634.

cause the Minots came late to Concord (about 1686), but widow Rachel Biggs, who died in 1646, was one of the incorporators of Concord, with large holdings south of Walden. Her son John's widow Mary Dossett Biggs was the second wife of Captain John Minot, the pioneer of Dorchester, and father of Captain James Minot who moved to Concord.

*Our worthy forefathers, let's give them a cheer*
*To climate unknown did courageously steer*
*Through oceans to deserts, for FREEDOM they came*
*And dying bequeathed us their FREEDOM and Fame.*
   Mercy Otis Warren: Liberty Song

The grant of six miles square to Concord established a standard size for towns in later grants throughout Massachusetts. Sixty families of about ten each, including servants and children, was considered the desirable number.

There is no record of the names of the incorporators; our only source, Winthrop's *Journal*, simply says that the town was granted to Mr. Bulkeley and [blank] merchant and about twelve families. Subconsciously, we picture a little procession of twelve men with their women and children making their way through the trackless woods with their clergyman at their head, but this I am sure is a completely false picture. The twelve, and Governor Winthrop was indefinite as to the number, refers to the petitioners, who never moved here in a body. Instead, they were the preferred stockholders, as it were, who invested some capital and promoted the settlement from Cambridge. Mr. William Spencer lived out his life in Cambridge. Mrs. Biggs, so far as we know, remained in Dorchester. There would have been little point in moving a family here before shelter could be found and crops planted.

What probably happened was this. The new arrival, or the dissatisfied inhabitant of one of the seacoast towns, heard about Simon Willard's plan for a new town. He traveled out to Musketaquid, and if he liked the look of it, he went to work on the central building which was to become the meetinghouse and meanwhile would serve to keep one's goods dry while a house was being built. This had been the method used in Watertown as described in John Master's letter to Lady Barrington. They blazed out a road from Watertown using what paths existed and by-passing the swamps.[2]

*Bulkeley, Hunt, Willard, Hosmer, Meriam, Flint,*
*Possessed the land which rendered to their toil*
*Hay, corn, roots, hemp, flax, apples, wool and wood.*
　　*Emerson:* Hamatreya

The standard checkerboard pattern of town planning was never considered here since the natural contours provided a better plan. The meetinghouse was built above the Bay Road up against the southeast corner of the ridge which became the burial hill. The millsite was granted to Mr. Bulkeley who paid for erecting a mill and settled the miller near it. Lots were laid out on both sides of the millpond and along the Bay Road extending about a mile eastward. Another ridge allowed for four lots to the north and about a dozen lots could be laid out south of the millpond. A small group, including Thomas Flint, William Buttrick, John Heald, William Spencer, Walter Edmunds, Robert Tomlin, and Baptist Smedley, crossed the river to choose sightly lots on the ridge above our north bridge while Simon Willard himself took Nashawtuc hill between the rivers.

As soon as they could get oxen from Watertown farmers to carry their goods, they made the move, a few at a time, depending on their urgency to leave their temporary quarters. Two years after the incorporation, Watertown farmers were complaining to the General Court at having to rent their oxen, which they could ill spare, to Concord settlers. Those who ventured out first are said to have dug caves in the gravel hillside, framing a doorway with logs and putting sods above the door to keep out some of the rain until their houses were built.

---

[2] The road was traced by Albert E. Wood, a Concord civil engineer, in 1900, who found the most likely route to be Orchard Street in Watertown through the village of Waverly, toward East Lexington, then skirting Vine Brook near the present Middle Street, Lexington, and over Mill Street in Lincoln toward Virginia Road. It then, I think, came from the old Woburn road at what we now call Bloody Curve between the present Lexington Road and Virginia Road to avoid the Elm Brook on the south, and the Shawshine headwaters on the north, to Meriam's Corner, where narrow old paths suggest its course. Thence in to town it was called the Bay Road and its course was never changed, though its name is now Lexington Road instead of Bay Road.

Accounts of the expulsion of Roger Williams agree that the winter of 1635–36 was very severe.

*Of all the four parts of the world that I have yet seen,*
*I should rather live here than anywhere.*
    Captain John Smith: A Description of New England 1614

The names of the investors who secured the incorporation of Concord can be inferred from the names of the large landholders. Bulkeley had a large grant in present-day Lincoln, south of Flint's Pond, while Thomas Flint had land east of Bulkeley running to the town line. William Spencer had the Spencer Brook valley and Robert Blood land north of Punkatasset Hill. Another grant of 1,000 acres, usually spoken of as Stow's, was also in present-day Lincoln, east of the river running to the Sudbury (now Wayland) town line. Recent research shows that the Stows got the land from their uncle John Biggs, a fellow-townsman of Simon Willard in Horsmonden, Kent. His mother, widow of John Biggs, Sr., came over in the same ship with Simon Willard in 1634. She settled in Roxbury with her daughter Elizabeth, wife of John Stow, and mother of six children one of whom, Nathaniel, was an early settler in Concord. Thomas Stow sold his share of the Biggs inheritance, 333 acres, to Thomas Goble and Daniel Dean in 1660. Samuel Stow sold 666 acres to Henry Woodis who in turn sold to Goble and Dean. Evidence may yet be found that there were one or two other investors with land grants in the outlying northeast part of town belonging later to the Meriam, Wheeler, and Wooley families, but proof is now lacking. The Smedleys may have owned 200 acres in the Nashoba Brook valley, later owned by John Hoar and by him sold to Edward Wright.

It is even more difficult to try to list the ordinary settlers. Many came and went without leaving any record. Mr. Bulkeley often bought land from those who left and his next deed may tell from whom. Other names can be gleaned from the incomplete registers of births, marriages, and deaths. [See Appendix A.]

The places in England from which they came were widely scattered. Hartwell, Bulkeley, and Wheeler were from Bedfordshire; Willard, Stow and Hosmer from Kent; Flint and Wood from Derbyshire; Hunt from York; Heald from Northumberland; and Heaward from Yorkshire.

William Buttrick came from Surrey; Edward Wright from Stafford; and Thomas Brown from Lavenham, Sussex. Charles E. Banks in *Planters of the Commonwealth* estimates that in the whole colony twenty per cent came from the East Anglia counties.

One need not share Sumner Powell's thesis (in his recent study of Sudbury) that the locale from which a settler came determined whether farming would be done in private fields or in common fields. It is more likely that the experience of Plymouth and the patterns followed in the seacoast towns would have outweighed the English experience of a few of the settlers. In Concord a second division of land was planned and promised from the beginning, but until it could be made, a common pasture was provided on the great meadows between the river and the north and east running ridges. The higher part of this land was a general planting field called the Cranefield, a name taken from a place near Odell in Bedfordshire but doubtless also because herons were found here. Another field, called the South Field, was set aside behind the house lots south of the millpond and another field for those beyond the river on the plains between our Lowell Road and Barnes Hill Road.

Later, two fields privately owned were used for common pasturage at so much per head. These were the "calf pasture" behind Main Street between the millbrook and the Sudbury River and the "ox pasture" near the top of Brooks's hill on the south side of the Bay Road.

The great meadows did not prove to be an ideal pasture. Aside from periodic flooding, there were quicksands from which a cow or horse could not be extricated, and poisonous plants, such as the water parsnip, which were fatal to cattle. Upland pastures were urgently needed. One such was the "twenty score," an area of 400 acres owned by twenty proprietors in lots of twenty acres each. This area on both sides of Estabrook Road continued to be pastured, in part, up to 1900. But in the early seventeenth century, the twenty owners pastured it, or parts of it, in common, by mutual agreement, specifying how many sheep each could send up and what trees were not to be cut down. Before the final division, which was made by lot, rights were bought and sold and divided like any other private property.

No mistake was made about the fertility of the fields above the flood plain. They remained among the most productive in the State for three centuries.

Merrick's pasture above Lowell Road called the calf pasture in the seventeenth century. This was part of Reverend Peter Bulkeley's estate.

*Their buildings were conveniently placed on one
straight street under a sunny bank.*
    Johnson: Wonder-working Providence

The earliest word picture of Concord is given by Edward Johnson of Woburn in 1656 in his book *Wonder-working Providence,* a quotation from which will be found in Appendix B, but unfortunately parts of it are too confused to be taken literally.

Reverend Peter Bulkeley, as has been said, employed a carpenter, Thomas Dane, to build his house and mill. The frame was set up first, without a cellar. The heavy sills, beams, and posts were hand-hewn from selected oak and were pinned together on the ground with trunnels (wooden pins) driven through auger holes. Then the frame was raised with the help of neighbors and was boarded and roofed. Most of the first houses were of one room with a loft. The boards had to be sawn at first by hand labor, one man standing below in a pit and a second man standing above with a two-handled saw. The early roof was thatched but it proved unsatisfactory in this climate with its long-lasting winter snows. Chimneys were catted, at first, of wood plastered thickly with wet clay, but both the extreme cold and the abundance of wood tempted the settler to have a hot fire which soon turned these chimneys and the thatch into an extreme fire danger.

In April, 1641, two Concord parents had left their children at home while they went to church. A little girl accidentally burned a cloth and, thinking to hide it from her mother, ran out and stuffed it into a hay stack near the door which set the hay on fire. The thatch caught and burned down the house with the baby in its cradle.

Just as soon as possible, bricks were made here and used for chimneys. A bed of suitable clay was located north of the Bay Road and a kiln built on a little hill rising out of the swamp there. This was called brick-kiln island. Wood chunks which could be readily split were used to make riven shingles.

Peter Bulkeley's house was still standing in 1775 when Ralph Earl made his sketch of Concord center on the Nineteenth. At that time the house was a two-story house, directly in the center of town near Jethro's oak.

Mather says Bulkeley was the student, as well as the owner, of a good library. It was his custom to catechize the young people every Sunday after the sermon. He was exact in the observance of the Sabbath. Even when it was fashionable to be a round head, he did not cut his hair short. He was immediately useful in the colony as presiding officer at the trial of Ann Hutchinson and in working out a codification of religious beliefs and a body of laws. He carried on an extensive correspondence with his colleagues in other churches after he moved to Concord, and finally published a book of sermons called *The Covenant of Grace Opened.* More than a hundred years later, President Stiles of Yale read the book and said that he considered Bulkeley one of the three or four most valuable ministers in the early days of the colony.

He constantly reminded his parish:

There is no people but will strive to excell in something. What can we excell in if not in holiness? If we look to number, we are the fewest. If to strength, we are the weakest. If to wealth and riches, we are the poorest of all the people of God through the whole world. We can not excell, nor so much as equal other people in these things. And if we come short in Grace and Holiness too, we are the most despicable people under heaven. True holiness toward God is ever accompanied by righteousness toward men. There is a true holiness and there is a false dissembling holiness. How is one to be discerned from the other? Holiness of truth hath righteousness going with it. But false holiness thinks it enough to seem holy toward God, neglecting duties of righteousness and justice toward men.

But Peter Bulkeley was an aristocrat, not a democrat. In April, 1650, he wrote to Reverend John Cotton that in England, where matters were swayed by the wisdom of the minister, matters went on with strength and power for good, "but here, where the heady or headless multitude have gotten the power, there is insolency and confusion. And I know not how it can be avoided unless we should make the doors of the church narrower than we have warrant for from the Word."

He wrote to Governor Endicott in 1655 to report that servants and some children under their parents' government

. . . yet take liberty to be abroad in the nights and run into other sinful mis-carriages, not to be suffered under a Christian government. This is to desire that you would make some order by which a magistrate may correct such offenses in the parent or master by laying a fine or pecuniary mulct upon them and by whipping or otherwise, the younger sort. It is time to begin with more severity than hath been, unless we would see a confusion and ruin coming upon all.


*And yet, in the eternity of nature,*
*how recent our antiquities appear.*
    *Emerson:* Historical Discourse


Concord was the first town carved out of the wilderness. Every other town in all America had been close to the ocean or a tidal river, where goods could be transported by boat and natural features would mark the bounds with a minimum of exploration. Thus the bounds of Watertown were well marked where they touched Cambridge and where they had the Charles River, except for a fish weir, as boundary on the south, but the Watertown grant was to extend eight miles up into the country from the meetinghouse to meet a line from the west border of Watertown near Nonesuch Pond, making a triangle with the first line. After the Concord grant was surveyed, Watertown surveyed its bounds and this point was found to be well within the Concord six miles square (near the northwest bounds of the present town forest). This land had not been divided out to individuals by Watertown, so her proprietors were compensated in 1638 by the grant of a whole new town to be called Sudbury, on Concord's south boundary. Sudbury was soon settled by Watertown people and by newcomers, who later spread to Marlborough. Next, Cambridge got from the General Court an extension of her bounds ". . . as far as Concord bounds give leave." These Cambridge farms later became Lexington. A black pine stump was found by survey to mark the corner where Watertown and Cambridge met on Concord's east line. Since each town later granted its land to individuals who built stone walls, those walls on the east side of the Rice and Flint farms (now in Lincoln) mark this ancient boundary. The bound stone on the Bay Road was called the "C," having Cambridge on one side and Concord on the other. When this east line is extended, it coincides with part of the present boundary between Lexington and Bedford, which was the ancient Concord–Cambridge boundary before Bedford was set off from Concord. The original south boundary is found by extending the present Concord–Sudbury line to meet this line. Concord's southwest corner is unchanged and the present Acton–Concord line can be extended up into Carlisle to find "Berry Corner," still marked with a stone land bound, a short distance southwest of Cross Street, Carlisle. Before the Concord–Carlisle boundary was straightened out in 1903, the old line coincided with the north bounds of farmers who chose to stay with Concord, as may be seen on the maps of 1830 and 1852. It crossed the river and crossed Concord Road, Bedford, at its northerly intersection with Davis Road, passed about a quarter-mile south of Bedford's Great Road to Shawshine Corner just east of that river, where it met the east line of old Concord. Walcott had the engineer-surveyor William Wheeler make a map showing these old bounds for his *Concord in the Colonial Period*, published in 1884.

It may be noted that regular perambulation of the town bounds and renewal of markers was a duty enjoined on Selectmen in the first Body of Laws.

Even today, if one attempted to follow this line on a compass course, part of it would be obstructed with swamps full of horse brier and parts would be hot and sandy and redolent of sweet fern. A hurricane in 1635 had knocked over many old trees and branches, making the walking even more difficult, so that Johnson's description becomes more credible if we allow that he confused several surveying trips at different times of the year. His description is of interest because it is almost the only one we have. (See Appendix B.)

*The righteous Puritans, their heads as dry*
*As the remainder biscuit.*
*Such bred the deeds of witchcraft, that his Muse,*
*Our gentle-hearted Hawthorne touched so well,*
*Drawing a beauty out of all their cant*
*And the self-lauding sect, moral in sin.*
    *Ellery Channing:* Hillside

References to Concord are disappointingly few in Governor John Winthrop's *Journal.* After the brief notice of the incorporation and the ordination of the two ministers, the next item about Concord is dated July 28, 1642.

Some of the elders went to Concord, being sent for by the church there to advise them about the maintenance of their elders, etc. They found them wavering about removal not finding their plantation answerable to their expectation, and the maintenance of two elders too heavy a burden for them. The elders' advice was that they should continue and wait upon God and be helpful to their elders in labor and what they could, and all to be ordered by the deacons (whose office had not formerly been improved this way amongst them) and that the elders should be content with what means the church was able at present to afford them, and if either of them should be called to some other place, then to advise with other churches about removal.

The split was inevitable. There was a constant shift in population as newly arrived immigrants came, stayed a while, then went to Connecticut or returned to the coastal towns, where those with a trade but no knowledge of farming could hope to make a living. Almost every deed to land in Concord listed the buyer as yeoman, except for the few gentlemen, but in Charlestown the identifying word would be that of a trade: glover, tanner, brickmaker, mason, shoemaker, doctor in physic, tobacco merchant, cooper, maltster, feltmaker, mariner, joiner, distiller, woolen draper, dishturner, to quote a few from early Middlesex deedbooks. In other words, the seacoast was a better location for tradesmen. This shifting of population made the Concord community unstable and increased the difficulty of collecting the taxes necessary to support two ministers. The facts were that one minister was wealthy and the other poor, that one was ten years older than the other, one higher in rank and deferred to more often by the Boston authorities; both were stubborn, independent men, attaching great importance to the minutest details of doctrine. Separatism is itself divisive, since it substitutes the individual conscience for centralized authority. The case of Ambrose Martin, which occurred at this time, was probably not the cause of Jones' removal, for John Jones' signature is directly below Bulkeley's on the petition, but it illustrates this divisiveness.

Ambrose Martin had said that the covenant of the Boston church was no better than a stinking carrion, a human invention, and that the ministers did dethrone Christ and set up themselves. Martin was fined £10, his cow was sold, and a further levy made on his house and land in Concord; but their value was double the fine. Martin refused to take back the difference, since he considered the whole fine illegal, even some years later, when he was poor and ill. The court records have a petition in Mr. Bulkeley's handwriting asking that the whole sum be returned to Martin. The petition was denied by Governor Endicott on June 4, 1644, in these words: "The case appears to be now past help, through his own obstinacy, but for the overplus on sale of the distress, he or his wife may have it when they will call for it."

Cotton Mather's *Magnalia*, written many years later, says, without specifying what caused the disagreement: "Upon Mr. Bulkeley pressing a piece of charity, disagreeable to the will of the ruling elder, an unhappy disCORD in the church of ConCORD."

Whatever the cause, the final break came in the summer of 1644 when Mr. Jones took his family and fifteen Concord men to Fairfield, Connecticut, on Long Island Sound.[3]

---

[3] When John Jones left in 1644 he probably sold his Concord property to Mr. John Strange, a merchant of Boston who sold it in turn to William Alline of Concord. Both went back to London and found a third buyer. We have their instructions to Alline's representatives in Concord, Richard Griffin and William Buttrick, dated 1659, to pay to Mr. Jones thirty pounds, ten shillings, to pay two pounds, ten shillings to the college and ten pounds to the Indians. In other words, Jones was not paid until this third sale of his Concord house. John Jones, son of Reverend John, graduated from Harvard in 1643 and became minister at Nevis in the Lee-

*Where are these men? Asleep beneath their grounds*
*And strangers, fond as they, their furrows plough.*
*They added ridge to valley, brook to pond*
*And sighed for all that bounded their domain.*
  Emerson: Hamatreya

In 1636, in order to make their land titles doubly secure, the first settlers called the remnants of the Massachusetts tribe to a meeting under
the big oak which stood near Mr. Bulkeley's house and solemnly purchased the six miles square. Present were Simon Willard, already
known to the Indians as a fur buyer, Mr. Jones, William Buttrick,
Richard Rice, Mr. Spencer and others, and the Squaw Sachem, who
was head of the tribe after her first husband's death; also Tahattawan,
the sagamore, Nimrod, Waban, Jehoiakim, Jethro, his son Jethro, and
other Indians. A quantity of wampompeag, hatchets, hoes, knives, cotton cloth, and shirts were given, and Webcowet, now husband to the
Squaw Sachem, received a new suit of cotton cloth, a linen band, hat,
shoes, stockings, and a great coat. After the bargain was concluded,
Simon Willard pointed to the four quarters of the world and declared
that they had bought three miles from that place, east, west, north,
and south, the said place being accounted about the center. The Indians declared themselves satisfied. They had received things they
really wanted. They retained their hunting rights which constituted
the chief value of the land to them. As for the colonists, since they
believed their titles secured through the Royal Charter and the grant
from the Massachusetts Legislature, the treaty was really intended at

---

ward Islands. Perhaps Harvard also waited for the tuition. The Jones lot, I believe,
was next to the Main Street burying place and was owned for a time by George
Wheeler whose first lot had been on the opposite side of Main street on the corner
of Walden Street. Wheeler sold it to Jonathan Prescott in 1678. (George Wheeler
died in 1687. His will is in the Suffolk Co. Registry of Deeds but does not give
the location of his "mansion house," which he had probably built on his original
lot after the 1676 sale to Prescott. The town records of 1693 refer to Jonathan
Prescott's lot as "formerly George Wheeler's." It is now the Savings Bank lot.)
In Fairfield, Mr. Jones's will, dated January 17, 1665, gave his second wife,
Susanna, the fifty pounds he had promised her, and named his children: John
Jones, Eliphalet, Sarah Wilson, Ruth James, Rebecca Hull, and Elizabeth Hill.
Theophilus had died, Eliphalet was settled as pastor at Huntington, L.I. Sarah
Wilson, as widow of Thomas Bulkeley, had married again.

Reverend John Jones house (Wheeler-Prescott-Bliss house), from a drawing by Henry Wilder in 1801.

the time to establish friendly relations with the Indians and it was successful for the lifetime of most of the party. When the Massachusetts Charter was revoked in 1689, those witnesses still living were called upon to make sworn depositions as to the agreement, and it is from the depositions of William Buttrick, Richard Rice, and Jehoiakim that these details are taken.

Soon the brook had been dammed and a corn mill built at Mr. Bulkeley's expense and a millpond was formed. Around the pond was a cluster of little houses with Mr. Bulkeley at one end of the horseshoe and Mr. Jones at the other. There was no road over the milldam until 1742 when the town meeting asked Mr. Timothy Minott to build a bridge over the flume at his mill. Behind the meetinghouse was the burial hill. The most important people would be buried nearest the meetinghouse. The graves of Peter Bulkeley and his son Edward would have been there although there were either no stones to mark the earliest graves, or the stones were too crude to endure. Such a spot may be readily identified in the lower east corner where sod covers a brick vault in which human remains and the remains of coffins were found. There was a strong English superstition against carrying a corpse across a running stream; indeed, as a practical matter, it would have been hard to carry a bier over the millbrook, so the burying ground for the south quarter was established at the same time. Joseph Meriam's stone, dated 1677 in the hill burying-place, is the oldest stone now extant there and one dated 1693 is the oldest in the south burial

Simon Willard house. This is a view of the house as it was enlarged by Woodis Lee and Joseph Lee before the fire of 1857.

place. Between Mr. Bulkeley's and the meetinghouse was the open field used as a training place. Eight training days per year were required by the Body of Laws.

Near the burial hill began the house lots of the first settlers, extending down the Bay Road for a mile and circling the pond to the south.

To the north there were four houses against the north ridge, and across the river, half a dozen had settled. The town very early built the north bridge leading to these lots and the south bridge leading to Simon Willard's farm on the slope of Nashawtuc hill. Although the bridges required constant repair, wood was plentiful. Keeping up the causeways leading to them was a serious problem with the frequent floods and without any machinery, even a tipcart.

East of the meetinghouse on Bay Road was Thomas Dane's lot, sold to the carpenter by his employer, Mr. Bulkeley, who had purchased it from George Heaward and Michael Wood when the former moved beyond the falls of the Assabet and the latter moved across the south bridge. Dane was to pay for it in boards, delivered in Cambridge or Charlestown, as Mr. Bulkeley should direct. This stipulation reminds us that wood, so plentiful in Concord, was very scarce on the Charlestown and Boston peninsulas and became a valuable source of income to Concord farmers, who made the slow trip with oxen and sleds in the winter carrying firewood, or boards or timber for housebuilding or shipbuilding, and bringing back what luxuries they needed from mer-

The ridge above the Bay Road, the Farwell house lot, and the Beatton house lot at the left.

chants in the seaports. Charlestown was the nearer by land, but a ferry ran from East Cambridge to Boston, with the tolls going to Harvard College, which had been founded in the same year as Concord.

During the first century there were no merchants and few taverns in Concord; in fact the selectmen had to beg Sergeant Buss in 1660 to keep an ordinary, and since he was unwilling to serve anything but beer or cider, the selectmen asked that Robert Meriam be impowered to ". . . sell wine and strong waters to such as stand in need in our town and are weak and sick and to strangers that want." John Heywood, who lived next door to Buss, succeeded him as innkeeper in 1666. The jail was next to the Inn.

Some of the stone walls bounding these original house lots may still be seen along the Bay Road. The lots were of three to eight acres, depending on the number in the family, including servants, for some of the families had paid the passage of able young men and women in exchange for a few years service. The Bay Road lots ran from the crest of the sheltering ridge to the millbrook, with a house site against the ridge for shelter from the winter wind. The well was dug out front by the roadside, one well sometimes serving two or three houses. The barns were built below the road so that the cows could walk down to the brook for water. Whenever possible all these houses faced south, even if it meant putting the gable end to the road.

Concord at its incorporation was excused from taxes for three years but not from training, for military service was accepted as a primary duty of citizenship with only the minister, schoolmaster, magistrates, physicians, and Harvard students excepted. The students were potential ministers. We have seen the difficulty of raising money by taxation to support two ministers. Those who had bought house lots after the first settlement petitioned the General Court in 1643 for more land to the northwest of the town, saying that after four years' trial they found the land barren, the meadows wet.

Again in 1645, the leading citizens petitioned to have their colony tax reduced ". . . both because of the poverty and meanness of the place and the wetness of the meadows," and because the last summer a seventh or eighth part of the town went to the southward with Mr. Jones and many more resolved to go after them. These figures, incidentally, fix the 1644 population at 100 families, or seven or eight times the fifteen Concord planters in Fairfield. The Court reduced the tax, but at the same time inhabitants were forbidden to remove without the consent of the magistrates. This last proviso soon became a dead letter.

The petition for more land was granted in 1651 and Concord Village (now Acton) was surveyed, but the new grant was not divided among the inhabitants of Concord for another fifty years, although each property owner had "rights" in the Village which could be bought and sold or transferred by will. This new grant was also ceremoniously bought from the Indians.

As the accessible wilderness was thus granted to towns, some of the wealthier people in Boston who had been promised land petitioned for farms to the north of Concord. John Winthrop and his son-in-law, Thomas Dudley, received in 1638 about twenty-five hundred acres north of the Concord boundary and east of the river, and divided it so amicably near two large rocks that the stones have ever since been called "the two brothers." They may still be seen on the edge of a river meadow in Bedford. Grants west of the river to Thomas Allen of 500 acres, to Increase Nowell of 500 acres, to Atherton Hough and to Simon Willard of 400 acres, were later bought by John and Robert Blood, whose wife was Elizabeth, one of the daughters of Major

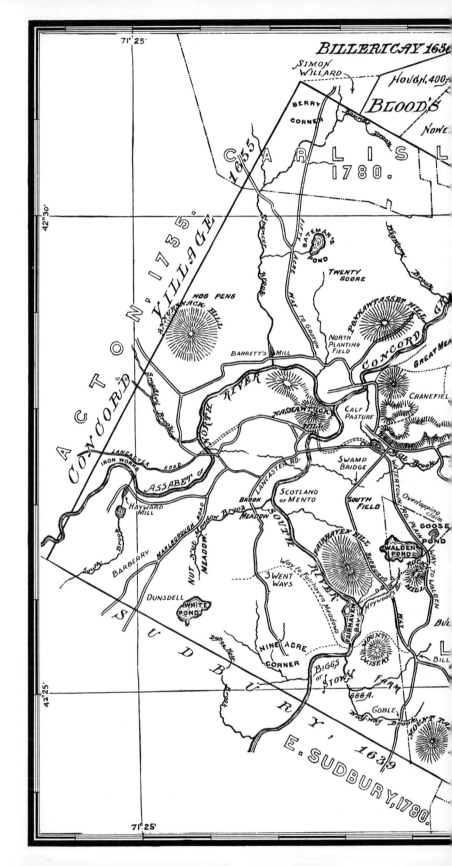

# Map of Concord
## IN THE
## COLONIAL · PERIOD.
### (Not including the New Grant.)

Drawn expressly For
*Walcott's 'Concord' in the Colonial Period.'*
By Wm. Wheeler
Engineer

REVISED *for*
Ruth R. Wheeler's
CONCORD: CLIMATE
FOR FREEDOM
1967
Henry B. Kane

DUDLEY'S FARM
Two Brothers
FARM

BILLERICAY 1655

CEDAR OR
SANCTO DOMINGO
SWAMP

B E D F O R D, 1729.

WHEELER'S MILL
BLIND PLAINS
PINE HILL
SHAWSHINE CORNER
Old Woburn Road
SHAWSHINE RIVER

LEXINGTON, 1712.

BLOODY CURVE
CONCORD CORNER

The C

CAMBRIDGE FARMS

THOMAS WHEELER
FLINT'S FARM.
750 A.
Black Pine Stump

N

LOLN,
4.

BEAVER POND

WATERTOWNE
WALTHAM 1737.
1630

ESTON, 1712.

### REFERENCES.
Boundary of Original Grant.
Highways.
Abandoned Highways.
Bridle Roads.
Town Lines (Modern.)
Meeting-houses, Concord.
Meeting-houses, Bedford and Lincoln (Modern.)

Willard. Much of Blood's land inside the six miles square he left to two daughters who had married Buttricks. Joseph Wheeler had a large grant in a triangle north of Lake Nagog above the Acton line, part of which he sold to the Shepards. It was many years before Concord came to an agreement with the Bloods about taxes, which were also claimed by Billerica. The Bloods were often involved in litigation. The Middlesex County records have the sworn testimony of witnesses in a suit brought against Robert Blood in 1654 by Samuel Hunt for damages for slander and saying evil against him in the course of accusing him, Hunt, of mowing Blood's meadow. John Blood was also presented for refusing to take the oath of fidelity to the Commonwealth.

*Here the free spirit of mankind, at length*
*Throws its last fetters off: and who shall place*
*A limit to the giant's unchained strength,*
*Or curb his swiftness in the forward race.*
    *William Cullen Bryant:* The Ages

Even back in 1645, taxes were not always paid cheerfully and promptly. The Concord constable in that year was summoned into court to answer to a complaint by William Symons that the said constable had distrained his featherbed. The six Selectmen of that year wrote an explanation:

To our Honored Governor and the rest of the Magistrates in Court Assembled.

Whereas the Constable of our Town of Concord is summoned to appear at the Court to Answer one William Symons in an Action of the case for distrainment of a featherbed of his lying at our Town. We whose names are underwritten have made bold hereby to Certify to the Court that said Constable was thereto necessitated, the said William Symons having lived in our Town almost since the first planting of it and having had as good accommodations as most have had, of his quality, and having earned as much money in the Town, hath notwithstanding paid nothing as we can hear to the upholding of Ordinances nor gave anything to the use of the Commonwealth, but what he hath been constrained to, but hath rather at all times showed his unwillingness upon demand having been made of him. And the Goods Distrained were not all used by him this long time for anything we can understand.

To our Honored Governor and the rest of
the Magistrates in Court Assembled.

Whereas the Constable of our Towne of Concord is summoned
to appeare at the Court to Answer one William Symonds
in an Action of the case for distrayneing of a ffeatherbed of
his lyeing at our Towne, Wee (whose names are under written)
have made bold hereby to Certify the Court, the said Constable
was hereto Necessitated, The said William Symonds haveing
lived in our Towne almost since the first Planting of it, and
haveing had as good accomodatione as most have had of his quality,
and haveing earned much money in the Towne, hath not withstanding
payd nothing as wee can heare to the upholding of Ordinances,
and scarce anything to the use of the Common wealth, but what
hee hath beene Constrayned to, ————————, but hath rather at all
times showed his unwillingnes upon demand hath beene made
of him. And the Goods distrayned, were not at all used by
him this long time for any thing wee can understand

Firs. Griffin.
Simon Willard
william wood
Robert ffloyer
Eli Brooks
Geo. Heaward

The six Selectmen who signed the petition were Richard Griffin, Simon Willard, William Wood, Robert Fletcher, Thomas Brooks, and George Heaward. Richard Griffin was deacon of the Concord church from its founding until his death in 1661. William Wood's lot was listed on Walden Street between Joseph Estabrook and Samuel Meriam. He died in 1671. Wood, father of Michael Wood whose descendants are still numerous here, was also an early settler. He is believed by some to have been the author of *The New England Prospect*, a promotional pamphlet full of useful information for the would-be migrant, ". . . laying down that which may both enrich the knowledge of the mind-travelling reader or benefit the future voyager." The map published with it shows our river with its branches and islands and uses the name "Musketaquid" for the first time in print. Thomas Brooks was also a first settler with a house lot south of the mill pond. Robert Fletcher was a first settler with his lot on the Bay Road near Ridge Road. He died in 1677. George Heaward (later spelled Hayward) was an enterprising first settler who sold his lot near the meetinghouse and moved out beyond the Assabet to start a mill. He died in 1671, ". . . by drowning overthrown by the force of the stream after setting William Frizzel across in his canoe." His resolute independence is shown by a petition he sent to the General Court in 1668:

Honored Sir.

I was told by some from our Constable that I must go to Court but for what they could not tell and I have seen no warrant. So that if critical business may pass in the court I hope I may be excused but such occasions as I understand are used as doth obstruct the honest intent of law and government and put both Court and private persons to much needless trouble. I guess that my sending for may be to make good some former presentment concerning Concord which if it be this, I say that what was done was by virtue of an oath of fifteen men chosen by the County to present the breach of the laws of the Country all which laws are either injunctions or prohibitions and so to be looked upon under a various notion, the one negative and the other affirmative all things enjoined and not performed must be presented by virtue of a negative oath which if not valid the grand jury hath little work to do. This I write with regard to the trouble the Court hath with persons often presented and sympathizing.

Concord being presented for want of something enjoined not by virtue of a negative oath. Inquiry being made whether such things were I must either excuse or arrange the excuses which I was able to make did neither satisfy the rest of the jury nor myself but if the Honored Court desire further intelligence the present grandjury man for Concord can inform as well as

myself and thus entreating you to pardon my rude boldness I rest desiring
not to be tedious. Your humble and obedient servant
Concord 6.1.68                                                    Geo. Hayward

*Taking into consideration the useful parts and abilities of divers
inhabitants which are not Freemen.*
     Body of Liberties

The codification of colony laws which the ordinary citizens regarded
as their *Magna Carta* was called the Body of Liberties. This expressly
permitted every man (except apprentices and bound servants) to vote
in town meeting, after taking an oath of fidelity. In colony affairs one
had to be a church member to vote. These were called freemen. Church
membership, after the first signing in 1636, was difficult, involving a
public confession of sins and statement of repentance. Consequently,
by 1685 only a third of the eligible citizens were church members in
full communion. Town meeting with its wider franchise became a
school of democracy, remarkable both for the training it gave and for
the ideas it tested. Here everyone was on an equal footing. In England
there were many classes, here only two: gentlemen and yeomen, and
there was little to differentiate them except that the former were always
designated "mister." This was the title used by ministers, magistrates,
and a few wealthy merchants. The overwhelming number of Concord
citizens were yeomen—land-owning farmers—called by their first
names. However, military titles were always used if possible. Thus
Simon Willard, as a magistrate, was entitled to be called "Mister," but
he was called "Captain" in 1634 when first chosen by the train band,
and when promoted to major in 1653, he was ever after known as
Major Willard. He was often away and moved to Lancaster in 1659.
Even a minor title was prized. William Buss, sergeant of the train band,
was never called anything but Sergeant Buss. The train bands elected
their own officers but sent the list in to Boston to be confirmed by the
magistrates there, usually a matter of form. Re-election year after year
was the custom.
     There was not much interference with Concord by the colony govern-
ment in the seventeenth century, but the town was overruled when it
tried to make Sergeant Buss a constable. He complained that he was
already a militia officer and too busy to be constable. Constable was

the hardest office to fill, for it involved collecting taxes and since these could be paid in cattle, grain, wood, or work on the roads or bridges, they were indeed complicated.

The town was also fined for the undue election of Mr. Thomas Flint as a magistrate. The exact offense is not specified, but it may have been for voting in a town meeting rather than in the more restricted freemen's meeting. In any case, Flint was a representative for four years and a governor's assistant for eleven, until his death in 1653. He had been the largest investor in the town, after Peter Bulkeley. His son, John, inherited his house above the north bridge. His second son, Captain Ephraim Flint, inherited the big grant between the pond and the Watertown line. The latter married Edward Bulkeley's daughter, Jane, and lacking children, left all this property to Edward, son of his brother John.

Concord men were soon busy with their second division of land. As owners came and went and rights changed hands before the actual allotments took place, some deeds were recorded in the new county registry, and more were entered in the town books; the confusion had to be resolved. The town voted in 1653 to have each property owner get his list of possessions approved by his neighbors and entered in a new town book.

The town was divided into quarters or sections, three in number, to make this easier. The East Quarter included all the land east of the immediate vicinity of the meetinghouse and north of the millbrook and a line running above Mr. Flint's farm. The North Quarter included the ridge west and north of the meetinghouse and all the land west of the Concord River and north of the Assabet. The South Quarter included the land between the rivers and south of the millbrook and East Quarter line to the Sudbury line. Land deeds always specified which quarter of Concord the land was situated in. In choosing their second division of land, Michael Wood and George Hayward, whose house lots had been close to the meetinghouse, asked to have their allotments in the South Quarter, as did Thomas Dane and Luke Potter, while Richard Rice, Robert and George Meriam, Thomas Brooks, and Ensign Timothy Wheeler asked to go with the East Quarter.

Some moved out to their farms as soon as a house could be built but others gave the new land to their sons. Soon houses were strung along each of the roads leading to the surrounding towns. Many of these houses have survived to the present day even though altered to suit later generations. When built, they were of the familiar salt-box

Second generation house of Richard Rice near the old town bounds. Richard Rice was the last survivor of the first settlers and died here June, 1709. (Photograph by Harriette M. Forbes.)

Seventeenth-century house on Virginia Road owned by Timothy Wheeler, Josiah Meriam, and Joseph Algeo. (Photograph by Harriette M. Forbes.)

type, two stories in front and one story in the rear under a long sloping roof. They invariably faced south, so that they were all built on the upper side of the Bay Road which ran to the east; on the north- or south-running roads, the houses on both sides of the road had one end toward the road so that the house itself could still face the sun and be sheltered by its long rear roof from the cold north winds.

By mid-century a brickkiln had been started so that a big central chimney could now be built of brick and radiate its heat. In front of the chimney was the steep stair with two landings leading up to the bedrooms. Across the rear was the kitchen which sometimes had its ends partitioned off, one for a warm bedroom for old folks, invalids or new mothers, the other a buttery or storeroom. (The name "borning room," so pleasing to Realtors, was not found in any Concord deed.) Laths to hold plastering were boards with the center split roughly into strips. Many houses had double walls downstairs with the space between filled with broken brick and plaster. When an earlier house survived on the spot where the new one was built, it became an ell or even one room of the new house, which retained the low ceilings of the earliest houses.

Occasionally, Concord people were closely connected with English events. John Hoar's brother, Leonard, had married Bridget Lisle, daughter of a regicide, one of those who had condemned Charles I to death. At the Restoration in 1660, Charles II put a price on his head. Lisle fled to Switzerland but was murdered there. Leonard Hoar had graduated from Harvard in 1650 and had gone back to England to marry and become the minister of the parish of Wanstead in Essex. Hoar lost this parish at the Restoration and retired to Cambridge, England, to study medicine but was searching for an opportunity to come to New England when friends in Boston wrote him that the presidency of Harvard College was open. He arrived in Boston on July 8, 1672, and on July 13 was elected by the General Court, the first president to be a graduate. The Cambridge minister, Urian Oakes, had expected to be chosen and immediately fomented trouble which resulted in Hoar's resignation in 1675; the latter died within the year. He had owned land in Concord near Meriam's Corner with a cowhouse on it, though strictly speaking he could not be called a citizen. His widow married Hezekiah Usher, a Boston merchant and bookseller. Her mother, Lady Lisle, suffered a dreadful fate. After the accession of James II in 1685, the Duke of Monmouth led an unsuccessful rebellion and two fugitives from his followers were given shelter by Lady Lisle.

Town meadow. This was the site of Leonard Hoar's cowhouse.

She was found out, tried for treason, and beheaded.[4] When William and Mary succeeded in 1688 where Monmouth had failed, Bridget Usher returned to London and secured a posthumous pardon for her mother. Bridget came back to Boston in 1697 and lived until 1723, giving much of her first husband's library to Increase Mather after a fire in his house, and some books to the children of his brother, John Hoar, in Concord.

[4] "Mercifully beheaded" says the record, a quick death, instead of the usual penalty for treason, to be hanged until not quite dead, then to be drawn and quartered.

*Then in what time the primal icy years*
*Scraped slowly o'r the Puritan's hopes and fears*
*Like as great glaciers built of frozen tears.*
    Lanier: Psalm of the West

What records were kept in those first years in Concord must have included land transactions, but they were only paper books and became so worn that the town voted in 1664 to order a new leather-bound book and that ". . . what is useful in the old book be transcribed in the new." Unfortunately, only a few items were considered worthy. This old book is identical in binding and paper with one used in Bedfordshire, England, at the same time.

Of over-riding importance in 1664 was the record of land ownership. A committee was set up in each quarter of town, each owner brought in a transcript of his possessions, this was looked over and approved by his neighbors and then entered in the book. To help with the handwriting, Edward Bulkeley, Joseph Wheeler, and Thomas Brooks were appointed to assist. County government had been set up in 1639 with courts in Charlestown and Cambridge and a registry of deeds, but many transactions had been made which were never recorded, or recorded only in the paper books. Usually, a deed had been given and sworn to before a magistrate, but this town record book served to validate ownership up to this date. A deed from a New Hampshire attic, dated 1686, to Nathaniel Ball of the Wayside property but never recorded saw the light only recently. However, the Ball ownership had been included in the town book and was therefore never questioned. The authority of the towns to give valid deeds was voted by the Court of Assistants in September, 1630, and was based on the Colony charter. There were no private King's grants here except the grant to the whole colony by King Charles I in the charter of 1629. The transcript of what was useful in the old books follows:

INSTRUCTIONS GIVEN TO THE SELECTMEN OF CONCORD
FOR THE YEAR 1672

1. To see that the ministers' rates be discharged according to time.

2. To examine whether the meetinghouse, be finished according to agreement, & if not, that it may be; but if the agreement be fulfilled, then to take

Know whome it may concerne ... James Taillor sone in Concord sold to
Nathaniel Ball sone of the same Town of Concord two house lots: the first lot I
sold to said Ball in ye year: 1648 ye second lot in ye year: 1652 also twenty acres
of second division land aboute ye year 1672 or there about: I being fully satisfied
by ye sd Ball I signe & seal this ensuing deed: —

To all people to whome these presents may come to be seen or read: Know ye
that I James Taillor sone in the Town of Concord in the County of Middlesex in the
Massachusetts Colony in new england planter: for ye in consideration of a valuable
some of pay to me the sd James Taillor well & truly paid by Nathaniel Ball of
the same Town of Concord ... the receite whereof I ye sd James Taillor & doe
by these presents acknowledge & thereof ... of every parte & parcell thereof & doe
... fully & clearly & absolutely aquite ... & discharge him ye said
Nathaniel Ball his heirs executors administrators ... & sold & by these presents doe fully & clearly given
these presents have granted bargained & sold & by these presents doe fully & clearly given
bargained sold & confirmed unto him ye sd Nathaniel Ball a house lot of eight acres be
it more or less ... with all the right I ye sd Taillor bought
of sd ... it was formerly Goody Doubtyes ... be it more or less joyning to the ...
said ... also a house lot of five acres be it more or less joyning to the ...
to the sd five acre lot: more Nathaniel Ball to have the second division land: twoo to the
sd Taillor in the east quarter of ye Town of Concord I sd Ball to receive it ...
house lot of five acres more or less with ye second adition of land to it was for
mostly John Richardsons: both lots joyning as bounded on the south ends by the
mill brooke & on the east side by William Hartwell lot & on the north ends
by land formerly Obadiah Wheelers: & on the right side by Eliphalot Hopos
lot & ye high way going over the brooke: To have & to hold the above grant
one ... premises be & ye same more or less with all the issues & pro
fits thereof & all the housing their on standing & trees their on growing
... their in ... & fence their to be longing unto him the said
Nathaniel Ball his heirs & assignes for ever to his or their onely proper
use & behoofe: & I ye above named James Taillor for me my heirs executors
& administrators doe covenant promise & grante to & with ye above said
Nathaniel Ball his heirs executors administrators & assignes by these
presents: ... I ye sd James Taillor have good right full power &
lawful authority to grant bargaine & confirme the above said two lots
lyeing in the east quarter of ye Town of Concord with ye twenty acres of se
cond division land unto him ye sd Nathaniel Ball his heirs & assignes for ever
... sd Nathaniel Ball his heirs & assignes shall & may by force
of these presents for ever have after peaceably & quietly have hold
use occupy possesse & enjoy the above granted premises with all
the issues & profits thereof: without the let denial disturbance con ...
adition molestation or incombrance of me ye said James Taillor
my heirs executors administrators & assignes them or any of them
lawfully claiming & having any right title or interest their in or...
any parte or parcell thereof by from or under me or by any other
lawful wayes or meanes whatsoever. In witnes whereof I the
above named James Taillor sone in ... acknowledgment of my free
consent to this my ... & doe have here unto put my hand & seal
this first day of February in the year one thousand six hundred
eighty & six —

Signed Sealed &
Delivered in presence of

Christopher Woolley

Samuel Woolley

Thomas Woolley

James ✝ Taylor
his Marke

Original deed to Wayside. Courtesy of the Minuteman National Historical Park.

care that something be done to keep the water out, and that the pulpit be altered.

3. That care be taken of the books of martyrs & other books, that belong to the Town, that they be kept from abusive usage, & not to be lent to any person more than one month at one time.[5]

4. That speedy care be taken to mend or demolish the footbridge over the north River at the Iron works;

5. To treat with Capt. Thomas Wheeler about his lease of the Town's farm & if it may be upon Reasonable terms to alter that particular wherein the Town is enjoined to send such a number of cattle yearly to be herded by him;

6. To let out the land & housing where now John Law dwells; for the benefit of the town,

7. To take order that all corn fields be sufficiently fenced in season, the crane field & brick-kiln field especially;

8. And that encouragement be given for the destroying of blackbirds & jays;

9. That special care be taken to prevent damage by swine in corn fields & meadows.

10. That sheep & lambs be kept from doing damage in cornfields;

11. To make a Record of all the habitations, that are privileged with liberty at Commons;

12. To take account of the last year's selectmen for what is due, to the Town by Rent by John Law, or by gift by Joseph Meriam; or otherwise of right due to the Town, not to restrain the selectmen from leniency towards John Law;[6]

13. To see that men's lands both improved and unimproved be truly brought [listed].

14. To take care that undesirable persons be not entertained; so as to become inhabitants.

15. To take care that persons do not overcharge their Commons with cattle,

16. That all persons that have taken the oath of fidelity be Recorded.

17. That care be taken that Cattle be herded, as much as may be, with convenience.

[5] This is the earliest mention known to us, of books owned by a town and lent out on a regular basis: A public library.

[6] John Law is believed to have been a Scottish prisoner, one of 277 captured by Cromwell in 1652 after the battles of Dunbar and Winchester and shipped to this country to serve as indentured servants. After the Restoration "leniency" toward him would have been politically expedient. The inventory of Law's estate lists a quantity of woolen cloth and a claim to the land on which he lived in Acton near the brook which bears his name. During the term of his indenture, he may have been a sheepherder and was probably also a weaver.

These particulars were agreed upon by us whose names are underwritten. dated 4:1.mo.   1671

1672   Nehemiah Hunt; John Flint; John Miles; Will Heartwell; Tho. Wheeler; Joshua Brooks; Joseph Heaward; Gershom Brooks; Humphry Barrett; John Billings

*Let us cultivate a grateful remembrance of our pious ancestors and sedulously imitate their amiable virtues while we quietly enjoy the fruit of their singular toils.*

*Ezra Ripley:* Sermon at the Dedication of his Meeting House 1792

Instead of dividing the grazing land in the new grant (Acton), the town leased it to Captain Thomas Wheeler in 1669 in an elaborate document in which he agreed to pasture cattle for his fellow-townsmen at so much a head. He would build a house forty feet in length, eighteen feet wide and twelve feet stud, covered with shingles and with a pair of chimneys. This last meant a chimney with two flues (as in a pair of trousers). The number of cattle sent to board with him did not meet his expectations so the contract was revised in 1673. The owners of the cattle were to take care of them in turn on twelve Sabbath days yearly so that Wheeler could attend church. However, he was soon occupied with military affairs. He recruited a Middlesex troop of horse by selecting from the train bands those who owned horses and could supply their own equipment and gear. When King Philip's war began a few years later these troops proved invaluable. Thomas Wheeler led his troop to the defense of Brookfield, and before he died six months later as a result of his wounds, he had written an account of the campaign. His first house lot had been on the Bay Road between the lots of Joshua and Moses Wheat, a lot which included, below the road, the site of the Concord Antiquarian House. His heirs sold it to Peter Harwood. His wife was Ruth Wood, daughter of William Wood, who left her in his will "two cows of a brown color now in Thomas Wheeler's hands" and the balance to his son Michael except for one brindle cow to his granddaughter Abigail Hosmer. Two of Wheeler's sons died in 1676; another, Joseph, removed to Stratfield, Connecticut, with eight children. Another son, Deliverance, moved to Stow.

Reverend Edward Bulkeley's house. This was moved from Main Street to Sudbury Road.

Captain Thomas Wheeler was the brother of Timothy who bought from Reverend Peter Bulkeley's widow in 1660 three-fourths of the minister's Concord property. A quarter interest was bought by George Wheeler, uncle to Timothy and Thomas. Mrs. Bulkeley then moved to Connecticut with her own children. Reverend Peter had died in 1659 leaving an estate valued at thirteen hundred pounds of which one hundred and thirty-two pounds were in books. He had previously given part of his library to Harvard College. The town chose his son, Reverend Edward Bulkeley, to succeed him. Edward had been educated in England, had come to Boston in 1634 and was soon installed as minister in Marshfield. He was already forty-five years old when he was installed in Concord, but lived until 1696. He built his house on what is now Concord Academy property on Main Street, a house which I believe was moved over to Sudbury Road in 1826 and is still standing as Number 10. He suffered from illness and lameness in his old age so that the town installed Reverend Joseph Estabrook to assist him and later to succeed him. Estabrook bought the Billings house lot south of the millbrook. The only printed work of Edward Bulkeley's

House of Reverend Joseph Estabrook and Reverend John Whiting as it looked in 1880. (Photograph by Alfred Hosmer.)

to survive is the sermon of Thanksgiving which he preached on the return of Captain Thomas Wheeler from Quabaug. Thomas Wheeler's narrative of fourteen pages and Edward Bulkeley's sermon of thirty-two pages were printed in a pamphlet together. The sermon makes dull reading since there is a Bible reference and quotation for almost every sentence:

Firstly, let our praises be CORDIAL with the heart, yea the whole heart as in Psalm 34:1. Secondly let them be verbal as in Hosea 14:2. Thirdly in declaring God's goodness to others Psalm 34:1. Fourthly let our praises be continual Psalm 145: Luke 8:38. Fifthly God smelled a sweet savour in Noah's sacrifice after that wonderful preservation from the flood of waters Genesis 8:20.

Not all of his hearers suffered in silence. John Hoar was fined ten pounds in 1668 for saying at Buss's tavern that the blessing which Master Bulkeley pronounced in dismissing the assembly in the Meeting-house was no better than vain babbling. John Hoar had been interested at first in the fur trade and had a house near Nashoba Brook at the west boundary of the town. This he exchanged with Edward Wright in 1672 for the property we now call Orchard House on the Bay Road. Another outspoken dissident was Dr. Philip Reed who lived at the east end of town near Richard Rice, his father-in-law. He said he could preach as well as Mr. Bulkeley, who was called by none but a company of blockheads who followed the plowtail and was not worthy to carry Mr. Estabrook's books after him. He also said he thought the illness of a woman patient was caused by standing too long during the administering of the Lord's Supper. He was fined twenty pounds.

Life was indeed hard during the thirty years after John Jones's departure. Cromwell's successful war in England stopped the flood of migration and some men returned to England (as did Joshua Wheat and William Alline), but the ready market for cattle and grain which newcomers had supplied was suddenly cut off, and prices fell disastrously. Education was the first to suffer. Parents could not afford to let their boys have the time for schooling and the town found it hard to pay a schoolmaster although liable to a fine by the General Court for not maintaining one. Soon there was the threat of losing the Colony charter.

*Instead of purging out Popery, a further compliance was sought,*
*not only in vain idolatrous ceremonies but also in*
*profaning the Sabbath.*
    *Johnson:* Wonder-working Providence

When Charles II returned to his father's throne, one of his first cares was to try to cut down the Puritan monopoly in New England. These colonists had supported Cromwell's Commonwealth, now they were harboring two regicides, Whalley and Goffe. Members of the Church of England complained that they had no place to worship. Undoubtedly, King Charles thought that his father's charter gave Massachusetts too much liberty. Four warships came into Boston Harbor in 1664 with orders to take back the charter. By what evasions the Massachusetts Council managed to postpone the issue for twenty-five years is not part of the Concord story, but the declaration drawn up in Concord in town meeting assembled breathes such determination and willingness to fight, if necessary, that it might well have been written in 1774 instead of in 1664. It is just as resolute.

To the honored General Court of the Massachusetts Colony held at Boston October 19, 1664: the humble representation of the Inhabitants of the Town of Concord, both freemen and others:

Forasmuch as we understand there have been complaints made unto his Majesty concerning divisions among us, and dissatisfaction about the present Government of this Colony; we whose names are underwritten do hereby testify our unanimous satisfaction in, and adhering to, the present Government, so long and orderly established, and our earnest desire of the continuance thereof, and of all the liberties and privileges appertaining thereunto, which are contained in the charter granted by King James and King Charles the First of blessed memory, under the encouragement and security of which charter, we or our fathers, ventured over the ocean into this wilderness, through great hazards, charges and difficulties; and seeing our rightful Sovereign hath privileged you with power by force of arms to defend this place and people (we, having encouragement from the honored Council) cannot but acknowledge it a mercy of God that you so mind the good and preservation of this place and people according to oath, we do declare that we are ready to assist both with persons and estates, that so by the goodness and mercy of God we may still enjoy present privileges and remain yours in all humble observance.

Four columns of names follow on this yellowing sheet and they are the same ninety-three names that appear on lists of the Minutemen and on the names of our streets today: Brooks, Brown, Fletcher, Flint, Hosmer, Stow, Hayward, Heywood, Wheeler, Hunt, Miles, Hoar, Taylor, Baker, Heald, Hartwell, Davis, Barrett, Rice, Wood, Meriam, Dudley, Jones, Ball, Dakin, Buttrick, Billings, and Blood. [See Appendix A.]

Everything was not dark. As Emerson reminded his fellow-townsmen in 1835: "the landscape before them was fair. The little flower which stars our woods and road-sides might attract even eyes as stern as theirs with its humble beauty. The useful pine lifted its cones into the frosty air. The maple which will soon be making the forest gay with its orange hues, reddened over those houseless men. The majestic summits of Wachusett and Monadnock towering in the horizon invited the steps of adventure westward. . . ."

They also had land of their own, a town which they governed themselves, a religious establishment of their own choosing, and a college of their own to educate their ministers. A race relations problem still remained.

# Chapter II    Trial by Fire

A *nobler task was theirs who strove to win*
*The blood-stained heathen to the Christian fold*
*To free from Satan's clutch the slaves of sin.*
    *O. W. Holmes:* Francis Parkman

From the day the English Puritans landed on our shores, there were two opposing theories about how Indians should be treated, one group regarding them as immortal souls to be snatched if possible from the Devil, the other considering them as just dangerous nuisances if not actually agents of the Devil.

When the Pequots in 1637 murdered an English trader, the colonists did not seek out, arrest and punish the murderers, they held the whole tribe responsible. They surrounded and destroyed the whole village and actually thereby won the respect of the other Indians themselves. Thirty-eight years later in 1675, the surviving Pequots were faithful allies. Less fortunate was the moral effect on the English. Savage conduct had worked, so the common people believed it was the right policy. Others considered it unchristian and the feeling of guilt was especially strong among the clergy. This group was led by John Eliot, Daniel Gookin, and others, who had worked to convert the Indians to Christianity. They had taught several Indians to read and write. They had translated and printed a Bible. They wrote pamphlets describing their work to encourage contributions in England to the Society for the Propagation of the Gospel.

They got the General Court to set aside a series of villages for the Christian Indians. In a half circle beyond Concord were Natick, Nashoba, and Wamesit. Here they were supposed to live peacefully, cultivate the soil and become good sober industrious citizens like their white neighbors in Sudbury, Concord, and Chelmsford. Meanwhile, the English colonists had pushed up the Connecticut valley. Springfield, Hatfield, Deerfield, and Northfield surrounded the Massachusetts and Nipmuck tribes on a third side, while Marlborough, Lancaster, Groton, and Brookfield pushed into the heart of their territory and foreshadowed complete white settlement.

Those Indians who submitted to baptism because they had observed the power of the white man's God were willing to preach, go scouting, even to build and live in houses; but steady work, which was the foundation of English morality, was impossible for the Indian. The gap between the two civilizations was too great. Had the Indians been able to become farmers these settlements would have supported them, supplementing the fur trade. We should give the Bay Colony some credit for their attempts to be fair. In all prior history—Egyptian, Roman, Moslem, Anglo-Saxon, Norman, and American Indian as well—death or serfdom had been the fate of conquered people.

Some of the Indians worked occasionally for their white neighbors and got English clothing or "strong waters" in exchange, or even muskets and powder, though this traffic was forbidden. Forty years had certainly not made them civilized in the view of their hard-working English neighbors. Side by side with John Eliot's ideal of happy, civilized Indians was the reality of idleness, dirt, and drunkenness.

Forty years had also made changes in the white population. The general level of education was lower among the clergy as well as among the common people. Cotton Mather as well as Edward Bulkeley were narrower and more superstitious than the first generation, so that at last Mather came to concern himself with witchcraft and other works of the Devil.

The citizens of Concord had got on fairly well with their Indian neighbors. The remnant of the tribe which had survived the great epidemics of 1617 and 1633 had lived on Nashawtuc Hill at first, but as furs became scarcer and their numbers increased, they moved out beyond Nagog. In 1659, Major Willard sold his farm here and moved to Lancaster. The Indians were in and out of town a lot, entering the houses without knocking, and sitting in silence by the fire until the gift of food or tobacco and the ceremonial silence had been observed; then it would come out in their halting English whether they had furs and game to trade, whether they wanted to work a few days on the farm, or whether they just wanted the white friend to share his food or cider or make him a present of an old coat or a baby's shirt. Their observant eyes learned the location and extent of every settler's possessions and the work habits of every man. By 1675, every Indian brave had learned the use of firearms and owned his own musket, some bought, some stolen, and some traded from the Dutch in Albany.

In 1675, Massasoit's son Philip turned against the English who had educated him, and decided to drive them back to the seacoast and then if possible beyond the sea. Some of the praying Indians were willing to help him. Others of them reported his messages back to their English friends in Plymouth and Boston. The Indian haters did not require much proof of treachery; in any case, Indians were potential spies. Equally sure of their ground were the missionaries. Now at last their friendly policy was paying off, it seemed, as their protégés brought in the information about Philip's plans and Jethro, Andrew Pittimee, and others offered to go out scouting.

*And Philip and his devils pour in their shot so fast*
  *From behind and before*
*That man after man is shot down and breathes his last*
  *Every man lies dead in his gore.*
    *E. E. Hale:* Ballad of Bloody Brook

The war began with a surprise attack on Swansea on June 24, 1675. Houses were burned, cattle were stolen, and eight settlers killed. The foot soldiers of Plymouth and Boston were promptly mustered for a punitive expedition against Philip's home settlement at Mt. Hope near Bristol, Rhode Island. The Middlesex troop of horse were called out and Thomas Goble, Daniel Dean, and Ebenezer Prout rode off from Concord. The Indians were apparently cornered on a peninsula in Narragansett Bay, but during the night they escaped across the water. The Boston troops returned after July 18.

Meanwhile, the Nipmuck Indians near Brookfield were being urged to keep their ancient treaties of friendship with the English, but word came through that Philip was corrupting them. The Governor and his Assistants in Boston then ordered Captain Thomas Wheeler of Concord to escort Captain Hutchinson, who was commissioned by them to treat with the sachems of the Nipmucks. The troop of horse made a reassuring sight as they jangled off. Since not everyone had a suitable mount, only the more prosperous farmers joined the horse troop. Among these were the big proprietors in the southeast part of town, the Gobles and Deans, who now owned the Stow land (originally Mrs. Biggs's), and Ebenezer Prout who had bought of Peter Bulkeley's son in London the Bulkeley grant south of Flint's Pond, and the Billings family who lived between Prout and the river, south of Walden Pond, and ran a mill on the north branch of Halfway Brook. Thomas Goble and Daniel Dean had already ridden off to Rhode Island, so Stephen Goble took his father's place on the Brookfield expedition.

The troop spent the first night in Sudbury and during the next three days got up to Brookfield after making several detours to visit Indian settlements; these they found deserted.

At Brookfield they found the settlers hopeful. They met some Indians who agreed to a further parley the next day on Quabaug plain, three miles from the settlement. The company rode out, but found no Indians at the agreed place. An argument ensued: should this be considered a failure of the attempt at peace or should the company look further for the Indians? They went on toward the head of Wickaboag Pond. Suddenly, as the narrow path skirted a hillside, they were fired on, eight were killed and five wounded, including Captain Wheeler and his son. By keeping to open meadows, they managed to get back to the partially fortified tavern in Brookfield where the Indians besieged them. Lieutenant Simon Davis of Concord took over the command and tried to get off a messenger.

On the third attempt, Ephraim Curtis of Sudbury got away at night. He found help at Marlborough. Major Simon Willard, with forty-six soldiers and five friendly Indian guides, hastened to the rescue. Meanwhile, the Indians used several ingenious methods to set the garrison house on fire, creeping up to place hay against the walls, shooting arrows tipped with flaming tow, and pushing a flaming barrel on wheels along from a distance with poles. Rain was the only salvation of the besieged troopers. Outside, the savages howled and paraded the mutilated bodies of their dead victims. At Willard's approach, they burned every vacant house and then melted away into the forest. Brookfield was abandoned, but Captain Wheeler came back to Concord with the other wounded to tell and retell his story. The Wheelers, father and son, died of their wounds within the year.

An attempt was made to separate the friendly Christian Indians from the wild savages, and some were brought in to Deer Island in Boston Harbor. Others were brought to Concord and entrusted to John Hoar, who built a workshop and stockade for them next to his own house, which is now known as Orchard House. This caused a furor in Concord. Many considered the Christian Indians just spies and informers. The town defenses were in a precarious state. By December, a second troop of horse had been raised to go toward Narragansett Bay under Captain Prentice, drawing away more men.

During the autumn of 1675 after the Brookfield fight, the Connecticut Valley Indians joined Philip. On September 1, Deerfield was attacked; on September 2, Northfield burned; on September 3, Captain Beers was ambushed near Northfield and the Captain and twenty men were killed. On September 12, the teamsters who were evacuating Deerfield and Hadley were ambushed at Bloody Brook, where eighty were killed. Captain Moseley retreated to Springfield with his foot company, which had been recruited from the jails and waterfront of Boston, but on September 26, West Springfield was destroyed and on October 5, Hadley was burned. In the east, after Swansea, six were killed at Mendon in July, while at work in the fields. In Lancaster, one Sunday in August, eight men were picked off one by one by Indians, who immediately disappeared. Now the authorities decided to raise a large number of soldiers to attack the Narragansett Indians in their winter quarters near Wickford, Rhode Island, before they could join Philip who, they heard, had gone toward Albany to get ammunition from the Dutch or aid from the Mohawks. The Indian braves were not on hand for the Narragansett fight. On December 19, the English troops surrounded the fort, set it afire and slaughtered all the Indians left there—the old men, women, and children. Daniel Dean, Thomas Goble, and Nathaniel Billings of Concord took part in this engagement and the latter was wounded.

The foot soldiers came north through the forest, driving the war parties of Indians ahead of them while the troops of horse took the direct road back to Boston. The foot soldiers had a terrible experience during that winter march. No supplies reached them, and storms left two or three feet of snow on the ground. During the slow advance, the Concord men—Samuel Hartwell, Ebenezer Prout, and Daniel Goble— must often have thought with envy of those Indian women safely housed in John Hoar's stockade in Concord with food and fuel supplied by the foresight and charity of the English. When they reached home, their "hungry March" was described in all its horror until it became a by-word for years after for hunger, cold, and lurking danger.

*The morning lifts in fury as they come with torch in hand*
  *And howl about the houses in the shrunken frontier town,*
*Our garrisons hold steady as the flames by breezes fanned*
  *Disclose the painted demons, fierce and cunning, lithe and brown.*
    *Wallace Rice:* The Sudbury Fight

As the Indians came north, there were more victims. Just over the Framingham line from Sudbury, Thomas Eames's house was burned and his wife and children slain. Then the Indians attacked the Shepard family near Lake Nagog, killing Isaac Shepard and taking his sister, Mary, a prisoner. She is said to have stolen a horse during the night and made her escape to Concord where her mother's family, the Smedleys, lived. Isaac's brother-in-law, John Smedley, had been killed at Quabaug (Brookfield). His mother was Sarah Goble, sister of Daniel Goble and of Mary Goble, Daniel Dean's wife, so the Gobles had a near acquaintance with this tragedy.

On February 10, Lancaster was again attacked and many were killed or taken prisoner. Among the captives was the minister's wife Mrs. Rowlandson, who later wrote a book about her experiences. Her maiden name was White and her sister had married a Concord Hosmer. About sunrise, she heard the noise of guns and looked out and saw the smoke of several houses burning. In those houses only one or two escaped, the others were quickly killed or taken prisoner. The Indians soon surrounded the Rowlandson house. Hiding behind the hill, upon whose edge the house stood, or in the barn, they fired at the house and quickly wounded three of the men who were sheltered there. After two hours, they succeeded in setting fire to the house. Out dashed a defender and quenched the blaze, but soon a second fire was started and then the women and children ventured to the door. They were met by a hail of bullets. Mrs. Rowlandson and the child of six in her arms were wounded. There were six watchdogs in the garrison, usually ready to attack any lurking Indian, but they now refused to stir. The fire increased and soon all were forced to the door. A wounded man, Mrs. Rowlandson's brother-in-law, fell, and the Indians with shouts and jeers, were upon him, stripping off his clothes and taking his scalp. Her little nephew was wounded and then knocked on the head. Her sister-in-law was killed but Mrs. Rowlandson herself was seized and told she would not be hurt if she would go along with them. Then she watched the slaughter of all their cattle, and, what seemed most sinful to her, the reckless waste of it. Twenty-four people were captured and twelve killed. Just one escaped from that garrison to take the alarm back to Concord.

Concord raised fifteen foot soldiers, including Daniel Goble and his nephew Stephen Goble, for scouting duty. They arrived at Lancaster in time to bury the mutilated bodies of the men, women, and children. Mrs. Rowlandson's brother buried his own wife without recognizing her body. Some of the inhabitants of Lancaster were in other garrison houses and had beaten off the Indian attacks. They now came back to Concord for safety. The Wilders went to live east of the river with the Dean, Goble, or Billings families. There were three young men in the Wilder family, Nathaniel, Jonathan, and Thomas, Jr. Jacob Farrar's widow came back to Concord where her father, George Hayward, lived. She apprenticed her son, George, to the Gobles and he later bought their farm near the Wayland boundary. Thus the Gobles learned at first hand the horrors of Indian warfare and when the captives were ransomed and brought back to Concord they learned more. Widow Kettle and Widow Devens came in later in the summer to live here. Mrs. Rowlandson was ransomed in May and some of her children were recovered from tribes in Rhode Island and New Hampshire. She stopped in Concord with her sister when John Hoar brought her in. He was the only person who could be found to effect the ransom. The Indians knew him as a trader, but they gave him some anxious moments as he arrived at the rendezvous, Redemption Rock in Lancaster, firing their guns above and beside him.

Mrs. Rowlandson was asked about the Christian Indians and about the part Indian women played in the cruelty to prisoners. It was the Indian women who had starved her, she said. As to the Christian Indians, she said:

Those seven that were killed at Lancaster the summer before upon a Sabbath day, and the one that was afterward killed upon a week day, were slain and mangled in a barbarous manner by Marlborough's praying Indians.

One day she was begging for food:

Then one of the company drew his sword and told me he would run me through. Mine eyes have afterwards seen that fellow walking up and down in Boston under the appearance of a friendly Indian, and several others of the like cut.

When the time came to send a message about her ransom to Boston:

. . . it was a praying Indian that wrote the letter for them. There was another praying Indian, who when he had done all the mischief that he could, betrayed his own father into the English's hands, thereby to purchase his own life. Another praying Indian was at Sudbury fight though as he deserved, he was afterwards hanged for it. There was another praying Indian, when they went to Sudbury fight, went with them and his squaw with him with her papoose at her back. Before they went to that fight they got a company together to powwow.

*They fell upon us in the field*
  *And by the cradle head*
*And they were lucky who died the first*
  *For they were quickly dead.*
    *S. V. Benet:* Western Star

While Mrs. Rowlandson was still in captivity, a group of Concord men went over to reinforce the Marlborough garrison. In that month of March, 1676, Groton was plundered and all but the four garrison houses burned. On March 26, sixteen houses were burned at Marlborough. Every available man was sent scouting through the woods, but they never found the guilty Indians. The council had passed an order on August 30, 1675: "That any Indians found more than a mile from the center of their villages, except in the company of the English or on service, the English are at liberty to shoot them down or arrest them." Two such groups were found and brought in to Marlborough. Now in March, the authorities allowed some of the Indians at Deer Island to go out as scouts. Two of them claimed that the Indians at Marlborough were their families. Major Savage ordered them cared for, but the women of Marlborough rioted, in an attempt to kill the Indian women.

Over in Concord, dissatisfaction with the Christian Indians living at John Hoar's mounted until one Sunday Captain Moseley was invited over from Marlborough with his hard-bitten veterans of the Deerfield campaign. He packed up all the Indians on his own authority over John Hoar's protest and took them in to Boston where the Council put them on Deer Island. Though he acted contrary to official orders, public opinion was so heated that the Council did not dare to reprove

Old Minot house, Lexington Road. The frame of this house was built by John Hoar and used as a stockade for the Christian Indians in 1676.

him. After a successful search for Biblical precedents, these poor Indians were sold into slavery.

On April 20, a large body of Indians was reported just west of Concord headed for Sudbury. Ten men went over from Concord next morning to help Sudbury. They went on the east side of the flooding river. Seeing in the meadows some Indian women engaged in a pow-wow they crept up, as they thought, unobserved. They had been lured into ambush, and all were killed. The Indians then crossed to the west side of the river and attacked the English in the Haines garrison house all day. Captain Wadsworth and his men, marching over from Marl-borough, were ambushed and slain to a man. All the unprotected houses west of the river were looted and burned, including John Brewers'. He was Daniel Goble's wife's father. Daniel and Stephen Goble were both in active service during this period of Concord's greatest danger. Most of the scouting was completely frustrating be-cause the Indians were so superior at surprise attacks and escaped so readily through the woods. The names of the eight known dead from Concord are James Hosmer, John Barnes, Samuel Potter, Daniel

Comy, Joseph Buttrick, David Curry, Josiah Wheeler, and William Hayward. The next morning reinforcements came and spent the day burying the dead. Bodies of five Concord men were found in the high water on the meadow and brought by canoe to the bridge-foot in Sudbury to be buried. Thirty-six bodies were buried in one grave on the hill where Captain Wadsworth was killed.

The Indians now split up into small groups. It was time to plant corn, but small parties continued to make raids. On May 12, cattle were destroyed at Hatfield. June 3, Indian women who were not supposed to be out of custody were captured near Concord and locked up in the town jail. Only the very old men and the very young were left in town and they did not relish the job of guarding the women. Others feared that if they were released they would report how lightly Concord was defended. They did escape after ten days and Concord's dismay is reflected in a letter from Constable John Heywood to Governor Leverett on June 13, 1676.

Inasmuch as there has been a sad accident befallen us through the occasion of negligent persons that had trust imposed to them to keep sentry over three old squaws and one papoose; these watchmen fell all asleep, and in the meantime the squaws made their escape, which may produce a great deal of damage to us that are resident in Concord, because we are afraid that they are acquainted with the condition of our town and what quantity of men are gone out. I hope your Honor will send us more strength to support us from our enemies, for we are in daily fear that they will make an assault upon the town.

This was the background of fear and revenge in the hearts of Daniel Goble and his nephew Stephen, of Daniel Hoar and of Nathaniel Wilder as they scouted through the Concord woods on August 7. The presence of Indian women on Hurtleberry hill[1] might be to lure them into ambush as their friends had been lured three months and a half before, just a couple of miles up the river in Sudbury. These women might be spying to see whether any of the outlying houses were unprotected and could be looted and burned. According to last year's law, they could be arrested or shot on sight. Arrest just meant more trouble as had been proved in June. There were dead relatives to avenge. In the sudden surprise of finding three Indian women and three children on the hill, all were killed.

[1] I believe that Hurtleberry hill is the hill rising on the east side of Fairhaven Bay in Lincoln near the old Dean farm, now called Mount Misery.

Goble farm house, later owned by Farrar, near the old Sudbury bound, on Wayland Road, Lincoln.

From the safe vantage of Boston, it was now seen that the war was shifting toward Maine and New Hampshire. Many small groups of Massachusetts Indians sent in messages pledging peace and friendship and some in authority felt that peace could be made if the Indians were promised equal treatment before the law. On August 11, in Maine, Falmouth was burned, but on August 12, Philip himself was killed in Rhode Island and that ended the war to the west and south.

With this good news, the attitude in Boston shifted. One of the murdered squaws was the wife of Andrew Pittimee, who had been one of Major Savage's most loyal guides. Then Jethro, another loyal Indian, brought in his own father, who had been accused of the Eames murders in Framingham. Now, it was argued, if he is to be hung, we must mete out the same punishment to white men who murder Indian women. An indictment was drawn up against Stephen and Daniel Goble, Nathaniel Wilder, and Daniel Hoar. They were promptly arrested, tried, and found guilty. The Reverend Mr. Rowlandson attended them in gaol, and wrote and witnessed their wills. Stephen Goble was the first to be made an example of. On a cloudy and raw day in September, Stephen Goble was hanged and with him three Indians ". . . for firing Eames his house and murder." All Boston turned

Nathaniel Billings house, Lincoln, later owned by Nathaniel Baker and Charles Francis Adams. (Photograph by Harriette M. Forbes.)

out to see the spectacle including Samuel Sewell who has left a description of it. "Mr. Mighil prayed. Four others sat on the gallows, two men and two impudent women, one of which at least, laughed on the gallows." She was there to be whipped for adultery. The Hangman read the record which was the same for all four men, except for their names:

Stephen Goble of Concord, thou art indicted by the name of Stephen Goble for not having the fear of God before thy eyes and being instigated by the devil, with others thy complices, at or on the seventh day of August last, near Hurtleberry hill in the woods in the bounds of Concord, or there or thereabouts, did murder and kill three Indian women and three Indian children, contrary to the grace of our sovereign Lord the King, his Crown and Dignity, the Law of God and of this jurisdiction. Also the libel and evidence in the case were presented to the jury and remain on file with the records of this court. The jury brought in their verdict: they found him guilty and accordingly sentence of death was pronounced against him and that he should go from hence to the place from whence he came and thence to the gallows and there be hanged till thou beest dead and the Lord be merciful to thy soul.

I Comit my soule to God who gaue it, & my body to the dust from whence it was taken. And as for my Estate It is my will and that Hannah my wife together with my brother Thomas Goble be Joynt Executors. & that my deare wife fortwithmioned be in pease & full possession of my House & Roome & Effects for the comfort & maintenance of hir & our foure childeron duing the time of hir widdowhood, & in case shee change hir con- dition by marriage, or in state of hir widdow-hood & changed by death my will is that the estate be Reserued for & in time Distributed Conandiently amongst my foure childeron that is Daniel & John, Hannа & Elis: Goble acording to the discretion of my brother Thomas Goble or as also of John Bur- on & Jacob Moore whom I appoynt overseers of this my Last will, & Esta- ment allwayes to be and also that the thirds of my estate being in case shee remayne that Hom is he for my beloued wife duing hir naturell life & then to returne to my childeron.

This to my Last will, witnes my hand

The marke of

Daniel + Goble

In presence of us
Joseph Rowlandson

Thomas + Joy
his marke

Thomas Goble

Daniel Goble's will witnessed by Reverend Joseph Rowlandson.

A week later, Daniel Goble, too ill to walk, was drawn upon a cart to the place of execution and hanged in company with five Indians. Perhaps wondering whether Indians were made like white men, Sewell tried to find out.

Sept. 22: Spent the day from 9 in the M with Mr. Brakenbury, Mr. Thomson, Butler, Hooper, Cragg, Pemberton dissecting the middle-most of the Indian executed the day before. X taking the heart in his hand, affirmed it to be the stomach. I spent 18s, 6d in ale, 6d in Madiera wine, and 6d I gave to the maid.

Dr. Brakenbury was the Sewell family physician.

Sept. 26 Tuesday: Sagamore Sam goes and Daniel Goble is drawn on a cart upon bed-clothes to the execution. One-eyed John, Maliompe, Sagamore of Quabaug, General at Lancaster etc., Jethro, the father walk to the gallows. Note. One-eyed John accuses Sagamore John to have fired the first at Quabaug and killed Captain Hutchinson.

This Jethro had been present at the purchase of Concord from the Indians, and was a Christian convert.

*For the Indian there is no safety but in the plow. A race of hunters can never withstand the inroads of a race of husbandmen. Even if the hunter is brave enough to resist, his game is timid and has already fled. We have forgotten the Indians' hostility as well as their friendship.*
   *Henry Thoreau:* Journal I 446

Now, however, the lust for hanging had been somewhat sated. Daniel Hoar had powerful friends, since his father was noted as a champion of the Christian Indians and had risked his life to ransom Mrs. Rowlandson. Nathaniel Wilder, too, was a parishioner of Rowlandson's and his young wife was from Sudbury. Neither the Sudbury nor the Lancaster people had any reason to condemn the killing of Indians. King Philip's head had been brought in and news had come of the final annihilation of the tribe of Weetamoe, Squaw Sachem of the Pocassets. About the seventh of August, a small company went out from Taunton and captured the remainder of her tribe. She was drowned in trying to escape, and when her body was found, the head was severed and exhibited in triumph in the streets of Taunton. Thus what was a hanging matter in Concord was a military triumph in Taunton on the same day. The war was now over in Massachusetts. The Court was ready on October 11, 1676, to listen to a petition:

> Upon the humble petition of Daniel Hoar and Nathaniel Wilder presented to this Court, acknowledging the justice of this Court and begging pardon for their lives, the Court have granted their petition and accordingly do remit the sentence of death passed upon them and order, that they pay prison charges and ten pounds apiece money, half towards the charge of witnesses, to be paid to the treasurer of the country, and the other half to Andrew Pittimee and Swagon, the Indians prosecuting against them, on payment whereof they are discharged.

There is one more item on the record—the payment of costs in "the Gobley case" to the witnesses: Daniel Dean, William Hunt, Thomas Wilder, Jonathan Wilder, Stephen Muttock, and Thomas Goble, Jr., amounting to five pounds, four shillings.

A few years later, every soldier who had taken part in the Narragansett campaign, when the Indian stockade had been burned and all the Indian women and children slain, was awarded a soldier's bonus, a share of land in one of the new "Narragansett" townships laid out in central New England, on the land wrested from the Indians. Daniel Goble's son Daniel inherited and sold his father's right in what was later called Voluntown. Daniel Senior's widow had forfeited the inheritance because she married Ephraim Roper in 1677, and moved to Lancaster. There she and her second husband were killed twenty years later in a new Indian war. Roper had already suffered at the hands of the Indians. His first wife and baby daughter had been killed in the Rowlandson garrison in 1676.

Daniel Hoar married Mary Stratton in 1677 and had eight sons and two daughters, born in the old house on the Bay Road, and they in turn have numerous distinguished descendants. One of them was the leading lawyer at the Middlesex County bar in 1812. Squire Samuel Hoar won a pardon for a murder offense for his client, Alpheus Livermore, guilty of killing an Indian, on the plea that an Indian was a wild creature, so his killing could not be considered murder. Some of Daniel Hoar's other descendants settled on his bonus land, the "Narragansett grant," in what is now the town of Westminster, Massachusetts.

Nathaniel Wilder returned to Lancaster and lived as one of its most honored founders, only to die in the Indian raid of 1705.

Thus the example of fair dealing made to the savages by the hanging of the two Gobles had no permanent salutary effect on relations with the Indians. Equally, the terrorism, of which the Hurtleberry hill murders were a part, had no permanent restraining effect.

During King Philip's War, 600 settlers had been killed, 600 houses burned and twelve towns destroyed. The summer must have been a hard one in Concord, with most of the men away on military duty and farm chores left to the women and children. There was constant anxiety and when there was an alarm, all gathered in a house in the neighborhood which had been designated as a garrison because of its size and location and the nearness of the well.[2] Shattuck says the chosen garrison houses were the house next to the south burying-place bought from George Wheeler by Jonathan Prescott, who had taken refuge here from Lancaster; the house at Meriam's Corner; the house on Bedford road just over the present Bedford line, a second in present-day Bedford; one at John Hosmer's (opposite the entrance to Emerson Hospital); one at John Flint's beyond the north bridge, and one at Silas Holden's in Nine Acre Corner.

We can be sure that the fate of Stephen and Daniel Goble was the subject of frequent debate in Concord, though curiously, History is silent on the subject.

It is often remarked that our ancestors had unusual powers of endurance to sit through the long church services. The service was varied because they stood for prayers and for hymns. Official notices were read including marriage intentions, making it a center for news, and in the sermons any unusual happening in the town or in the colony was described and a lesson drawn from it, because they all firmly believed that every event was ordered by Divine Providence. Thus the slight earthquakes of 1638 and 1653 and the severe ones of 1717 and 1755 were plainly meant as warnings but it was harder to explain the ice-storm of 1659:

Near the town of Concord that which is somewhat rare and therefore to be reckoned among remarkable accidents. In the month of February, it having rained a great part of the night, it froze extremely so that many limbs were broken off from many trees by the weight of the ice caused by the sudden freezing of the rain upon the boughs. It was somewhat formidable to hear the crackings made a good part of the night by the falling of so much wood (thousands of cords) as was by that means occasioned.[3]

---

[2] Because the first settlers did not fear the Indians, no house in Concord had been *built* as a garrison. The nearest *fort* was at Littleton. It was later Walter Powers' house. If one of these houses had an overhanging second story, it was simply because the carpenter who built it had learned in England to build houses that way.

[3] Increase Mather's *Illustrious Providences*, Boston, 1684.

Thomas Pellett's kitchen where his dinner was spoiled. (Photograph by Keith Martin.)

Mrs. Mary (Chandler) Heald whose husband had settled in present-day Carlisle near the Acton line refused to move back to town during the Indian wars. She said her husband and sons could go if they wished but as for her, she would not leave her own house. She was never called on to shoot an Indian but she is said to have shot a bear, an exploit which has lost nothing in the re-telling.

*There is a sense of terror in the air and apparitions of things*
*horrible are seen by many; from the sky above us the*
*stars fall and beneath us the earth quakes.*
   *Henry Wadsworth Longfellow:* The New England Tragedy

After the aridity of Edward Bulkeley, Mr. Estabrook was more inspiring, encouraging his hearers to think of themselves as a chosen people who had come into this uncultivated wilderness not to gain great estates but to promote religion. He seems to have anticipated *Walden* by one hundred and fifty years when he added: "indeed the shortest way to be rich is not by enlarging our estates, but by contracting our desires."

Thomas Pellet in 1678 was sexton of the meetinghouse. He lived on a small lot between the Bay Road and the burying place which had been given to his wife, Mary, by her father, Thomas Dane. It was a convenient place for children to wait while their parents attended the communion service. One Sunday they tried a practical joke and their parents were brought into court where eight of them were fined. The court record tells the story:

For spoiling Pellet's dinner.

Thomas Pellet and Mary his wife appearing in court do upon their oaths say and attest that the last Sabbath day was a fortnight, some young persons being at their house at noontime when the Sacrament was administering, their pot being boiling over their fire, when they came to take of the same, they found it much abused, and that tobacco smaller and greater pieces they found therein, whereby the provisions therein was made unfit to be eaten, and that some of their children tasting of some little thereof, became sick and vomited. Also they both add that when they came to take notice of their pot, they observed that Mary Power, Hannah Stannup and Peter Rice did laugh and nicker.

# Chapter III   Division

*Let us be thankful that we have our titles to our houses and
lands confirmed to us. Surely it was not to gain great estates,
but for the promotion of religion that made our pious
predecessors come into this uncultivated wilderness.*
    Rev. Joseph Estabrook: Election Sermon 1705

The leading citizen of Concord in midcentury was Peter Bulkeley,
Esq., son of Edward, the second minister. Born in 1641, he graduated from Harvard in 1660 and married Rebecca, only daughter of
Lieutenant Joseph Wheeler, in 1667. He built a house across the millpond from his father-in-law which is still standing at 25 Lexington
Road. Its paneling is more elaborate than that of most Concord houses
of the period and artisans from the Bay were employed in the building. Peter Bulkeley, Esq., represented the town in the General Court
and in 1676 was chosen Speaker. He was also Major of the Middlesex
militia and in 1677 was chosen a magistrate or member of the Court
of Assistants. He was sent to London in 1676 to represent the colony
in settling the Mason and Gorges claims. He found it easy to fit into
fashionable London, where his cousin had been Lord Mayor. Though
the courts ultimately decided against Massachusetts, the Gorges heirs
were bought out so that the colony added Maine to its territory. When
James II at last revoked the charter and sent over Andros as governor
in 1685, Peter Bulkeley became a member of his council, and was
severely condemned by his fellow townsmen for helping the man they
considered a tyrant. He died May 24, 1688, leaving his affairs in disorder. The papers in the Registry of Probate concerning the settlement
of his estate give us some knowledge of how business was conducted.
He had both a Negro and an Indian servant. There was a bill owed to
Jonathan Prescott for his services as a physician and also as a blacksmith. Prescott had been a leading citizen of Lancaster before the
Indians destroyed it. He had bought here from George Wheeler the
house next to the south burying-place and added Edward Bulkeley's

Peter Bulkeley, Esq. Portrait by Kneller. Signature is from a deed to Wayside. He was a member of His Majesty's Council. (Courtesy of the Concord Antiquarian Society.)

Peter Bulkeley, Esq., house, later owned by Reuben Brown. First home of the Concord Antiquarian Society.

land further up Main Street with much outlying land, and soon became one of the town's largest landholders. He later collected his bill in full from the Bulkeley estate, because he married Peter Bulkeley's widow and his son, Jonathan, Jr., married Peter's only daughter, Rebecca. Peter Bulkeley's estate had an account with James Russell, a merchant in Charlestown. The latter imported for him a sword, a periwig, and books, and credited him with onions and a horse exported to the West Indies, among other products. Major Bulkeley was also interested in the ironworks. The proprietors of the Saugus iron furnace had undertaken a second iron smelter at the falls of the Assabet. Started in 1660, the business had failed by 1701 when James Russell, this same merchant, liquidated the company, selling off sixteen hundred acres in Concord, Concord Village, and in Sudbury. Bog iron ore may still be found in our meadows underlying the surface peat, but the quality, quantity, or the price paid did not meet expectations. Purchasers of the ironworks land were Samuel Wright, John Barker, Jr., Samuel Jones, Ephraim Jones, and Jonathan Knight. Hezekiah Usher backed an attempt to mine copper at Nine Acre Corner before 1700 and built a bridge and a house for the workmen. The bridge had disappeared by 1740. The bridge was, I believe, halfway between the present Lee's bridge and Fairhaven Bay, just below the then mouth of Halfway Brook at a spot called phonetically Knakers (nine acres) Point in a later deed. A road still runs to the river here, kept open for hauling ice until 1900.

A lime kiln was built in the north part of town in the Estabrook woods, that region of rugged pastures once called the twenty score. Lime for Watertown's west meetinghouse was bought here and of course it was used with the Concord bricks for Concord chimneys.

The old quarry and Thomas Estabrook's house cellar may still be seen.

The revocation of the Massachusetts charter in 1685 and the appointment of a governor by King James II precipitated a crisis. For fifty years the colony had developed almost without interference. The most precious privileges of individual land ownership and the single religion of Puritanism were now threatened. The King demanded through Governor Andros that a church be found in Boston for Episcopalian services; since there was no empty church, he ordered the Old South congregation to wait every Sunday in the street until a prior Episcopal service was dismissed inside the meetinghouse. Simon Willard's son, Samuel, was minister of this Boston church and he did not enjoy the sharing. All land titles were declared null and void unless they were registered with the Andros government. In Concord, only Rebecca, widow of Peter Bulkeley, and her father, Joseph Wheeler, registered their land and paid the heavy fee. The original charter provided that only church members in full communion could vote in colony affairs although no distinction was made in town affairs. This rule was now to be enforced and it was found that Concord had only seventeen church members to thirty-five freeholders who were not in full communion. The General Court, already in revolt against the abrogation of the charter, voted on March 21, 1689, to make the thirty-five freemen, without any religious qualification.

Now too they gathered those witnesses still living who were present at the purchase from the Indians and they made sworn depositions about the purchase in order to strengthen their land titles. One of the deponents was the Christian Indian, Jethro, who had turned in his father, Jethro, Sr., thirteen years before for the Eames murder. His testimony locates the site of the bargain as the house of Peter Bulkeley *which now Captain Timothy Wheeler liveth in.*[1]

An Indian title was a poor thing to depend on, but Andros went much farther. He suspended the right of *habeas corpus* and took away from town meetings their long-established right of taxation. When Ipswich, led by its minister, John Wise, protested, he was imprisoned, fined, and suspended from the ministry in complete disregard of colony law and custom. On April 4, 1689, news came to Boston that James II had fled to France. When this news reached Concord, the militia assembled under Captain John Heald and marched to Boston where, with the other train bands, they arrested Andros, locked him up on Castle Island, and restored to the office the eighty-seven-year-old Simon Bradstreet. The order for Andros's arrest was signed by Ebenezer Prout, a Concord man who was Clerk of the House of Representatives. William and Mary soon issued a new charter to the province of Massachusetts which confirmed the old land titles and once more allowed local governments to impose taxation but allowed the King to appoint the Governor. Episcopalians now had their own King's Chapel in Boston and the colony was now called a province.

---

[1] Since we have recorded transfers from Timothy Wheeler to his daughter, Rebecca Minot, and from her to her Minot descendants, this proves beyond question that Peter Bulkeley's house and Jethro's oak were side by side in the town square and the bronze tablet placed on Lowell Road in 1885 is misplaced, although undoubtedly on Bulkeley land.

Now the subjects of debate became civil liberty, keeping the judiciary independent, and keeping their time-honored right to tax themselves.

*Philip Reed said that Mr. Bulkeley was called by none but a*
*company of blockheads who followed the plowtail and was*
*not worthy to carry Mr. Estabrook's books after him.*
    Charles H. Walcott: Concord in the Colonial Period

Reverend Joseph Estabrook, born in England but a graduate of Harvard in 1664, had come to Concord in 1665 as colleague to Edward Bulkeley and succeeded him in 1694. To his influence may be attributed the fact that Concord never shared the witchcraft delusion nor suffered under the dominance of the clergy. His wife was Mary, daughter of Captain Hugh Mason of Watertown. They had six children, one of whom, Benjamin, was to be the first minister in Lexington after that parish was organized from the west part of Cambridge in 1691. Another son, Joseph, also settled in Lexington where his family became prominent. The Concord minister's brother, Thomas, as has been said, married Sarah Temple, daughter of that Richard Temple who had bought the William Spencer property in Concord. Thomas Estabrook settled in the north part of town. Reverend Joseph Estabrook came to Concord just when the first meetinghouse was abandoned for a larger one with a bell turret surmounting a beveled roof, built nearer the milldam than the first. When he died in 1711 the town had just completed its third meetinghouse, with an English roof, a barnlike structure without a tower but large enough for the provincial Congress to meet in sixty-four years later. The old meetinghouse became the town house after whatever was useful of it was moved to the present site of Monument Hall, and the bell continued to be hung in its turret. Mr. Estabrook lived in the Nathaniel Billings house at 48 Walden Street and his sons sold it to his successor in 1711.

There was a real contest in the choice of his successor. Benjamin Prescott had just graduated from Harvard in 1709 and had not yet found a parish. It was customary to offer a settlement to a new minister, that is, money enough to pay for a house as well as a stated salary. Captain Prescott offered to pay his son's settlement and declined to serve in his usual post as moderator of the town meeting where the choice was to be made, in fairness to the other candidates. Edward Holyoke, later president of Harvard, and John Whiting were also candidates. Whiting's mother was a daughter of Honorable Thomas Danforth, once deputy governor of the colony, and Thomas Whiting inherited some wealth from her. He also was connected with the Bulkeley family. Since graduating from Harvard in 1700 he had been a fellow and tutor there. He was a man, says Shattuck, of wealth, learning, influence and talents. His wife, Mary Cotton, was granddaughter of Reverend John Cotton of Boston and great-granddaughter of Governors Simon Bradstreet and Thomas Dudley. A meeting of church members gave him a call and then the town meeting concurred and fixed his settlement at one hundred pounds and his salary at the same amount. The town paid the expenses of his ordination which drew a great many delegates, for the ministers by this time were a closely knit group, many related to each other by marriage, sharing the same education and meeting frequently at such occasions as this ordination. Judge Samuel Sewell, now a Boston deacon, rode out in a borrowed calash, leaving Boston at five A.M. and arriving five hours later. Benjamin Prescott soon got a call to Salem Village where he lived to be ninety and was a distinguished and eloquent patriot. Three of his grandchildren lived in New Haven where one granddaughter married Roger Sherman, a signer of the Declaration of Independence. Her mother had been Rebecca Minot of Concord and her brother, James Prescott, married Rebecca Barrett of Concord. Roger Sherman's daughter married Samuel Hoar of Concord in 1812.

*May 14, 1712.    Mr. Whiting preached from I Tim.3*
*(A bishop must be blameless, vigilant, sober, given*
*   to hospitality, apt to teach.)*
*   Samuel Sewell: Diary*

The choice of John Whiting had far-reaching consequences for it began fifty years of dissension in the church. There is nothing of the dissatisfaction on the record, however, for the next twenty years during which the Whitings had four sons and four daughters. No sermon of John Whiting's is extant. Mr. Whiting's trouble, which appears to have become most serious after the first Mrs. Whiting's death in 1731, was that he often had such a severe hangover on Sunday mornings that he was unable to preach. Often the schoolmaster, Timothy Minot—an ordained Harvard graduate—was sent for to take his place, and if the town paid the substitute, questions arose about deducting the amount from Mr.

Whiting's salary. Ministers of other churches were called in consultation and in the end Mr. Whiting agreed to resign and allow the town to call another minister. This time, in 1738, Daniel Bliss of Connecticut and of Yale College was called by a vote of seventy to thirty-two, and he turned out to be a crusading evangelist. Many in the parish and some liberal ministers in surrounding towns objected to his theology and his revivalist style. He held outdoor mass meetings, sometimes several in a week, and sinners became hysterical. The British evangelist George Whitfield came here to preach and reported that the hearers were sweetly melted down. "Brother Bliss broke into floods of tears and we had a sweet refreshing in our way to the heavenly Canaan," wrote Whitfield.

A sermon preached by Bliss in 1755 in Concord gives a view of Hell just as vivid as Jonathan Edwards's more famous sermons. "The torments of the damned would never cease," he thundered.

Now they will be in blackness of darkness where their companions will be damned devils, their tormentors. The evils here inflicted . . . under which they could by no means exist were they not continued by the same Power. God supports them under the weight of his wrath, neither will his eye spare nor his heart pity, so that when they shall have suffered as many ages as there shall have been moments from the beginning to the end of time, they will be nothing nearer to the end of their torments but will be even then beginning to make their bed in Hell, never to rise therefrom whereby they are crushed and broken beyond all our thoughts.

A group of the more liberal parishioners, who had been friends of Mr. Whiting, found Mr. Bliss's opinions impossible to listen to. More councils were called but they came to no agreement. The dissenters began to have church meetings of their own. The town meeting refused to excuse them from church taxes and refused them permission to meet in the town house. They held their services in a new tavern called the Black Horse which had been built on the corner of Main Street and Sudbury Road. This was a square building built by John Holden, who came to Concord from Weston about this time. John married Mary Jones, whose parents lived across the way. The house later belonged to Judge Nathan Brooks and was moved to Hubbard Street in 1870 to make way for the Library. Among the members of the Black Horse church were Honorable James Minott,[2] the town's wealthiest citizen,

[2] Some members of the Minott family spelled the name with one "t," others with two. As with other family names, there were many variants which are without significance.

Reverend Daniel Bliss from a crayon portrait owned by the First Parish in Concord.

Jonathan Buttrick and Samuel Miles who were deacons; Josiah Hosmer and Ezekiel Miles, the choristers; Stephen Hosmer, Nathaniel Colburn and Charles Prescott, brother of the defeated candidate, Benjamin Prescott. There were twenty members in all.

Peter Bulkeley's daughter, Rebecca, had married Jonathan Prescott, Jr., and after she became a widow in 1729 and Mr. Whiting's wife died in 1731, she married Whiting. Mr. Whiting proved an embarrassing layman in his old church. He first insisted on sitting in the pulpit where he could gaze at friends and enemies during Mr. Bliss's sermon. By this time a few of the wealthier members of the parish had been voted the privilege of building their own pews. These had turned posts and railings, curtains and cushions, and were far more comfortable than the wooden benches where most sat. The town now built an elaborate pew for Mr. Whiting, hiring an out-of-town cabinet maker and paying his board while he installed forty-five bannisters at a cost of three pounds, thirteen shillings. A special town meeting was called on November 27, 1739 ". . . to see what the town will do about Mr. John Whiting's sitting in the pulpit," but some arrangement must have been reached, because the article was dismissed without a vote.

Suitable entertainment for the Bliss ordination cost sixty pounds, most of it paid to the tavern keeper. When Mr. Whiting died in 1751, his friends erected a white marble shaft in the south burying-ground which tells the truth if not the whole truth: "he was a gentleman of singular hospitality and generosity, who never detracted from the character of any man and was a universal lover of mankind."

*And in the extreme difficult seasons of heat and cold, we were ready to say of the Sabbath "Behold what a weariness it is."*
　　Petition of sundry inhabitants of the northeast part of
　　Concord to be set off as a distinct town.

A lasting consequence of the church dissension was the setting-up of separate church services in Bedford in 1725 and a request to be set off as a separate town with part of Billerica, claiming with some justice that besides the long trip to Concord or to Billerica these farmers had the expense of nooning—"refreshing themselves and their families between services." Billerica at first objected, but Concord gave consent and the new town was incorporated September 23, 1729. Farmers along the proposed boundary elected which town to choose. Concord lost a Selectman and deacon in Samuel Meriam and outlying farmers named French, Dean, Fassett, Davis, Cheever, Wooley, Bacon, Colburn, Stearns, Taylor, and Richard Wheeler.

The division of the land in Concord Village was well underway by 1734 and the town of Acton was set off as a separate town in 1735, a true daughter-town since every farm was granted to a Concord resident or the representative of one. Deacon Hunt, for example, owned a pew in Acton Meetinghouse (as well as one in Concord) and left it in his will to the sons who had settled on his land in Acton.

With Lincoln a real struggle took place. A separate parish was asked for several times. The Lincoln meetinghouse was built in 1747 and a church gathered, which included some farmers from Weston and Lexington as well as all those southeast of Walden Pond. The Brooks family on the Bay Road was divided. Reverend William Lawrence was chosen as minister and efforts to be set off as a town continued until the act of incorporation was secured in 1754, not without political bargaining. Governor Shirley had taken a position against dividing towns any further, but he wanted the legislature to build a fort on the Kennebec River so he gave in to Judge Chambers Russell and signed the act separating Lincoln, in exchange for Judge Russell's support in the Kennebec project.

The Lincoln area's leading citizens were the retired merchant James Russell, formerly of Charlestown, and his brother, Chambers, himself representative of Concord in the General Court. He tried repeatedly to get Concord to build a bridge at "Sandy Point" in the Nine Acre Corner area, and in spite of negative votes at Concord town meetings, the General Court ordered one built in 1742. Chambers Russell presented his Concord pew to the town and they were able to sell it at auction for eleven pounds, a poor recompense for the loss of Lincoln.

Carlisle at the same time began petitioning to be set off, and started a separate meeting, on April 19, 1754, suggesting that the Assabet River and the mouth of Ralph's Brook be the boundaries. A substantial number of residents on Barrett's Mill Road and near the river objected and filed their protest with a map which survives in the State Archives as the oldest map of any part of Concord. The whole project of a precinct was given up in 1757, but the separation was finally made in 1780. The boundary line was again determined by the wishes of the individual farmers, the Hodgmans on the River Road electing to be included in Carlisle although surrounded by Concord, and the Kibbes, whose pasture was surrounded by Carlisle, choosing to remain in Concord. The first meetings had been held at Joseph Adams's house and had been attended by Deacon Ephraim Brown of the Concord church. After Bliss's death, when the final separation came, the Adams and Brown farms remained in Concord. Jonathan Buttrick (1695–1767) who had planned to give the land for a Carlisle church was dead by the time a decision was reached and all the Buttrick land remained in Concord. After the separation from Concord in 1780, Carlisle remained a District of Acton until its final independence in 1805.

Reverend Daniel Bliss died in 1764 leaving a son, Daniel, who became a lawyer and was the only Tory in Concord whose property was confiscated in the Revolution. He became a judge in New Brunswick. The minister's son, Thomas Theodore, moved to Brimfield and became an officer in the Revolutionary Army. Samuel, another son, was a British officer to whom an island in the Bay of Fundy was granted

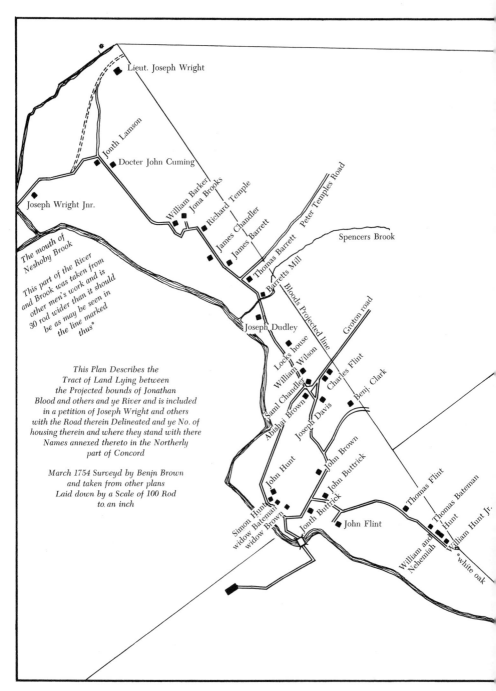

Lieut. Joseph Wright

Jonth Lamson

Docter John Cuming

Joseph Wright Jnr.

William Barker
Jona Brooks
Richard Temple
James Chandler
James Barrett

Peter Temples Road

Thomas Barrett
Spencers Brook

Barretts Mill

The mouth of
Neshoby Brook

This part of the River
and Brook was taken from
other men's work and is
30 rod wider than it should
be as may be seen in
the line marked
thus°

Joseph Dudley

Bloods Projected line

Groton road

Locks house
William Wilson
Charles Flint

This Plan Describes the
Tract of Land Lying between
the Projected bounds of Jonathan
Blood and others and ye River and is included
in a petition of Joseph Wright and others
with the Road therein Delineated and ye No. of
housing therein and where they stand with there
Names annexed thereto in the Northerly
part of Concord

March 1754 Surveyd by Benjn Brown
and taken from other plans
Laid down by a Scale of 100 Rod
to an inch

Saml Chandler
Abishai Brown
Joseph Davis
Benj. Clark

John Hunt
John Brown
John Buttrick

Simon Hunt
widow Bateman
widow Brown
Jonth Buttrick
John Flint

Thomas Flint
Thomas Bateman
Hunt
William and
Nehemiah
William Hunt Jr.
white oak

1754 map of North Quarter.

after the war. The fourth son, Joseph, was an ardent Whig. One daughter married Isaac Hoar who inherited Orchard House; the elder, Phebe, married her father's successor, Reverend William Emerson and later his successor Reverend Ezra Ripley and lived in the old manse until she died at eighty-three, a loving grandmother to her son William's children, Ralph Waldo Emerson and his brothers.

The dissension in the church continued for a while through Mr. Emerson's pastorate focusing on the re-admission to the church of Joseph Lee into full communion, but his supporters lost interest as his Tory opinions became more and more unpopular. Lee finally signed a satisfactory confession of faith. Just before Mr. Emerson left for Ticonderoga in 1776, the church covenant was renewed and he recorded with satisfaction that it was signed by everyone except Timothy Wheeler.

# Chapter IV   Education and Trade

From Autumn frost to April rain
Too long her winter woods complain.
From budding flower to falling leaf
Her summer time is all too brief,
Yet on her rocks and on her sands
And wintry hills, the school-house stands,
And what her rugged soil denies
The harvest of the mind supplies.
    John Greenleaf Whittier: Our State

Harvard College in retrospect appears to us to have been a narrow institution of learning, yet it represented the most enlightened thought of the day. It had a good library, and youth being what it is, the very gathering in Cambridge of sons of the ministers and merchants must have had a broadening effect on the students. Harvard had an important influence on Concord. Year after year, the town meeting would authorize two of the town fathers to go down to the College to arrange for a teacher for the town school. Many a student would interrupt his college course for a year or two to earn money and his influence in the town would extend beyond his pupils to the families where he boarded round. The title "Sir" was given to these Harvard youths, and their presence kept the town from becoming as ingrown and backward as inland small towns were supposed to be. Thus in the first twenty years of the eighteenth century the teachers were Robert Breck, Samuel Burr, Grindall Rawson, Jr., Samuel Parris, Samuel Aspinwall, and Nathaniel Sparhawk, besides the native college youths, Sir Prescott, Sir Timothy Minott, and Sir Samuel Estabrook, who was engaged to help his father in the ministry as well as to teach. When Timothy Minott was engaged in 1712 at the age of nineteen, his father, Captain James Minott, agreed that if ". . . any come for larning exceeding his son's ability the said captain doth agree to instruct them himself in the tongues." Ten years later, after his graduation, Timothy Minott was hired to teach and also to assist Mr. Whiting, "on extraordinary occasions," as the Town Records politely put it. At the same time that this special attention was given to the teaching in the center school, improvements were needed in the outlying schools where elementary classes had been held in private houses. Some schoolhouses were built at the expense of the Quarters and half the school tax was divided among the Quarters. More than one neighborhood school was sometimes needed in a Quarter. The South Quarter had a school at Billings End east of the river before Lincoln was set off, as well as one at Nine Acre Corner, and the North Quarter had a school on Punkatasset as well as another near Barrett's Mill. The East Quarter built a schoolhouse where Virginia Road met the old Bedford Road as well as one on Brooks's Hill. In the seventeenth century women taught reading and writing to the neighbors' children, but with the beginning of the eighteenth century probably few were qualified to teach. In the town records almost all the paid teachers were men, but on the one or two occasions when a woman was paid, the amount was half that allowed a man, or less. Thus in 1740 the town paid Daniel Wheeler "four pounds for his wife's keeping school ten weeks in Billings End in the summer last past." A man would have received a pound and a half a week.

Citizens proposed several times to have the grammar school kept in the outlying areas in turn, but the town denied the request and the upper school remained in the center on land in Monument Square given to the town by Timothy Wheeler (the first) in his will in 1687. The town, however, cut the size of the schoolyard in 1726, selling a house lot to Timothy Minott beyond the school. This house is still standing after being moved to Bedford Street. The Selectmen had charge of the schools except for a certain amount of autonomy which they gradually gave to separate committees in each Quarter.

The Selectmen also had charge of the valuation of estates for tax assessments, committing the list for collection to a constable who sometimes had a deputy in each Quarter. It was so difficult to get anyone to serve as constable that the man who refused to serve was fined as much as five pounds by the town. Gershom Heald had his fine remitted in 1738 on the reasonable plea that he could not read or write. Money from fines was used toward the support of the poor. One sometimes wonders whether certain men were elected constable because of their ability to pay the fine. Practical jokes were not unknown. It became the custom to elect each newly married man a hogreeve. Sometimes a name

Mr. and Mrs. Timothy Minot. Portraits attributed to Smibert and bequeathed by Mary (Brooks) Buttrick to Stedman Buttrick. (Photograph by Henry D. Childs.)

would be proposed for whom no marriage record appeared, and the election would be debated with sly solemnity. The Selectmen were unpaid but met regularly at the newest tavern. In 1707, they met at Jonathan Hubbard's, then with John Holden, Jonathan Prescott, Jonathan Ball, Ephraim Jones, John Holden, Jr., Ebenezer Hubbard, and Thomas Munroe, each of whom was paid for a few successive years for entertaining the Selectmen. Gravel had been taken without permission from the common to widen the milldam so the town sold the land where the Wright Tavern stands to Ephraim Jones ". . . to prevent its further wasting away." He built the tavern in 1747, but soon sold it to Thomas Munroe (1751) and built a larger tavern beyond the south burying-place.

There can be little doubt that drinking increased during this period. Beer and hard cider were everyday drinks in the seventeenth century. Now the importation of molasses, the establishment of distilleries in Medford and elsewhere on the seacoast, and the improvement of roads made rum readily available and it was widely used. Every trade was followed by a drink to seal the bargain. Every gathering from a minister's ordination to a house-raising meant a treat, and soon the records

Timothy Minot house. This house is now on Bedford Street.

show substantial amounts spent, even at a pauper's funeral, for rum. As Henry Thoreau wrote after seeing the frame built to hold eight barrels in the cellar of Stephen Hosmer's house: "the first settlers made preparations to drink a good deal, and they did not disappoint themselves."

Soon after Daniel Bliss's ordination, there was one case, the only one in the records, where Justice Minott collected fines for drunkenness from sundry persons amounting to one pound, ten shillings, and then fined Samuel Willis three pounds, six shillings and eightpence for selling strong drink, the fine to go to the town's poor.

Black Horse Tavern, later used as a residence and post office by John L. Tuttle. Later it was the residence of Judge Nathan Brooks. Beyond it, on the right, is William Parkman's house and store in which he kept the first post office. The Parkman house was later the Thoreau family home.

*The Town Meetings educated the people to self-government.*
*They are to Liberty what primary schools are to science.*
    Senator George F. Hoar: Oration 1885

The care of the poor occupied part of the attention of the Selectmen. The town customarily warned out new residents so that it would not be liable in case these persons ever became public charges and also went to great lengths to collect from other towns in such cases. Several legacies were made to aid the poor. William Halsted, dying in 1645, left to the town five pounds ". . . to be laid out for a cow to be a continual help to such as are in need." When the cow got old she would be turned in for a fresh one, the town paying something to boot, and this continued for a long time, apparently, for in 1698 the Selectmen ordered Stephen Hosmer to deliver a cow to Thomas Pellet, he being in great present want, ". . . which cow is of a black color, a white face with black spots around each eye." As late as 1767, the French family got the town cow. Other bequests for the poor came from time to time. In 1682, Robert Meriam left four pounds in corn for the poor, and when Peter Wright died in 1718 he made the town residuary legatee of a substantial estate after provision for his wife and his apprentices. He was a weaver and was one of the victims of an epidemic. Thomas Brown, the town clerk, records at the end of Book I of the town records:

Whereas the hand of God hath come forth against the inhabitants of Concord in a very awful manner, sending a malign and fatal distemper amongst us whereby there hath been a considerable number of persons of all qualities, sexes and ages that hath been removed from among us by death.

He records the names of those who died in the ten weeks between December 1 and February 20. The next page, in the handwriting of a new clerk, William Wilson, records the deaths of Thomas Brown and of his son, Thomas, Jr., in the same epidemic, in March and April, 1718. Brown had made out and witnessed Peter Wright's will, unaware of contagion. After the receipt of Peter Wright's legacy in 1730, the Selectmen paid out the income of about ten pounds more liberally. This became the Silent Poor Fund to distinguish its recipients from the Town Poor, whose support was a matter of public debate. People were paid for subsisting relatives, even a mother or sister.

The proposal to build a house for the poor was considered several times before it was finally adopted in 1758. The location must have been in dispute because the town then voted ". . . to build the house where people with ease may attend public worship rather than if it were two miles off." Accordingly, it was built on the North Road beyond Captain's Hollow (Court Lane), adjoining John Beatton's orchard.

The period of peace with the Indians after 1677 came to an end with the use after 1700 by the French in Canada of Indian allies in the American extensions of European wars between England and France. The presence of Catholic priests with the Indians during these raids served to reinforce the previous hostility toward that religion. Some of the captives were ransomed and treated kindly by the French in Montreal and Quebec where they were later exchanged. Others adopted by the Indians or the nuns never came back. Attacks by the savages came as near to Concord as Marlborough, Lancaster, Groton, and Haverhill. Captain Joseph Bulkeley, son of Major Peter Bulkeley, was captain of a company of fifty-one men engaged in scouting duty after 1704. In 1725, Captain Lovewell took forty-seven men including seven from the North Quarter of Concord to fight Paugus near Fryeburg, Maine. Josiah Davis and Jacob Farrar were killed, Eleazer Davis and Josiah Jones were wounded. Other veterans were Joseph Farrar, David and Eleazer Melvin. In 1729, the town of Pembroke, New Hampshire was granted to them as a soldier's bonus, while the wounded received Province pensions.

For a war with Spain in 1740, Captain John Prescott of Concord, a physician and son of Dr. Jonathan Prescott, Jr., was put in charge of 500 men enlisted from the Province to go to Cuba, of whom all but fifty died of disease. Prescott himself died later of smallpox while on a trip to London. Of fifteen from Concord, only three returned. John Prescott's widow continued to receive a pension from the British government until her death long after American independence. Soldiers from Concord took part in all the expeditions against Canada, Louisburg, Fort Edward, Crown Point, and Nova Scotia. Fighting side by side with the British, they were shocked at the harsh discipline and not impressed by British military skill. Their own officers, however experienced, were always subordinate to British officers of equal rank. British historians on the other hand have little good to say about the provincial troops. This attitude of contempt by the British for the fighting ability of the Americans was a distinct advantage to the Americans during the Revolution.

The wide-ranging travel to the west and north during these years by the soldiers led to petitions to the General Court for grants of new townships. Sometimes a single individual, Peter Prescott, Samuel Chandler, John Cuming or Samuel Whittemore, organized a group for colonization, meeting in a Concord tavern to get men to sign up. John Flint organized Walpole, New Hampshire, in a Concord tavern. Prescott started Peterboro, Chandler and Whittemore started Lunenburg and Fitchburg, while Cuming started Cummington and Plainfield. Some of the land was given free to bona fide settlers while the proprietor kept a large acreage to sell when it became more valuable. Soon almost every Concord family had relatives in these towns helped by capital, stock, and tools from home. There were little enclaves of Concord children and grandchildren in a score of communities in Maine, New Hampshire, and Vermont. New Ipswich, New Hampshire, prides itself on making the first arrival in Concord on April 20, 1775, to help the Minutemen, but half the population bore Concord names; they were coming down to help their brothers and cousins. The other half bore Ipswich names and were almost equally concerned. These "lower tier" towns had been colonized by Massachusetts to reinforce her claim to the land which later had to be ceded to New Hampshire.

Flint lost money at Walpole. After he had paid to have a road surveyed from Keene, jurisdiction was given to New Hampshire, which refused to confirm his charter.

*Louisburg is not forgotten, nor Beau Séjour nor Port Royal.*
   *Longfellow: Evangeline*

When war was declared between the French and English in 1755, the first act of the General Court was to order all the French subjects in this Province interned in Concord in the custody of the jailkeeper. The number could not have been large, but it caused Concord to supplant Jonathan Heywood's old jail with a new one behind the Main Street burying-place where the prisoners could be fed from Ephraim Jones's new tavern next door. This jail was a two-story wooden building partitioned into four cells on each floor with an outside wooden stair. A stockaded yard supplied the only facilities for exercise and sanitation. Fortunately, the French were soon allowed to sail for London.

Meanwhile, in Nova Scotia twelve to fourteen thousand people, farmers and their families, were dispossessed. The French habitants believed that the treaty of Utrecht in 1715 had given them the right to remain neutral and had relieved them of the obligation to bear arms, an exemption that no other British colonist enjoyed, but one which French Canadians tried to enjoy as late as World War I. The English believed that when the French ceded Acadia to them, the citizens had the same obligation as any other British subject and that, in any case, if they would not fight for, they must not fight against Britain. Most of their priests refused to accept the treaty and the loyalty of the Acadians to their religion aggravated the trouble. When the English took the fort of Beau Séjour they claimed to have found fifty or more so-called neutrals under arms. They were told they would not be punished if they took an oath of loyalty to the English King. When they refused, Governor Lawrence ordered Colonel Winslow to evict them. They were loaded on every available ship, their houses and barns were burned, and without any warning to Massachusetts, shiploads began to arrive in Boston in November, 1755. Some of the French were supposed to be sent on to the south, but the vessels were too crowded, provisions were short and the water bad. Two Boston merchants were asked to provision the ships, but many French came ashore and could not be forced back on board. The Massachusetts authorities ordered them dispersed to be taken care of by the separate towns, advising each town to find a house for its family and to try to provide work. In 1761, Simon Landry and his family were housed near Barrett's Mill; the town paid for grain and wood and medical expenses and for carrying the family back to Boston. In the same year another French family, spelled "Trayhorn" in the records, came to Concord. They were housed on Jonas Bateman's vacant farm on Punkatasset Hill and John Flint, Jr., did their plowing, Nehemiah Hunt supplied wood, a live pig and two cows, and David Whittaker an axe. Deacon Barrett supplied grain and pork and Joseph Buttrick made a coffin for one of Trayhorn's children. Colonel Cuming visited them when sick and delivered baby Georges in 1766; and finally in May, 1767, James Chandler procured bread for Trayhorn and his family on their voyage to Canada, and Ephraim Whittaker carted their goods to Boston. One can only hope they arrived back safely after six years in Concord.

*Each of these landlords walked amidst his farm*
*Saying 'T'is mine, my children's and my name's.*
    *Emerson:* Hamatreya

The period from 1700 to 1750 was of the utmost importance to Concord. The farms steadily grew more self-sufficient and a sideline of small specialties developed on almost every farm. New towns upcountry and improved roads led to a great increase in trade; better education and more independence in religion widened horizons. The experience of self-government increased the sturdy independence of the citizens who bore without question the responsibilities of citizenship, paying their self-imposed taxes, serving in the militia, caring for the poor and educating the young, and arguing out every item in town meeting.

The oldest extant assessors' list is that of 1717. It shows that after eighty years there was surprising equality in the population. There were 293 polls, the average assessment value for house and land was twelve pounds and for the wealthiest men, of whom there were scarcely a dozen, it would be twenty-four pounds. Captain Ephraim Flint had a real estate valuation of twenty-four pounds and had two horses, four oxen, five cows, and ten sheep. The smaller assessments were on sons of larger proprietors, most of whom had one horse, two oxen, two or three cows, and a few sheep. Those who had a trade and few livestock paid a tax on "faculty." A blacksmith, for instance, paid on a valuation of four pounds for faculty. Only three farms had as many as twenty sheep, only six had as many as eight cows, and only one had four horses.

The improvement in highways was steady as most farmers worked out part of their taxes on the roads and could have another part "crossed" by teaching in the elementary schools, supplying plank for bridges or stone for causeways or board to the poor or, in the case of the parish tax, by supplying grain, meat or wood to the minister. The usual credit for supplying two oxen and a man for road work was four shillings a day in the summer or half that in the off season on the farm. Now began the construction of "causeys" over the wet spots or culverts over the small brooks which made it possible to straighten the roads which in the first century had skirted the wet spots. When the old right of way reverted to the abuttor, no payment was made for the land taken in for the new one. Old land grants had often been bounded by a road; now if a road crossed a pasture, the owner was given the right to set up gates. Sergeant Thomas Wheeler's descendants had four houses on Virginia Road and could set up gates as needed. John Hunt could set up gates on the little-used lower road from the north bridge to the corner of Barrett's Mill Road.

When a road led to a neighboring town, representatives of the towns concerned would lay out the road together. The road from Concord to Lancaster was laid out before 1654 by George Wheeler and John Smedley on the part of Concord and by John Roper and Ralph Houghton for Lancaster. They set the place for the first south bridge downstream and around the bend from the present bridge so that the road would pass directly by Simon Willard's house which stood above the bend until burned to the ground in 1857. The road then followed our Wood Street and Main Street and Old Road to Nine Acre Corner to Marlboro Road. At Old Bridge Road, one turned to cross Darby's Bridge over the Assabet or continued by our Harrington Avenue south of the Assabet to Hayward's mill. Near town, the Lancaster road began at a zero milestone at the east end of the church green, turned to cross

Benjamin Barron house on Lexington Road. Here John Jack earned his freedom

the millbrook at Ford or Potter's bridge, turned back on Walden Street and wound around the south burying-place, then followed in the general course of Main Street curving to the east toward Scotchfords Lane and again toward Jonas Heywood's house on Cottage Lane, then took the railroad right of way toward the south bridge.

On a lane between Meriam's Corner and the north bridge, one or two free Negroes had built cabins with the tacit permission of the landowners. Negroes were not usually allowed to own land. One of these was Caesar Robbins, succeeded in the early nineteenth century by Peter Hutchinson. This house was later moved to Bedford Street after that road was built in 1855. Another cabin close to the ridge and not far from Meriam's Corner on this path was the home of John Jack and Old Violet, former slaves of Benjamin Barron, a cordwainer, or shoemaker, whose house and shop were at 53 Lexington Road. After Barron's death in 1754, Jack earned enough money, doubtless with the permission of the widow, to buy his freedom in 1761 and retire to an easier life, solaced by alcohol. He asked Daniel Bliss, Concord's Tory lawyer, to draw up his will, leaving what was left after Bliss had paid his burial expenses to Old Violet; and Bliss made him immortal by composing an epitaph in the prevailing balanced style of the day, which had a barb for the liberty-loving patriots who nevertheless kept slaves. One of Bliss's Tory friends sent it to England to be printed in a

Grave of John Jack. The stone was replaced by the lawyers of Concord about 1830.

London newspaper as an ironic comment on the pretensions of the Sons of Liberty:

> God wills us free; man wills us slaves.
> I will as God wills; God's will be done.
> Here lies the body of
> JOHN JACK
> a native of Africa who died
> March 1773 aged about 60 years
> Tho' born in a land of slavery,
> He was born free.
> Tho' he lived in a land of liberty,
> He lived a slave.
> Till by his honest, tho' stolen labors,
> He acquired the source of slavery,
> Which gave him his freedom;
> Tho' not long before
> Death, the grand tyrant
> Gave him his final emancipation,
> And set him on a footing with kings.
> Tho' a slave to vice,
> He practised those virtues
> Without which kings are but slaves.

Cottages on the church green.

Of the greatest importance in the development of the town was the growth of trade along the Bay Road which took place in the eighteenth century. As towns were settled to the west of Concord, traffic increased and farmers began to develop profitable sidelines which in a favorable location soon became their mainstay. Thus on the Bay Road on the church green was the Wright tavern and its bake shop and east of the green the trader, Robert Cuming, who had come over from Scotland, after the troubles of 1715, with enough capital to set himself up in business and send his son, John, to Harvard. His store was in the white block facing the Wright tavern across the church green.

Opposite the meetinghouse was Benjamin Barrett's blacksmith shop, John Ball's goldsmith shop, Thomas Munroe's tavern, Seth Ross's cooperage, and Jonathan Fiske, saddler in Peter Bulkeley's house which was owned thereafter by a succession of saddlers of whom the last was Reuben Brown. Next to him John Beatton, another Scot, had his first store and made enough to buy considerable land, including the big lot to his east which had been the home and tailor shop of John Jones. Jones had inherited it from his mother, Sarah (Farwell) Jones. Then came the dwelling and shop of Nathaniel Harwood, then Benjamin

Barron and his shoeshop, and Dr. Abel Prescott with his sons, Dr.
Samuel and young Dr. Abel; then Daniel Hoar, gentleman and farmer,
and Henry Yours, worsted weaver. Next was Caleb Ball, whose house
was sold in 1769 to Samuel Whitney, a patriot from Boston who took
a prominent part here as a member of the Committee of Correspondence and the Committee of Safety, and became muster master of the
Minutemen. There followed in the East Quarter a blacksmith, a housewright, a joiner, a gunsmith, a weaver, a currier, a cordwainer, a tanner—a succession of shops supplying almost every need. As Salem and
Boston grew, demand grew for salt beef and flour to provision the
ships, for barrels and casks to pack these supplies, and for lumber, firewood, and cider as well as butter, lard, onions, and root vegetables.
Concord was a convenient distance from the hill towns for the sale of
cattle and the purchase of a return load. Traders' account books of the
period show that a large part of the business was done on credit and
by swapping, with some accounts never settled until the buyer died.
It will be noticed that Concord lagged a century behind the seacoast
in this growth of trade.

There were two or three slaughter houses near town, and a large
tannery in the center below the milldam, rivaled by the Brooks tannery
near the present Lincoln town line which used Elm Brook for soaking
the hides.

Elnathan Jones, Jr. (1737-1793), was a successful trader who built
himself a fine house at 60 Main Street with a store adjoining, which
was moved after his death to the town house site and moved again in
1850 around the corner for a house that is now part of a modern
"country store."

Another successful trader was the Scot, John Beatton. He became
town treasurer and was such a careful and exact figurer that the books
were kept in pounds, shillings, pence and farthings; but in his store
accounts he went a step farther and split the farthing into so many
common pins, so that a little girl, sent to get a jug of molasses filled,
would come home with the change in pennies, farthings, and the right
number of common pins in her coat. Other merchants threw in the
fractions, but Beatton's exactness was preferred to their generosity. He
had a reputation far and wide as Honest John Beatton, but he also
knew how to be generous. Having no children, he made the town
residuary legatee, after taking thought for his wife, his relatives at
home in the Orkney Islands, and his apprentices here. He gave, in his
lifetime, land to enlarge the hill burying-ground, while Dr. Cuming
paid to have the new part fenced. For some reason, his wife was never

John Beatton house, later Heywood house. (1880 photograph by Alfred Hosmer.)

allowed to join the church. Henry Thoreau heard the story from old George Minott, grandson of Dr. Abel Prescott, Sr., who had married the widow Beatton:

> Beatton used to say of Deacon Brown, who usually dined at his house between services on Sundays, and highly praised his wife's dinners, but yet prevented her being admitted to the church, that "his tongue was like a coo's [cow's] tongue, rough on one side and smooth the other!" (Thoreau's *Journal,* Jan. 6, 1857.)

This increase in the number of shops resulted in an increase in the number of apprentices, a new element of ambitious and hard-working young men. Most were from outlying towns, but some were sons of Concord farmers, whose fathers or widowed mothers were glad to place them where they could learn a trade.

Mrs. John Beatton, later wife of Dr. Abel Prescott, Sr. (Courtesy of the Concord Antiquarian Society.)

*Such perpetual discussion afforded in itself no mean school of
intellectual training. Viewed in relation to the subsequent
mental activity of New England, it may be said to have
occupied a position somewhat similar to that which the polemics
of the mediaeval schoolmen occupied in relation to the
European thought of the Renaissance.*

    *John Fiske:* The Beginnings of New England

We have seen how the migration to Massachusetts had necessarily attracted the more independent and adventurous Englishmen and how the choice of an inland location had winnowed from them the more independent of these immigrants. The attention given to the fine distinctions of their theology and the stimulus of an education under the most enlightened young men of the day had developed a group of citizens with a keen interest in public affairs and the ability to express themselves. To them was added in the early eighteenth century a number of Scots, fleeing from "the troubles" caused by James Stuart's and Bonnie Prince Charlie's attempts to regain the throne of England for the Stuarts. These were people with no love for the English and no fear of armed revolt, and though they were not many, they, too, had an influence on Concord. One French family, called in the records Shevally, came here after 1685.

Citizens gain a certain self-confidence from the knowledge that one has had one's say, regardless of the decision. The school began the training in its Friday afternoon declamations, when every boy had to stand on his feet before an audience and speak. A second training-place was the country store or tavern where, quite informally, among his neighbors, there was opportunity for opinions to be asked and given. At the town meeting, there was always a chance to be heard. Governor Andros recognized their importance when he tried to limit town meetings to one a year, for the election of officers. Emerson noted with admiration that at the Concord town meeting the worst was heard as well as the best. Every opinion was aired and when the decision was made, it was the result of hearing all sides. Edmund Burke told Parliament that the American colony was a nation of lawyers. Its people were certainly articulate. Books on law had an extraordinary sale here and fine points of law were considered important and frequently discussed. "Townships in New England," wrote Thomas Jefferson in advocating a similar government for Virginia, "are the vital principle of their government and have proved themselves the wisest invention ever devised by the wit of man for the perfect exercise of self-government, giving to every citizen, personally, a part in the administration of public affairs."

Emerson wrote:

In this institution the great secret of political science was uncovered and the problem solved how to give every individual his fair weight in the government without any disorder from numbers. The roots of society were reached. Here the rich gave counsel, but the poor also and moreover the just and the unjust.

Many purely local matters were discussed at town meetings. There were the improved roads to be newly laid out, the care of the poor to be authorized, the fishing privilege to be sold at auction with Deacon Samuel Minot as vendue master and Colonel Cuming the purchaser, with decisions to be taken about the sale of pews to the increasing number of people who wanted to own separate family pews or who wanted to build separate horse stables (not over nine feet wide) behind the meetinghouse, to shelter their horses during the long church services.

The increased attention paid to funerals is very noticeable in the town records. The town more than once had to renew the burying cloth which covered the bier as it was carried to the burying place, and pay the sexton for taking care of it. The town bought four white wands probably to be carried at the head of the funeral procession. If the family boasted a coat-of-arms, it was painted on a square piece of wood, called a hatchment, hung diagonally above the door after a death and taken on the bier to the grave. Rum was required, even for a pauper's funeral. The town paid for two quarts for the widow Allen's funeral and two quarts for those who laid out Sarah Temple. For twenty years orders were made and bills paid for fencing the burying places and for building gates with expensive iron latches and hinges. Stray animals had been knocking over the stones and users of gravel had been encroaching on the hill as the milldam was widened. The stones and inscriptions became more elaborate. If the earliest graves were marked at all, they had native stone markers, crudely lettered, which did not survive. Our earliest surviving stone is dated 1677. Slate was found in several places in Massachusetts and since it was easily quarried in flat slabs, soon came into general use. There is no record of the importation of grave markers from England except when the Pepperell family of Boston imported marble in 1737. A white stone was erected in 1812 to Miss Abigail Dudley ". . . designed by its color to signify the moral character . . ." of the spinster who left to the church a fund for the encouragement of singing.

Gravestones were the first attempts at sculpture here and original work was widely admired. In 1717, a stone was ordered in Boston from the stonecutter, Joseph Lamson, at a cost (with carting) of two pounds, twelve shillings, for the grave of Richard Kaets who moved out to Concord in his old age after making a living in Boston as a mason and a constable. In his will he had left to the Concord church six pounds for a silver communion cup. His stone has rosettes at the head of the side borders, characteristic of Lamson, as well as a border on the bottom and the usual death's head at the top. In 1720, few Concord people could afford such a stone, but by the latter part of the century much more elaborate stones were the rule. A quarry of close-grained durable dark blue slate was opened at Pin Hill in Harvard and a family of stonecutters named Park settled in nearby Groton in 1756. William Park was succeeded by his sons, John and Thomas, and the latter was the sculptor of the elaborate stones with coats-of-arms put up for the Barretts and Lieutenant Daniel Hoar. Colonel Barrett's cost 540 pounds in depreciated currency during the Revolution. The Park

Gravestone of Daniel Hoar, Jr., in Hill Burying Ground.

Gravestone of Major John Buttrick wh gave the command to fire.

Gravestone of Colonel James Barrett.

Mary Brooks' grave with her stone repo card: "She was very Excellent for Readin and Soberness."

South or Main Street Burying Ground with the old Block House.

stones have delicate tracery of vines and flowers in the side panels, and above, a constantly improving series of death's heads with wings denoting immortality. The skulls gradually give way to angel's heads or even to small portraits, like the one on Deacon Thomas Barrett's grave. We do not know how lifelike the portrait was, but the coat and waistcoat were done with great fidelity. The ugly skull on little Helen Cuming's grave of 1757 has rosebuds tucked behind it. At the turn of the century the winged figures on the stones give place to the urn and weeping willow. A new burying-place was opened in 1823 at the west end of our present Sleepy Hollow.

Since the graveyard was the only place where it was proper to walk on Sunday, save to church, the stones were inspected and admired by all, and therefore the inscriptions were chosen to point a moral for the living, as well as to memorialize the dead. Ezra Ripley liked to suggest such epitaphs and doubtless drew up many. The most important were on the raised brick tombs with large slate slabs on top which allowed for long eulogies; these were for ministers, deacons, and magistrates. The most pathetic stone is that for little Mary Brooks who died at eleven: "she was very excellent for reading and soberness." John Stone, who died in 1791, father-in-law of William Munroe, Sr., might be forgotten if we did not find here that "he was the Architect of that Modern and justly Celebrated Piece of Architecture Charles River Bridge. He was a man of good Natural abilities which seemed to be adorned with Moral Virtues And Christian Graces."

# Chapter V    Against the Self-will of England

*Here English law and English thought*
  *Gainst the self-will of England fought.*
  *James Russell Lowell:* Ode Read in Concord April 19, 1875

In the midst of these local matters the town began to be concerned with larger questions. In 1754, the record says that the town considered

. . . the act of the general court granting unto his Majesty an excise upon wines and spirits distilled and sold by retail within this province, and upon limes, lemons and oranges, and his Excellency's speech thereon the seventeenth of June last, and after a considerable debate thereon, the question was put whether the town are in favor of said bill and it was passed by a very great majority.

This bill had been passed by the House of Representatives in order to raise money for the French war effort without adding to the burden on polls and real estate, but had not been concurred in by the Governor's Council—the wealthy—who disliked a tax on commerce. Governor Shirley had suggested that the bill be printed and sent out to the towns for their opinion ". . . so that he might be informed of the general sentiments of the country concerning a matter of this importance and difficulty which so nearly touches the natural rights of every individual member. . . ."

The Governor thus committed himself to having due regard, in a question of taxation, to the voice of the people. This was not the first instance of taking an opinion poll in order to break a deadlock between the House of Representatives and the Governor's Council. It expresses, twenty years before the Revolution, an acknowledgment of the natural rights of citizens and of their interest in matters of taxation.

Next, the Stamp Act was to be enforced. In October, 1765, a special town meeting discussed the article: "to see if the Town will give any instructions to the representative about any important affair that may be transacted at the General Court concerning the Stamp Act." A set of instructions was read and discussed and it was voted ". . . to accept the Instructions." Duly recorded is the town's vote to enter these in-

Doctor John Cuming house at the Reformatory Circle.

structions on the record. Jonas Heywood, the town clerk, was cautious, and in spite of the vote, these instructions do not appear in the town record book.

A year later, a Boston mob damaged the property of Andrew Oliver, the tax collector, and set fire to the house of Chief Justice Thomas Hutchinson, with damage estimated at 4000 pounds. On October 21, 1766, a meeting considered ". . . whether to pay their part to the sufferers by the late disturbances in the town of Boston relative to the Stamp Act." The town refused, but another special meeting was called in December, because now the town had been ordered to pay its share. The question was put whether they would reconsider their vote. It passed in the negative, so Concord allied itself with the Boston opponents of the Stamp Act, an overt act of disobedience.

The town of Boston a year later wrote to the other towns urging all to sign a non-importation agreement and in December, 1767, a Concord town meeting voted to make the Selectmen a committee to report their recommendations at the next meeting. Their report was accepted on February 22, 1768.

The growing importance of Concord is reflected in the vote of a special town meeting in December, 1767, naming Dr. Cuming and

Joseph Lee a committee to ask the General Court to set up courts of justice in Concord and in agitation to set up a separate county with Concord as the center.

In September, 1768, a special town meeting was held to discuss ". . . whether to choose any person or persons to meet a convention that may be held in Fannel Hall in Boston in order to consult the best measures for the good of the province in this critical day." Captain James Barrett was chosen. (The town clerk spelled Faneuil as he pronounced it.)

On May 13, 1771, there was a general town meeting in the town house but ". . . the house being too strait . . . ," the town adjourned to the meetinghouse. In the same way the Faneuil Hall meeting in Boston had adjourned to the Old South Meetinghouse because in the rising excitement, the hall first appointed had been too small.

Special town meetings were held frequently, but when these were forbidden by General Gage, the annual meeting was adjourned from March to May and May to November and November to January to give the appearance of legality to more frequent meetings. On December 31, 1772, the town met to see whether any particular instructions should be given to Captain James Barrett, the representative, regarding the infringements on the rights and privileges of this Province. The committee chosen contained all the best-educated men of the town: Dr. Joseph Lee, Charles Prescott, Esq., John Cuming, Esq., Daniel Bliss, Esq., Mr. John Flint, Deacon Thomas Barrett, Captain Stephen Hosmer, Captain James Barrett, and Ephraim Wood, Jr. This committee brought in a report which expressed loyalty to the King but insisted that the privileges of the Province were infringed on, unconstitutionally, and the judges should not be paid by the Crown lest they be influenced thereby. Daniel Bliss did not sign and thus openly allied himself with the Tories. The committee report "was read several times and coolly and deliberately considered," says the official record, "and debated upon and passed in the affirmative unanimously in a full town meeting." The meeting continued the next day and drew up a reply to the town of Boston.

On January 10, 1774, there was a meeting which set up a Committee of Correspondence to consider a letter from the town of Boston requesting Concord's sentiments respecting the late act of Parliament granting liberty to the East India Company to export their tea into this province and raise revenue contrary to the charter. It was voted that anyone purchasing tea would be deemed unfriendly and inimical to the happy constitution of this country. The non-importation pledge

Colonel Barrett's house about 70 years ago. (Photograph by Alfred Hosmer.)

is still in the town archives and contains the signatures of almost every man and five women. Among all the signers only Stephen Hosmer made a condition, that his signature would not obligate his wife to give up tea.

On January 24, 1774, the town met and voted to enroll the committee reports among the town records where seven resolves are recorded. On March 7, once more they adjourned to the meetinghouse for the election of officers; but every meeting was not devoted to public affairs. On May 16, they voted to new-seat the meetinghouse but not to appropriate any part of the meetinghouse to singers. The Black Horse church had had two choristers but the town as a whole was not yet ready for the innovation of a choir.

On June 27, the town met to consider the state of our liberties and voted not to purchase from any who had not taken the non-importation oath. On September 26, 1774, they elected Samuel Whitney and Ephraim Wood, Jr., representatives to a Provincial Congress and then voted to raise two companies to stand at a minute's warning in case of an alarm and to pay said companies, if called out of town. Tolman in his *Preliminaries of the Concord Fight* thinks this is the first use of the word "minute" in describing these men.

They voted to buy seven and a half barrels of powder in addition to the town's stock and appropriated seventeen pounds, three shillings, fourpence to pay for it. On October 24, they met and voted to mount the cannon. On November 15, they met and voted to pay the money collected for the Province taxes to Henry Gardner, treasurer of the illegal Provincial Congress instead of into the Province treasury. This of course was open rebellion.

On January 2, 1775, the town voted to pay the Minutemen for drilling once in a fortnight.

I have put these votes in succession to show the many slow steps by which the town brought itself, over a period of twenty years, to the point of open armed rebellion. The statement so often made that the Revolution was a civil war with as many Tories as Patriots certainly did not apply to Concord, if it applied anywhere in Massachusetts, except among Boston merchants. Only Daniel Bliss gave aid to the British by supplying information about the collection of arms in Concord, and remained a loyalist.

The meeting in Concord of the Provincial Congress did much, of course, to harden sentiment, but a Middlesex County convention held in the meetinghouse on August 30 and 31 was closer to the people. The county voted to support a Provincial Congress. Ephraim Wood, Jr., John Flint, and Nathan Meriam were the Concord delegates but the galleries were filled with Concord men. Here occurred the debate between Joseph Hosmer and Daniel Bliss which remained in the memories of all who heard it. Bliss gave a polished, reasoned, and witty argument with all the eloquence at his command, showing to all that open opposition to the might of Britain would be futile. A stunned silence was broken when the young and awkward cabinetmaker, Joseph Hosmer, rose to speak. Plainly dressed, hesitant at first and diffident, his speech became eloquent as he recited the hardships through which our ancestors had established their rights, and the illegal steps, contrary to our charter, by which Parliament was taking away those rights. As he recited these grievances, his voice rang with conviction until his audience was completely carried with him and resolved to maintain their rights at whatever cost.

It was not only taxation that inflamed public sentiment but the usurpation by Parliament and the military in Boston of direction of the courts. The County Convention voted to boycott the court and prevent its sitting if possible. Joseph Lee, one of the justices, who lived on the Willard farm, went down to Cambridge to report the intended disturbance, and so inflamed was public opinion that he was dragged out by a mob on his return and roughly treated. He signed a confession and apology and was eventually forgiven, though a shot was occasionally fired at his house by passing Patriots.

Colonel John Cuming was moderator of ninety town meetings between 1763 and 1788 and undoubtedly much of the patriotic fervor and resolution of Concord can be attributed to his influence. He was born in 1728, son of Robert and Hellen Cuming. His father had emigrated to Boston from Scotland after the rebellion of 1715 and must have been of some consequence there, since he used the coat-of-arms of the Comeyn family, allied with the Montrose clan. He soon moved to Concord and became a successful merchant on the church green, buying for his home in 1724 the former Hezekiah Fletcher place, still standing on the corner of the Cambridge Turnpike and Hawthorne Lane. John entered Harvard in 1744 with the class of 1748 but left to teach the town school in Nine Acre Corner for nine weeks in 1746. He enlisted in the French and Indian war and was wounded in the hip where the bullet remained until his death. He was captured by the Indians and carried to Montreal where, after a time, he was exchanged. He then studied medicine abroad, probably in Edinburgh, and returned to marry Abigail Wesson of Concord in 1753. He enlisted as a Lieutenant Colonel in the northern expedition in 1755, under Colonel Josiah Brown of Sudbury in Sir William Johnson's regiment, and went to Crown Point as a combat officer rather than as a physician. Harvard gave him an honorary degree of Master of Arts in 1771. John Adams went out to Cambridge to see the handsome pair of brass candelabra which he presented to the college chapel. He had a fine library of medical books, law books, sermons, works on agriculture, and miscellaneous books including Milton's works, Young's works in five volumes, and Butler's *Hudibras*. As we have seen, he was active as a physician and citizen and in the first year of the Revolution was named General in charge of the army which was to go up the Champlain Valley to reinforce Gates. His friend and minister William Emerson was going as chaplain and rushed over to congratulate him but found him ". . . in a very low condition as to health and everything else concerning the present day." Part of the trouble was that Mrs. Cuming was determined that her husband should not go.

He served out the war as member or chairman of the town Committees of Correspondence, Inspection, and Safety. He had been appointed a Justice of the Court of General Sessions by the Crown and received the same appointment from the Provincial Congress. The town sent him to the House of Representatives in 1776 and to the Constitutional Convention in 1779.

The town of Concord is credited by students of constitutional law as the first public body to suggest that a constitution should be drawn up not by a legislature but by a separate constitutional convention, especially elected for that one purpose, which could give each of the three branches—executive, legislative, and judicial—its fair share of power.

The Legislature of 1776 had drawn up a constitution and submitted it to the towns for ratification in October, 1776, but it was rejected by the Concord town meeting after hearing the report brought in by a committee consisting of Ephraim Wood, Nathan Bond, Colonel James Barrett, Major John Buttrick, and the Colonel's son, James Barrett, Jr. The committee's report was considered resolve by resolve and accepted unanimously. Other towns also rejected the legislative constitution. The principle of having a convention draw up a constitution was used as a pattern by several states and by the Federal Government and is an important fact in constitutional history.

Colonel Cuming invested extensively in land. He was a proprietor of Marlow, New Hampshire, of Brandon and Leicester, Vermont, and in 1762 he bought, in partnership with James Hayward and Charles Prescott, township number five in the Berkshires from the Province and sold it off to settlers. The initial meetings were held in his house. This purchase became the towns of Cummington and Plainfield. His own house was west of the Assabet, a house now standing at the Reformatory Circle, and his farm ran from the river to the Acton town line with some land also on the east side of the Assabet, over 200 acres in all.

He died while visiting his friend, Reverend Ebenezer Bridge, in Chelmsford in June, 1788. The Chelmsford doctor had bled him in spite of his objections. He left no children; the only one, a daughter, had died at the age of five. His will named his friend, Ephraim Wood, executor. To the son of his friend William Emerson, William, Jr., he left the one half of his wearing apparel and his military accoutrements and sash. One wonders what the young school teacher who became four years later minister in Harvard, Massachusetts, did with the military accoutrements, and whether the clothes were finally cut down for his son, Ralph Waldo, or one of his other boys. His medical books, instruments, and medicines he left to Dr. Joseph Hunt of Concord

Brister's Spring. Dr. Cuming's freed slave Scipio Brister lived here.

who had studied under him. He had two namesakes, John Cuming Flint and Cumming Wesson, who each received 100 acres in Cummington. His two former slaves, Bristo and Jem, were to have thirty-five pounds sterling each, to be expended under the direction of the Selectmen. Brister, as the town records spell the name, outlived a wife and three children and gave his name to the hill and spring near which he lived until 1822. The church was generously remembered with fifty pounds for communion silver, twenty-five pounds to the deacons for poor communicants, and twenty pounds to Reverend Ezra Ripley. The University in Cambridge and the town of Concord were each to receive 300 pounds and half the residue after his wife's death, which occurred in 1794. Concord used half its share for the schools and half for the poor; but Harvard, as Cuming instructed, used theirs with some other funds for a Professor of Physic and so began Harvard Medical School with Dr. Benjamin Waterhouse and Dr. John Warren as the first professors. When Shattuck wrote his history of Concord in 1835, Dr. Cuming had been its most eminent citizen over the two hundred years and received a separate biography, the only one so honored except for the ministers. Today he is unknown in the town for which he did so much, and his gravestone is only seen in passing, on the path to John Jack's. His life is a link between the frontier, the fight for liberty, and the genius of Emerson, and his death supplied the seed which became the vast humanitarian complex of Harvard Medical School. Surely his was no mean record.

*And here were men, co-equal with their fate*
*Who did great things, unconscious they were great.*
      Lowell: Ode Read in Concord April 19, 1875

The Minutemen met frequently for drills and in August, 1774, had their first alarm when word came that the British had marched out to Cambridge to look for powder and confiscate two cannon. Before the day was out, 20,000 men had gathered in Cambridge, but the British were safely back in Boston. The Powder Alarm, as it was called, showed the efficacy of the alarm system but made it evident that stores should be kept at a greater distance from Boston than Cambridge.

The first Provincial Congress met in Salem where the House of Representatives on October 5, 1774, finding that Governor Gage and his Council would not qualify them, voted to join the Provincial Congress and adjourned to Concord. This Congress in the Concord meetinghouse included both the delegates chosen by the separate towns and the duly elected members of the General Court. They chose John Hancock as President and Benjamin Lincoln as Secretary. Reverend William Emerson was chaplain. They adopted an address to General Gage and adjourned October 15 to convene in Cambridge from October 17 to 29 and again from November 23 to December 10.

The second Congress convened in Cambridge from February 1 to 16 and then adjourned to meet in Concord on March 22 where it sat until Saturday, April 15, 1775. These Congresses had ordered supplies to be bought and stored in Concord.

The stores were placed under the charge of Colonel James Barrett, whose notebook was copied by Lemuel Shattuck in the first *History of Concord*. Barrett had been Representative from Concord in the General Court since 1768. Barrett was instructed to set a guard every night, to have a number of teams in readiness on short notice to remove the stores, and to have couriers to alarm the neighboring towns.

The Barrett notebook[1] reports that there were received from David

---

[1] The Barrett notebook is not with the few Shattuck papers in the Massachusetts Historical Society. I have quoted it from Shattuck's *History of Concord*.

The old Barrett mill about 1860. Notice the hewn beams and trunnels and the chalk tallies.

Cheever of Charlestown twenty loads containing 20,000 pounds of musket balls and cartridges, fifty reams of cartridge paper, 206 tents, 113 iron spades, fifty-one wood axes, 201 billhooks, nineteen sets of harness, twenty-four boxes of candles, fourteen chests of medicine, twenty-seven hogsheads of wooden ware, one hogshead of matches, cords, iron cannon balls, twenty bushels of oatmeal, five iron worms for cannon, rammers, et cetera. These were stored at Captain Elnathan Jones's Joshua Bond's, Willoughby Prescott's, Jonas Heywood's, Colonel Barrett's and the town house.

From Moses Gill of Boston, eleven loads containing 150 tents, axes, pickaxes, hatchets, spades, wooden spoons and dishes, and canteens stored at Captain Thomas Hubbard's, Ephraim Wheeler's, Willoughby Prescott's, and Ephraim Potter's. Also received from R. Pierpont were forty-five firkins and two barrels of butter stored at Colonel James's and Mr. Humphrey Barrett's, and fifty-five barrels of beef stored at Thomas and Elisha Jones's, and twenty-five barrels at Daniel Cray's. From Colonel Lee of Marblehead, six hogsheads containing thirty-five half-barrels of powder stored at Colonel Barrett's, James Chandler's, James Barrett, Jr.'s, Ephraim Wood's, Joseph Hosmer's, and Jonas

Ephraim Wheeler house, Sudbury Road. (Photograph by Harriette Forbes.)

Heywood's. Another load of powder was sent on to Leicester. A load of tents, poles, axes and hatchets was stored at Abishai Brown's. Three hundred and eighteen barrels of flour were stored at Ebenezer Hubbard's, Captain Timothy Wheeler's, Samuel Jones's, Isaac Hubbard's, Jonas Heywood's, Samuel Whitney's, and Jonathan Heywood's.

From Marblehead came seven loads of salt fish (about 17,000 pounds), stored at Elisha Jones's, eighteen casks of wine, twenty casks of raisins and a quantity of oil, sent on to Stow, and fifty barrels of salt, stored in fifteen different places, four loads of tents, tow cloth, and canteens stored at Ephraim Potter's, one bundle sheet lead, several hogsheads of molasses, and a quantity of linen.

From Salem came twelve tierces (about 35,000 pounds) of rice stored at Ebenezer Hubbard's, Thomas Hosmer's, Thomas Davis's, Stephen Blood's, Edward Richardson's, Deacon George Minott's, and the town house.

Many other stores were prepared here. Firearms and gun-carriages were made at Barrett's mill; cartouch-boxes, holsters, belts, et cetera, at Reuben Brown's; saltpetre by Josiah Melvin; oatmeal by Captain Timothy Wheeler and quantities of wooden ware and barrels of beef and pork. Part of the building now occupied by the Colonial Inn was used as a public storehouse in 1776 and thereafter.

"Our operations depend upon secrecy," Colonel Barrett was warned.

Major Joseph Hosmer house. At right, old house of Obadiah Wheeler, Jr.

*They came three thousand miles and died*
*To keep the Past upon its throne.*
    *Lowell:* Lines Suggested by the Grave of the British Soldiers on Concord
        Battle-ground

It is doubtful if any general was ever better informed of the enemy activities than was General Gage. Sitting as a member of the Committee of Safety was Benjamin Church, a paid informer. He and Benjamin Thompson, who later became Count Rumford, between them knew everything that was going on. In the last weeks before he sent the expedition to Concord, Gage had reports every day or two. He had an accurate map of the town with all the principal hiding places marked. We know that De Berniere and Brown, the most notorious British spies, had stopped at Daniel Bliss's house on March 20 and he had guided them by the Watertown road to Boston where he could have given a verbal report to Gage to corroborate the report from

Mansion on Walden Street, formerly Duncan Ingraham's house.

Dr. Church. Bliss must have had a forewarning of what was to happen in Concord, for he went all the way with the two British officers and remained in Boston. A county committee had been visiting suspected Tories, intimidating them and trying to get them to recant, but had not yet visited Bliss, because of his previous popularity and his relationship as son of the former minister and brother-in-law of William Emerson. "Verily our enemies are of our own household," said Emerson. Townspeople did not prevent it when Daniel Bliss sent his brother, Samuel, a few weeks later to bring his family and a few valuables in to Boston. Samuel was questioned by Duncan Ingraham, a next-door neighbor, who was himself later suspected of Tory leanings. Bliss's house, the second on Walden Street, was confiscated and sold at auction in 1781 for 178 pounds.

Gage's informers told him just where the supplies were hidden, just when the order was given to ship them to other towns and later, just what remained. He was told on April 15 that the Provincial Congress was divided about taking any further warlike measures until they had consulted Rhode Island and New Hampshire. An immediate expedition was advised before all the provisions could be dispersed and support could come from the other colonies. Church offered to get the Congress to adjourn, if that would be agreeable to the General. Gage had been instructed from England to arrest Hancock and Adams. He must have decided to put this off. He gave no such orders to Lieutenant Colonel Francis Smith who was now chosen to head the expedition. Had he intended to arrest the ringleaders as they themselves believed and as historians have repeated ever since, he would have acted while the Congress was still in session.

His orders to Smith gave particular instructions about destroying the stores and supplied maps showing their exact location.

On the day the spy's letter arrived he took his grenadiers and light infantry off their regular duties saying that they were going to be taught special exercises.

The information which Gage received on March 9 was written in transparent French. Among other details it read:

Il-y-a sept toneaux de poudre a feu deposités chez un certain nommé Whitney, pres de l'entre du Vilage de Concord (dans un Maison Blanche Emplatree sur La Main droit, La maison ayant une petite Cour devant entouree des palisades).[2]

Il est a Soupçonner que les armes, et La poudre sont placés dans une Espece de magasin ou Boutique a coté de La Maison.

Il-y-a aussi dans le meme Vilage, et chez Le dit Barret, une quantité de poudre, des Balles, des Fusils et Bayonets. Il-y-a Cent Barriques de Farine avec une quantité considerable du Lard, et des pois depositees, dans une Espece de Brasserie, appartenant a un nommé Ebenezer Hubbard, dont La maison est située pres de L'Eglise, au centre du meme Vilage.[3]

Il-y-a aussi un quantité du Lard et des Pois dans un Magazin qui appartient au nommé Samuel Jones; sa demeure proche de celle du dit Hubbard.[4]

Il-y-a deux Routes d'ici a Concord. La premiere par Le passage a Charlestown Les vilages de Cambridge et de Lexington; La distance environ six Lieues ou dixneuf miles. La seconde par les Vilages de Roxbury de Watertown et une partie de Weston, sept Lieues ou environ 22 miles.

In Gage's instructions to Lieutenant Colonel Francis Smith who was to lead the expedition, Gage also mentions Butler; two men by the

---

[2] The white plastered house with the little fenced-in courtyard belonging to Whitney was doubtless our "The Wayside."

[3] Ebenezer Hubbard's house site was across the millpond from the church where Hubbard Street now meets Walden Street.

[4] Samuel Jones, a tailor (1707-1802), lived next door to Hubbard. His wife was Sarah Hubbard. He was uncle to Lieutenant Elisha Jones at the Bullet-hole House.

Ebenezer Hubbard and his old house on Walden Street, one of the store houses in 1775.

name of Bond; cannon hid in a wood a mile and a half from the center of the village between the river and Malden pond; the wood thick, a good deal of underwood; the ground no little wet but not a marsh; the medicine chests, and powder barrels, tents, et cetera, distributed in the chief houses, particularly Mr. Barrett's, Captain Wheeler's, Mr. Hubbard's stores and the two Bonds's.

Malden is of course Walden but there are several likely hiding places between Walden and the river. The two Bonds were Abijah and his sons, Nathan and Abijah, Jr., who had come up from Watertown and opened a store here on Main Street beyond Ephraim Jones's tavern, with its jail next to the south burying-place. They were soon active in town affairs. Nathan was a Harvard graduate and later prospered as a merchant in Boston. The widow of Abijah Bond, Jr., continued to run the store. The building is still in existence and has been moved up Main Street to #99 and used for a dwelling. She was also named Sarah Hubbard, a cousin of Sarah, wife of Jones the tailor. Captain

Wheeler was Timothy, called "Pond Tim" to distinguish him from four other Timothy Wheelers in the various branches of this many-branched family. Joseph Butler did not belong to an old Concord family. He was later captain of one of the two Concord companies which served under Major John Buttrick, enlisting April 20 for eight months service. Captain Butler and Sarah, his wife, had children here between 1772 and 1778 and the boy born January 12, 1776, was named George Washington Butler after his father's commanding officer, surely an early recognition of Washington's greatness. Butler had first come here to run the old Bateman-Munroe tavern on Lexington Road.

*Then haste thee, Prescott and Revere!*
*Bring all the men of Lincoln here:*
*Let Chelmsford, Littleton, Carlisle,*
*Let Acton, Bedford hither file,*
*Oh, hither file and plainly see*
*Out of a wound, leap Liberty.*
    *Lanier:* Psalm of the West

But if General Gage had accurate information about what was going on in Concord, Concord was just as well aware of what was going on in Boston. By April 18, a large number of small boats had been drawn up at the foot of the Common, and the light infantry and grenadiers had been excused from regular drill; there was no question but that an expedition into the country was afoot. Concord with its storehouse of supplies and its revolutionary sentiments was the most likely target. It only remained to confirm it and learn whether it would be by land over Boston neck and through Watertown or across the broad Charles estuary and through Lexington. When the presence of boats proved that the latter route would be taken, it was the mission of Paul Revere and William Dawes to warn the countryside and each left Boston by a different route. Concord had been busy moving what could be moved to other towns, but oxcarts were slow and not too numerous. Colonel James Barrett was in general charge. He had to send to the outlying farms to borrow the carts, arrange for their loading, and plan where to send them. Some of the carters had not got home when the alarm came on Wednesday, April 19.

Young Dr. Samuel Prescott had lingered late in Lexington on the

Paul Revere's lantern, bought from the sexton of the Old North Church for the Concord Antiquarian Society.

night of the eighteenth of April at the hospitable house of the widow of the clockmaker, Nathaniel Mulliken, which was on the main Boston road just east of the village. The widow was Lydia, daughter of Deacon John Stone. There were seven children in the family, the three oldest boys between nineteen and twenty-three and Nathaniel, the oldest, a member of Captain Parker's company, but it was the oldest daughter, Lydia, who particularly interested the young doctor. Rumors were flying in Lexington that night and it was natural for the doctor to wait for news until midnight when Revere arrived, soon followed by Dawes.

The Mulliken house was burned during the British retreat the next day. Dr. Prescott went on a privateer to sea, was captured and taken into Halifax where he died. Lydia waited until 1783 when the last hope of Dr. Samuel's return had faded, then married Joseph Burrill of Haverhill.

Hancock meanwhile sent Solomon Brown from Lexington to warn Concord, but he ran into a trap near the Concord–Lincoln town line and was detained. A group of six or eight horsemen had been sent out by Gage to prevent messengers from alarming the countryside and so far they had been successful.

Dr. Samuel Prescott lived here. Some of the ell remains of his father's house. He brought Paul Revere's message to Concord.

Revere, Dawes, and Prescott came along together, warning every house, where the fact that they all knew Dr. Abel Prescott's son made it easier to persuade the sleepy farmers that the British were coming in strength. Among those they warned was Josiah Nelson, who then dressed to take the news to Bedford, and afterwards said that he met the British patrol and they slashed him with a saber, thus shedding the first blood that day. Just west of Nelson's, the patrol, hidden in a pasture and on Mill Street across the way, intercepted the messengers and took them into a field to disarm and question them. Despite threats to blow his brains out, the young doctor spurred his horse over a wall and cut over to Virginia Road which was then, at that end, part of the main Bay Road. Here he warned the two Hartwell families who lived in houses beyond the present corner and they in turn warned Captain William Smith next door. Smith, the dashing young captain of the Lincoln Minutemen and Abigail Adams's brother, had lived in Boston, was a "high son of Liberty" there, and presumably one of the Indians in the Boston Tea Party.

Prescott got to Concord center soon after one o'clock, alerted Amos Melvin, on guard at the town house, who rang the alarm bell in the

Captain William Smith house on Virginia Road.

cupola of the old town hall. Plans had been made in advance for messengers to carry the word to other towns. As a doctor with two sons already learning his profession, Abel Prescott had four saddle horses, the largest number in any one household in Concord. Physicians were also exempt from training with the militia, so both the sons were messengers. Tradition has it that Samuel rode on to Acton and Stow while young Dr. Abel rode south to Sudbury and Framingham. Abel returned at noon along Walden Street to see the British starting their retreat along the Bay Road. A shot was fired from the millbrook meadow and he was wounded. He took refuge in the widow Heywood's house where his wound was treated but in his weakened condition he fell a prey to dysentery and died in August.

*Swift as their summons came they left*
*The plow mid-furrow standing still,*
*The half-ground corn-grist in the mill*
*The spade in earth, the axe in cleft.*
     *Whittier:* Lexington

On Wednesday, aroused by the bell in the town house turret, the Minutemen and militia gathered before dawn in the rutted training field near the Wright tavern but had no definite information about the progress of the British. They sent Reuben Brown, the saddler who lived in Peter Bulkeley Esquire's old house, to find out. He stopped on Concord Hill in Lexington when he heard the firing and brought back word that the British force was very large and that there had been shooting on Lexington Green but he did not know about casualties. "Did they fire ball?" he was asked. "I do not know but think it probable," was his cautious reply.

At early daylight, now, Major Buttrick sent the older men, who had been left in the militia when the Minutemen were recruited, up on the burial hill, where a flag was fluttering from the Liberty Pole as a symbol of their defiance to the illegal acts of Parliament. What the flag was, is not of record. The Concord Minutemen with the men from Lincoln, who had now arrived, marched down to Meriam's Corner and waited on the slope of the hill which marked the end of the long ridge from town. Their stand here was similar to Captain Parker's on Lexington Green, an assertion of their right to assemble, but they had some warning of what might happen. They numbered less than a hundred and fifty men at the most, even including the company from Lincoln under Captain Smith. Abijah Pierce of Lincoln had just been appointed Colonel of a Minuteman regiment, but since his commission had not arrived, he went that day as a private with the Lincoln company. Many of the militia that day marched with the Minute companies. The Concord men were led by Captain David Brown, whose farm faced the north bridge above the road fork, and by Captain Charles Miles, who lived at Nine Acre Corner at Williams Road. Friends had enlisted together so that Miles had more South Quarter and Brown more North Quarter men in his troop, including Brown's oldest son, Purchase, and three others named Brown, all related to him. The Lincoln men had heard that men were killed in Lexington but there were no details of the massacre that had already killed seven soldiers and one civilian and wounded eight. [ED. NOTE: J. S. Keyes says it was the Pine Tree flag.]

Although the British had marched five miles beyond Lexington, they came over Brook's Hill in glittering military array to the sound of fife and drum. There were fully seven hundred in Lieutenant Colonel Smith's force. The Minutemen saw themselves badly outnumbered; they turned and marched back to the center, with their own fifes and drums, warned the militia on the burial hill to follow, and took up for a short time a position on Windmill Hill, the high ground behind the old almshouse on the north bridge road, but as the British advanced, they retreated along the ridge, which had the traces of an earlier road along it. They crossed the bridge and went up the hill toward Captain Brown's pasture; then, collecting the women and children from the houses in the area hurried them along to Punkatasset Hill where reinforcements from Bedford and Acton and individuals in twos and threes joined them until between three and four hundred were gathered. Lanes through the Estabrook pastures connected the Hunt farm with roads from Acton and Carlisle. As they went, six British light infantry companies came along under Captain Parsons. These crossed the bridge and Captain Parsons left two companies under Captain Laurie at the bridgehead, one company, the 10th, under Lieutenant Kelly above the main road in Brown's pasture which the Minutemen had lately left, and another, the 4th company under Lieutenant Gould, above the lower road which led through a gate and around to the south of the hill toward Colonel Barrett's farm. Captain Parsons took this road with two companies, but was soon overtaken by one of the companies from the bridge and a seventh company which came along from town. He expected to find the most valuable stores at Colonel Barrett's.

Lieutenant Colonel Smith and Major Pitcairn had found all quiet in the center. They dispatched another company under Captain Mundy Pole to the south bridge and set the grenadiers to destroying stores in the center while they themselves relaxed with toddies, in chairs, in front of the tavern. Soon smoke was rising as tent pegs and wooden dishes found at Deacon David Wheeler's house on Sudbury Road were burned. The Liberty Pole was soon cut down and burned and gun carriages found in the town house were brought out and set afire.

At the bridge, a civilian on horseback came along from town and told Captain Laurie that he was a doctor going to see a patient, that he did not trouble himself with the disputes of the country nor did he in any shape belong to the militia. Laurie let him pass and saw him

Simon Hunt house near the North Bridge. (Photograph by Alessandro
Macone.)

go along the road that Parsons had taken and soon come back and
ride toward Punkatasset. This cool young man must have been young
Dr. Joseph Hunt, then studying medicine under Dr. Cuming, going
to the Simon Hunt house where his family lived, and finding them gone,
following over to his cousins' on Punkatasset Hill.

Soon the little group of officers on the Nehemiah Hunt doorstep on
that hilltop saw smoke rising from the various fires in town. "Will you
let them burn the town down?" cried Lieutenant Joseph Hosmer who
was acting as adjutant. The numerical odds were now the other way,
so the Americans marched back from Punkatasset Hill. As they came
around the corner by John Flint's, they looked to the British like a
very large army, perhaps 1,500 men by Sutherland's estimate, though
in actuality between 300 and 400. First the 10th company, who thought
they might be cut off, then the 4th, withdrew to the bridge while Laurie
sent one and then another urgent request to Smith for reinforcements.
Lieutenant Sutherland was the last to re-cross the bridge, stopping to
help tear up a few planks. He looked back and saw the Provincials
marching down in good military order by divisions, that is, four

The North Bridge and Minuteman Statue in 1965. (Photograph by Keith Martin.)

abreast, in the language of the day. (Cf. Allen French, *General Gage's Informers,* page 89, note 2.)

Adjutant Hosmer had directed the march to the bridge with Captain David Brown's company by twos, and the Acton company under Captain Isaac Davis by twos, beside them on their right. At the head were Major John Buttrick and Lieutenant Colonel Robinson of Westford, who had come down ahead of his men and volunteered to serve under Buttrick in spite of his superior rank. They were all still conscious of repeated orders not to fire first.

On the British side, Laurie tried to form his three companies (about 100 men) for street firing, then urged the crowding men to spread out. Lieutenant Sutherland obeyed, jumping over the wall into the Manse field, followed by a few men.

The main road to Groton from the north bridge in 1775 was three

Spring flood at North Bridge. This shows why the road made two angles to climb the hill.

rods wide and led up the hill between Captain Brown's land and Buttrick land, but it could not go straight up the hill from the bridge because there was a four-acre meadow directly west of the bridge which is flooded even today in the spring. So the road went around three sides of the meadow and on the side nearest the bridge ran parallel to and quite near the river for 400 feet opposite the Manse field. The so-called low road taken by Parsons and his troops toward Colonel Barrett's left this main Groton road at the second corner where the main road turned on the third side of a square to go up the hill. As the Provincials came down the hill, skirting the meadow on the upper side, Brown's men were nearest the enemy but they were out of effective gun shot. Then, as they rounded the last corner by the river, the Acton men were in the most exposed position and only the river's width away from the British soldiers who had leaped the wall with Sutherland. The British fired first, scattered shots went into the river and some shots were nearly spent; men asked each other jokingly

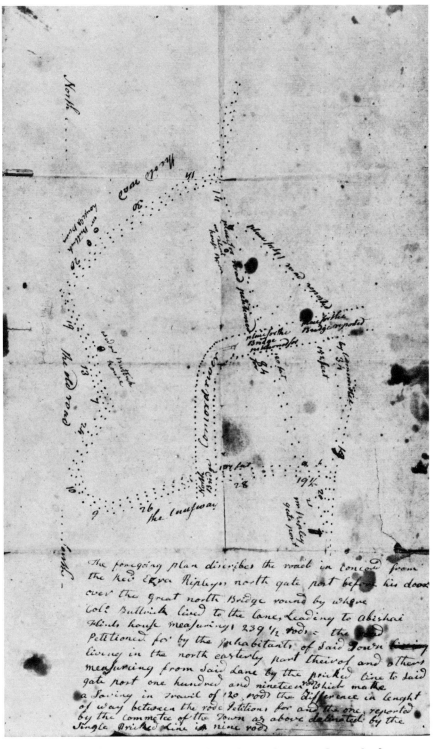

1790 plan showing the old North Bridge and proposed new bridge.

if the British were firing jackknives. Jonas Brown and Luther Blanchard were slightly wounded, but at the volley from the bridgehead or as the result of sharpshooting from the Manse field, Isaac Davis and Abner Hosmer, both of Acton, were instantly killed.

Now Major Buttrick cried: "Fire, fellow soldiers, for God's sake, fire!" The British were in each other's way and crowded in the narrow roadway. After the American volley, they fled, leaving one soldier from the 4th company instantly killed and two mortally wounded, one of whom was left for dead and one of whom was helped along almost to the center before he died. Nine others of the British were wounded: four officers, a sergeant, and four privates. That was the end of any organized fighting for the day on the part of the Americans. Some rushed after the British to discover that the grenadiers had come at length to help Captain Laurie, their pace slowed by the fat Lieutenant Colonel Smith who led them, so the Americans climbed the hill behind the Jones's house, which now got its bullet hole. They spent some time going back and forth along the ridge where they could watch the British who marched and countermarched in the road.

It was the end of discipline, too, for the British 4th company. "I do not believe it was collected again that day," reported Lister. Both sides apparently forgot Parsons and his four light infantry companies, the 5th, the 38th, the 52nd, and 23rd. They had found very little left at Colonel Barrett's and started back without hearing the firing at the bridge. They also failed to see the West Sudbury men under Deacon Haynes who followed them to the north bridge, too late for the fight there, but in time to join in the pursuit where Haynes was killed. He was eighty years old. Another delay had occurred when Parsons's men had paused at widow Brown's tavern at the corner of Lowell Road for rest and refreshment.

Some of the Americans had taken their dead and wounded up to the Buttrick house and the bridge was deserted when a young fellow of twenty-one from Captain Brown's company named Ammi White came along, hatchet in hand, and stopped to look at the two British soldiers. One was not quite dead, and as he stirred, White killed him with blows on the head. When Parsons came by and saw the mangled body he reported that one of his comrades had been scalped. This atrocity served to further inflame feeling and the truth of it was never admitted by the Americans. Captain Brown, whose family had been evacuated early in the day, brought them home and got his cousin,

Diorama of Concord Fight. (Courtesy of the Concord Antiquarian Society.)

Elisha Jones (bullet-hole) house. (Photograph by Alfred Hosmer.)

Widow Abishai Brown's tavern at Hildreth's Corner. (From the author's collection.)

Zachariah Brown and Isaac Davis's Concord cousin, Thomas Davis, Jr., to bury the British dead by the roadside. They testified later that neither had been scalped. The third soldier was buried near the square where his comrades left his body. Captain Brown wrote in his diary that night simply "had a sharp skirmish today." (See Appendix H.)

With Parsons back, some stores destroyed and everything apparently peaceful, Smith and Pitcairn put their wounded officers in carriages taken from the Beatton and Reuben Brown houses. They took Captain William Smith's horse for one of the wounded. Smith had left it in the center early that morning.

The British wounded had been treated by Dr. Timothy Minot, Jr., at his house in Monument Square and by Dr. Cuming in the Daniel Bliss house. One wounded soldier, Samuel Lee, of the Tenth Regiment, stayed behind and became a Concord citizen.

*You know the rest in the books you have read*
*How the British regulars fired and fled.*
*How the farmers gave them ball for ball*
*From behind each fence and farm yard wall,*
*Chasing the red-coats down the lane*
*Then crossing the fields to emerge again*
*Under the trees at the turn of the road*
*And only pausing to fire and load.*
  *Longfellow:* Paul Revere's Ride

The return began in good order. The shot at young Dr. Abel Prescott was made without command, probably by the flankers. Smith had every right to expect Lord Percy to arrive soon with reinforcements, having sent for them earlier. The British had flanking companies on the ridge and in the millbrook meadow, but when the ridge ended at Meriam's Corner, they joined the main body of troops to cross Elm Brook, a branch of the millbrook. Here the Minutemen from Reading and Billerica and those who had cut across behind the ridges from the north bridge were waiting, somewhat sheltered by the Meriam house and barn and a small hillock. Here occurred the first American attack of the day. No longer waiting for the British to fire first, they began the harassment which was to continue all the way to Charlestown. Some fired from the rear at the retreating British, others ran ahead to find

Meriam house where the pursuing minutemen in 1775 made the first attack on the British retreat. The house was built in part by the second generation and was designated a block house in King Philip's War.

shelters from which they could fire at the advancing column. The men from East Sudbury and Framingham had been waiting on the Brooks's hillside on the south side of the road. Sutherland thought he saw ". . . a vast number of Armed men drawn out in battalion order, I dare say near 1,000, who on our coming nearer, dispersed into the woods and came as close to the road and our flanking party as they possibly could and upon our ascending the height to the road, gave us a very heavy fire, but some shots from the left hand drew my attention that way, when I saw a much larger body drawn up to my left. This I take to be the party with whom those that attacked us at the bridge meant to join." Of course, Sutherland's numbers were greatly exaggerated, but Concord reports agree about the attack. Thaddeus Blood said he fired from behind Captain Minot's. This was the next farm east of Meriam's Corner. The Bedford, Billerica, and Reading men who had cut over behind the ridge made a second stand where the old Woburn Road joined the Bay Road in Lincoln. They had been joined

Virginia Road near Woburn Road at Bloody Curve. (Photograph by Alfred Hosmer.)

by late-comers from Woburn and Billerica. On the opposite side of the road in the swampy woods were the Sudbury and Framingham men who had hurried along from Brooks's hill. Here they fired with deadly effect and eight British were killed and several wounded, but the British flankers came up behind them and Captain Wilson of Bedford, Daniel Thompson of Woburn, and Nathaniel Wyman of Billerica were killed. The next day five of the British dead were buried in Lincoln cemetery. The place on the road has since been called "bloody curve."

The most courageous act of the day was the stand made by the Lexington men on a hill near the town's west boundary. For a little company of citizen soldiers that had lost seven killed and eight wounded in the morning, to regroup and march out against the enemy at noontime was a display of resolution that would be hard to match. [These figures are from *The History of Lexington*, Boston, 1913.] Three more were killed and one more wounded in the afternoon. The Lexington History reports that one British soldier was shot in the leg and Pitcairn's horse wounded on the Green and that Captain Nathan

Barrett, Captain George Minot, and Captain Charles Miles of Concord were wounded on the retreat. However, the fact is that Captain Minot lived until 1808 and Shattuck does not report that he was wounded. Hudson must have confused him with Ephraim Minot, wounded at Bunker Hill. The wounds of the other two captains must have been slight if any. Concord accounts agree that the last named was slightly wounded during the pursuit. Captain, later Colonel, Barrett died in 1791 and Captain Miles in 1827.

A strange encounter took place at the Fiske house in Lexington where James Hayward of Acton stopped at the well for water and saw a British soldier coming from the doorway. Both fired, the British soldier was instantly killed, Hayward died next day of his wound in his father's arms. Hayward was lame and a schoolmaster, exempt on either account from military service.

Captain Charles Miles of Concord was wounded during the British retreat and at first was reported killed. Asked afterward how he felt at the bridge, he said "as solemn as if I was going to church." In fact, Concord men realized fully the seriousness of the step they had taken. The decision to fight had been made and there was to be no turning back until Yorktown.

James Russell Lowell called it ". . . the era-parting bridge where the old world passed into the new" and mourned the British soldiers ". . . who came three thousand miles and died, to keep the past upon her throne."

Out of 1,800 British engaged that day, seventy-three were killed, 147 wounded and twenty-six reported missing. On the Colonial side, an unknown number took part (an estimate is 3,500), forty-nine were killed, forty-one wounded and five were missing. Although Earl Percy with his reinforcements were waiting in East Lexington, the running battle continued until the British reached Charlestown, to be ferried over to Boston. By far the greater part of the casualties occurred during the retreat, many in Arlington. The Concord men went along, each as far as his ammunition and strength allowed, a few even to Cambridge where the local soldiers became a besieging army of provincial troops, until, under the sponsorship of the Continental Congress, they were an American Army and so declared on July 2 by General Washington.

This was the day as Concord knew it. At Lexington a bloody massacre had taken place; at the north bridge, armed soldiers of several Middlesex towns had marched against armed soldiers of the Crown; at Meriam's Corner began the running battle, the first attack on the British with no question of who fired first; many separate acts of bravery followed, a day to celebrate as a whole, with glory enough for all.

The effect of the news on the other colonies was electric; companies from other colonies came to join the siege of Boston and the Continental Congress adopted the army and sent its best man as commander in chief. The Essex *Gazette* arrived in England on May 29 with the first news and sworn depositions. The Whig opposition in London was happy to have their prophecies fulfilled, while the party in power tried to make light of it. On June 13 the Earl of Suffolk, Secretary of State, hastened to reassure William Eden:

> For the soul of me I cannot see why Opposition should be so elated at what has happened in the Massachusetts. That affair has turned out exactly as was expected. A detachment was sent on a particular service; the service was performed; and on their return the troops were shot at from every place where there was cover, after having routed the only body of men who attempted to oppose them . . . and did there appear anything so terrible in this story when we reduced the exaggerated contents of the Salem Gazette into it? Or when people in opposition analyzed the first accounts, did they find much matter of triumph in them? Then what have they to crow about now? Or we to despond? I own it seems that Gage was betrayed; I mean that his design was divulged, and communicated to the rebels, by which means they had opportunity to remove the greatest part of their ammunition and stores from Concord, otherwise the General would not have risked anything for so inconsiderable a booty. To be sure it was to have been wished that the first blow should have been a hard one. This I trust will be the nature of the second and then perhaps a third will not be necessary. I cannot but believe that if these fanatical scoundrels are well drubbed at the next rencontre you'll hear no more of the great zeal and readiness of the Colonies to support their cause by arms . . . .[5]

The next rencontre was at Bunker Hill and only increased the zeal and readiness of the Colonies.

Many stories are told in Concord of the search by the British, and the destruction of the stores. The British were courteous on the whole and confined their destruction to the public stores, except for burning the Bible from the meetinghouse pulpit.

One of the early stories related that Pitcairn, at the Wright tavern, stirred his toddy with his finger and said he would so stir the Yankee blood that day. It was notable that they paid everywhere for the food and drink they took.

[5] From a manuscript letter in the Pierpont Morgan Library, used with permission.

The communion silver had been hidden in a barrel of soft soap, either in the Wright tavern or in the White Block opposite, east of the Green. Both stories are told but both agree that cleaning it later was no easy task. Martha Moulton, housekeeper for the old schoolmaster, Timothy Minot, begged the soldiers not to burn the town house while they were burning the gun carriages nearby, and they obligingly put out the flames. Timothy Wheeler saved some of the flour by holding a handful of his own flour over a barrel head and saying with every appearance of honesty "this is *my* flour." "We don't take private property" replied the grenadiers, but they rolled many barrels across the road into the millpond. Some of these barrels swelled and the flour caked near the outside so that much could be recovered next day. Many iron cannon balls and lead musket balls were also fished out to add to the stores which had been carted away to safety.

When Samuel Adams exclaimed in Lexington, "O what a glorious morning for America!" he was by no means the only one to recognize its importance. Reverend William Emerson, seeing it from his Manse, wrote an account in his diary.

During the siege of Boston, Ralph Earle, a Connecticut painter, and Amos Doolittle, an engraver, came out from Cambridge to Lexington and Concord to paint and publish their four scenes of the day for sale to patriots. Their backgrounds are surprisingly accurate and they must have heard eyewitness accounts.

Two years later Chastellux, a French ally, toured the battlefields and listened to the garrulous keeper of a tavern next to the south burying-place, Ephraim Jones, describe his own part in the day's events. A far less pleasant description of the tavern keeper came from Sir Archibald Campbell, who complained to General Washington of his treatment in the Concord jail in the tavern yard. Sir Archibald had been made a prisoner as he sailed into Boston Harbor, not suspecting that the city was held under siege. He or his companion James Wilson drew a sketch of the jail which is now in the Concord Public Library. Other evidence shows that the prisoners of war, like the poor debtors, were allowed the freedom of the "Jail Limits" during the day and were allowed to go anywhere from the milldam to Heywood Street and visit shops and houses on Walden Street or Lexington Road, in that area. Campbell was kindly treated by Mrs. Merrick, a daughter of Dr. Minot, and later in the war, when her son, Tilly, was captured at sea and taken in to a prison ship in Halifax Harbor, a much worse prison than Concord's, he was able to appeal to Campbell who had been exchanged and was then governor of Nova Scotia. Campbell soon managed Merrick's exchange. Merrick's mother became the second wife of the wealthy Duncan Ingraham.

When in 1785 the young John Quincy Adams came to Lincoln to visit his Aunt Smith (then, alas, deserted by her husband, Captain William), he visited the battlefield and predicted that some day "that hayfield would be as famous a shrine as the spot in Brussels where Egmont and Horn suffered"—surely a notable understatement.

Joseph Hosmer and Reverend Ezra Ripley had a standing arrangement with the innkeeper to send them word whenever an interesting war veteran came through. They repaired to the tavern to hear his story until the minister, at least, considered himself an authority on the war. When he came to write his story of the battle, which started a bitter controversy with Lexington, he drove about town with his stepgrandson, Ralph Waldo, to interview every living survivor and made each search his fading memory until he could corroborate Mr. Ripley's preconceived ideas, a method used by historians in other towns as well.

The real heights of tribute were reached, however, in the orations delivered at later anniversary celebrations, beginning in 1825 when Edward Everett, the most eloquent orator of the day, outreached himself in describing the bravery of the little band of patriots. But after all is read and spoken, the decision to fight, taken that day at the bridge, was indeed momentous. All the achievements of two centuries of America owe something to that brief fight which began the War of Independence. Without independence our experiment in government by the people would have been impossible. President Dwight of Yale wrote:

[These events] preface the history of a nation and the beginning of an empire and are themes of disquisition and astonishment to the civilized world. From the plains of Concord will henceforth be dated a change in human affairs, an alteration in the balance of human power, and a new direction to the course of human improvement. Man, from the events which have occurred here, will, in some respects, assume a new character, and experience in some respects a new destiny.

As Henry James put it in 1904 as he mused at the bridge: "the fight had been the hinge—so one saw it—on which the large revolving future was to turn."

For almost two hundred years Concord has concentrated to such an extent on the story of those few minutes at the bridge that the succeeding long hard years of discouraging effort are forgotten. On the day after the battle the town was a hive of activity. A few prisoners had to be guarded at Reuben Brown's, stores had to be retrieved from the millpond, a stream of recruits began coming through from upcountry and immediate plans had to be made for a besieging army. Here Reverend William Emerson took the lead. The meetinghouse was open for the groups who came through. Seven hundred were here on April 21, proof enough, if proof were needed, that the battle of the Nineteenth had been important. They could rest while they listened to words of encouragement. Mr. Emerson soon realized he must find out exactly what the situation was in Cambridge, so he rode down to see. When he found that Harvard Yard and Cambridge Common were full of soldiers in make-shift accommodations, he offered Concord as a refuge for the College and the offer was soon accepted. On the seventeenth of June, the College Library was being moved out here even while the battle of Bunker Hill was in progress. President Langdon had found quarters at Dr. Minott's, Professor Winthrop had hired Mr. Whitney's house (the Wayside), and Professor Wigglesworth had taken the house on Bedford Road built by Enos Fox and owned in 1775 by Jonas Minott, Jr. Stephen Jones, who had bought this house from Enos Fox and then sold it to young Minott, was overheard boasting in the tavern that he had put no stamps on the document and so could not be legally held to it. After the Revolution he was not only held to it, but also had to pay a penalty for his boasting.

The College reopened here in early October. The students were quartered in various places, some as far from the center as Joseph Lee's on Nashawtuc Hill. They walked in for classes at the town house and meetinghouse and of course added life to the village. Jonathan Fay, son of Westborough's leading family, fell in love with Lucy Prescott, sister of the young doctors, Samuel and Abel, and after the war, settled in Concord. Ezra Ripley was a graduate in 1776 and in 1778 became the Concord minister. The College was able to move back to Cambridge after the evacuation of Boston.

The county probate records were stored at Dr. Minott's, a house bought by the county a few years later.

Several patriot families moved out from Boston during the British occupation, enough so that a Boston town meeting was held here on July 18, 1775. Among those who came from Boston and remained to settle here were Samuel Bartlett, a goldsmith; Emerson Cogswell, a hatter; and Joseph Lasinby Brown, a goldsmith. Another to come was Samuel Parkman, brother to William Parkman of Concord and grandfather of Francis Parkman, the historian, who hired the brown plastered house at the head of the milldam which belonged to Ezekiel Brown. Ezekiel Brown, a cousin to Captain David Brown, had, as a storekeeper, run into debt to Frederick Geyer, a wholesaler in Boston. In 1773, he had been taken to Boston and imprisoned for debt but was allowed a limited freedom during the day. He used this time to assist a doctor in Boston until he had acquired enough medical knowledge so that, when he was freed after the evacuation of Boston, he could enlist in the Continental Army as a surgeon. Here he served three years. It is interesting to know that all the land now covered by the Catholic Church, the Town House, the Insurance buildings, the Dee Funeral buildings and six private houses was not considered enough security to cover a debt of less than a thousand dollars. Back from the army, Brown practiced in Concord until the peace treaty brought on a renewal of the claims, and a second imprisonment. After that Dr. Brown went to Benton, Maine, where he combined surgery with tavern-keeping and became a leading citizen. His wife was Mary Barron, a sister of Hannah Barron who saved the Province treasury when she worked at Ephraim Jones's tavern on April 19. She told the British that the room in which it was hidden was her room and so dissuaded them from searching it.

After the Nineteenth, the first concern was to recruit soldiers for the siege of Boston. As we have seen, the Provincial Congress had urged the towns to select from the ranks of the militia the younger men able to assemble at a minute's notice and Concord had enrolled about 100 men in two companies who had met and drilled together and been paid by the town. William Emerson's diary in January, 1775, calls them Minutemen. It appears that the name was used as early as November 24, 1774, in Leicester, Worcester County, but soon became popular and was applied everywhere to these selected companies, and then was used loosely to describe any man who marched on the Nineteenth of April. Not every town had Minutemen. In Lexington, it was the whole militia which assembled on the Green and Captain Parker, in his sworn deposition, alluded to himself as captain of the militia. Jonas Clarke says that there were sixty or seventy men gathered on the Green that morning. This is one-tenth of the entire population of Lexington; hence it must have included all the able-bodied men, that is, the militia. The roster of those who took part that morning in Lexington contains the names of many older men, who would not have belonged to a company of Minutemen had one been formed. It is a very small point whether the Lexington men were Minutemen or militia, but it indicates that patriotic fervor was not confined to the young and hot-headed. In any case the organization of Minutemen paid by the towns ceased next day when the Province adopted the besieging army and proceeded to enroll soldiers sworn into service for a limited, stated time. The first call in Concord was for eight months' service and two companies were enlisted on April 20, one under Captain Joseph Butler, a lieutenant in Captain Nathan Barrett's militia company, and one under Captain Abishai Brown who had been sergeant the day before in his cousin David Brown's Minute company. Before the war ended, he had become major in the Continental Army. The names of the Concord Minutemen are found in the town treasurer's lists and on old muster rolls (cf. Appendix H).

When a draft became necessary, the quotas of men needed were set by the Provincial Congress while it acted as a State government, and the needed men were taken from the militia by a local committee. When the fighting was close by, these brief enlistments relieved the army of the expense of providing winter quarters, but during the unexpectedly long war it often proved frustrating to General Washington who planned a campaign and then found that the terms of many enlistments had expired.

The advantage of a short term was proved when General Knox had mounted the guns from Ticonderoga on Dorchester Heights in March, 1776. Concord enlisted 145 men for ten days' service and they marched to Dorchester Heights where the sight of all these men and guns made the British evacuate Boston.

At the battle of Bunker Hill, Captain Butler's company was heavily engaged at the rail fence, which bore the brunt of the first two British attacks. Five Concord men were mortally wounded: Benjamin Ball, William Buttrick, Danforth Hayward, John Meers, and Amos Wheeler. Several others were wounded, including Ephraim Minot. As soon as news of the battle came, the women of Concord sent down a chest of hospital supplies while the whole reconstituted militia company marched down to Cambridge just in case they were needed. The British, however, were in no condition to follow up their costly victory on June 17.

In January, 1777, the town enlisted forty-four men for three years' service. The lieutenants were Nathan Wheeler, Ephraim Wheeler, Warham Wheeler, and Ephraim Minott.

The largest expedition of the whole war called for six months' enlistment and left with sixty-one men from Concord, twenty-seven from Weston, and two from Lexington under Captain Charles Miles with Jonas Brown, who had been slightly wounded on the Nineteenth, as

Ensign. This was the expedition to Ticonderoga with Mr. Emerson as chaplain, in which Dr. Cuming was to have gone as commander.

Before he left on August 16, 1776, the first anniversary of the fight at the bridge had come and Emerson told his flock:

> The anniversary of this day, my countrymen, though it can not be said to be a morning without clouds, yet, methinks, the clouds are morning ones that will soon pass away. Britain's tyrannic power, however hard to bear, has taught us lessons we should ne'er have learned without her, has taught us our own strength and how to live without her. She'll sway her IRON sceptre over this world no more; a glory this, too bright for all but those who hold the GOLDEN sceptre of peace and righteousness.

At his first stop after he left home he wrote to his wife:

> Dear Mrs. Emerson,
> I desire to leave you and our dear little ones to a kind and gracious Providence. Don't distrust God's power to make provision for you. I am willing to leave the matter with Him who does all things well.
>
> Your affectionate husband,<br>William Emerson

He died of fever in Rutland on October 20 at the age of thirty-three. In 1831, his grandsons, Ralph Waldo and Charles Chauncy Emerson, could not find his grave there, but he has an eloquent inscription on an empty brick tomb in the hill burying-ground.

Other companies were in the battle of White Plains and in the campaigns in New Jersey. A company of sixty-three men from Concord and Acton marched to Ford Edward and had the pleasure of watching the surrender of Burgoyne. They guarded the prisoners on the road back and thereafter in Cambridge. This company was commanded by John Buttrick, now promoted to colonel. An alarm at Rhode Island when Benedict Arnold invaded with the British fleet was the last large call-up of Concord men in the war.

In some of the later drafts, the town was divided into as many divisions as there were men to supply, and each division hired a man, paying him a bonus up to 180 pounds. If a slave enlisted, he was given his freedom. In some cases most of the bonus was contributed by a single individual. Unfortunately, so severe was the inflation of currency that Continental notes were not worth a fraction of their face value. Repeated efforts were made to stop inflation by controlling prices. Concord committees met to figure on fair prices and to get county-wide agreement only to find that the agreements could not be enforced. In the four years between 1777 and 1781 the exchange rate for $100 in silver went from $105 in paper currency to $7,500.

The cost of the war in money was high. In 1780, taxes were collected in silver and amounted to a pound for each of the 1,300 inhabitants. The town paid for aid to the families of soldiers. In the first winter the town contributed beef and firewood to the army in Cambridge. When General Washington set prices which did not equal the going price for commodities, the town voted to pay the difference. In January, 1776, Concord voted to send three cords of wood per day to the soldiers in Cambridge. Other particulars of the money and men contributed by Concord can be found in Shattuck's *History of Concord.*

# Chapter VI   Emigration and Consolidation

*Put green boughs in your hats and renew the old cause*
*Stop the Courts in each County and bully the laws.*
*Constitutions and oaths, sir, we mind not a rush*
*Such trifles must yield to the lads of the bush.*
    St. John Honeywood: 1786

Inflation did not stop with the peace treaty. It imposed serious hardships on many people—especially on those who could not use paper money to pay their debts and now found themselves sued and imprisoned. Farmers in the western counties under Daniel Shays and in Middlesex County west of Concord under Job Shattuck of Groton attempted to prevent the courts from sitting and so stop the actions for debt. On September 12, 1786, about two hundred identified by hemlock sprigs in their hats, gathered in Concord to prevent the court from opening next day. Concord had held a special town meeting on September 9 and adopted an address to circulate to other towns, in which they deplored the use of violent means to get redress of the very real grievances. They felt that legal and constitutional means should be used rather than take the risk of destroying the young government for which they had fought since April, 1775.

Some in Concord shared the farmers' hostility to Boston which was a carry-over from their old hostility toward the Tory merchants of Revolutionary days. This was expressed in a demand that the higher courts should be moved out of the city to Concord.

A compromise was reached in Concord on September 12 when the judges agreed that if they were allowed to meet as they were legally required to, they would immediately adjourn until November. Meanwhile, the General Court would consider the grievances. However, it did not do so, and in November when the adjourned session was held in Cambridge, 3,000 militia were called out to guard it, and warrants were issued for the arrest of the insurgent leaders. Sentiment here condemned the manner of Job Shattuck's arrest in Groton during which he was severely wounded. He was tried in Concord and condemned to death for treason, but the sentence was not carried out and in 1787, his attorney, Ephraim Wood, Esq., of Concord, obtained a full pardon for him. When the revolt continued under Daniel Shays in Pelham, the Concord militiamen were mobilized and some marched as far as Pittsfield before the rebellion subsided.

However, the town meeting instructed Isaac Hubbard, its representative in 1787, to aid in removing all the grievances complained of and to lighten the burden on local taxes by taxing foreign luxuries heavily and keeping public promises inviolable. Laws should be punctually executed, they said, and the constituents should have the fullest information about the doings of the Legislature. Thus the town carried out its agreement to work within the constitution for the redress of the grievances.

The instability of money was further aggravated by the circulation of large quantities of paper money and made unbearable by the circulation of counterfeit paper. In Concord, the little store on the future town house site was taken over by a Captain Daniel Smith who had come here originally as a journeyman tanner. He sold rum by the glass as well as groceries and medicines, and then made and passed counterfeit money. He was found out, arrested, and sent to State's Prison. Others were involved, either as part of his ring or in another group. Arrested were Tarrant P. Meriam of Meriam's Corner and Stephen and Amos Wheeler of Virginia Road and Captain William Smith, of Lincoln. The latter was found not guilty, although he had had counterfeit notes on his person when arrested.

The green store on the present Catholic Church site was run by Abel Barrett followed by Jarvis and Hammond and then by Burr and Prichard until the death of Mr. Burr in 1832. The latter had an arrangement by which people left their extra money with him at interest. He apparently paid back promptly whenever anyone asked. Without any careful accounting, the borrowed money was used in the business. Both were found to be completely bankrupt when Prichard had to settle up after Burr's death, although there was no accusation of embezzlement. The Parish lost one thousand dollars from its invested funds. The Parish funds had previously been lent in the main to farmers, whose land was security, and so the Ministerial Fund acquired a swamp or a woodlot from time to time. Everyone was glad to have the national bank started in 1832 and the savings bank in 1835. Even in those poor times $52,000.00 was deposited within five years in the savings bank, money which had been hidden in cracked teapots and behind the loose bricks of Concord houses. The unlimited credit given

Central part of Concord before the Court House fire of 1849. Part of the Court House is seen on the left. Burying Hill is seen a short distance beyond. The Unitarian Church and Middlesex Hotel are seen on the right. (Drawn by J. W. Barber. Engraved by J. Downes, Worcester.)

by the small merchants was the cause of many other store failures including that of the easygoing trader John Thoreau.

The farmers, whose wealth was in land, suffered less from inflation. After the Narragansett grants to veterans of King Philip's War, Concord farmers acquired pastures in New Ipswich, Ashburnham, Westminster, Templeton, and Holden, sometimes adjacent to farms owned by sons and cousins. Every May the dry cows and young stock were assembled and driven over the road to summer pasture. The men and boys made the drive on foot or on horseback and as roads improved a "democrat" or utility vehicle went along to hold oats for the horses, blankets, and a youngster or two. Farmers on the way would rent a fenced field to hold the stock at night and would allow the boys to sleep in the barn. Reciprocally, Concord farmers had fenced yards to hold overnight upcountry stock being driven to market. These were very small drives compared to those we see in pictures of the West, but they were usually a boy's first trip away from home: they stood for romance and adventure. During the nineteenth century, as Boston grew and became a busy seaport, traders gradually took over the business, buying up cows, driving them off to pasture, feeding them in the fall on the aftermath in Concord fields, and finally driving them down to stockyards in Watertown or dressing them off in Concord for salt beef. Of course, this gave farmers extra income as butchers, tanners, candlemakers, and coopers. Now picket fences became necessary in the village to keep stray animals out of one's yard.

Though important in the aggregate, each farmer was a small operator. In 1810, Colonel Buttrick, an average successful farmer, kept one horse, a yoke of oxen, four or five cows, and one or two hogs. He raised fifty bushels of corn yearly, and a little more hay than his animals consumed. He and his three sons did all the work. He had a few apple trees on which he grew as many russets as the family wanted and cider apples enough to make all the cider they drank. He sold some hay and corn, a few potatoes, and butter and cheese. The same farm fifty years later produced 300 bushels of corn, 600 barrels of apples, many bushels of pears and currants, and a large quantity of seeds for market. It had three horses, thirty cows and employed six men in the summer and two in the winter.[1]

The detailed listings in the assessors' books show but little variation in the possessions of the individual farmers in the first two hundred

---

[1] Says Jarvis's manuscript.

years. Among the neighbors at the north bridge in 1771, for example, John Flint had one horse, two oxen, five cows, no sheep, and two swine; Captain David Brown had one horse, four oxen, seven cows, nine sheep, and two swine; Jonas Bateman had one horse, two oxen, four cows, and one hog. One naturally wonders how these farmers could make a living even granting that they were self-sufficient as to food, raising their own rye and corn, their own cider and apples, meat, milk and butter, their own fuel, and wool and flax for clothing. They worked out their taxes at four shillings per man per day or eight shillings per day for man and yoke of oxen. Some families took in a little cash by teaching. In others, one man was a housewright, or a blacksmith, a furniture maker, a cooper, or a maltster. It appears from the records, however, that the sale of land was the usual source of cash. Almost every family, even after the distribution of second division grants in Concord and grants in Concord Village, had Narragansett grants, and later grants to veterans of the French and Indian wars. Although the sums made by these means appear small today, the amount would go far. Since they did not spend money themselves, very few of these farmers thought it was necessary to provide spending money for their widows. In 1790, Major Buttrick showed exceptional generosity by leaving two silver dollars yearly to his wife.

After the War of 1812, the stability of the new American government seemed assured. During that war, the militia was called on only for guard duty in Boston Harbor. In Shays's Rebellion the overriding argument had been the need to give the infant government a chance. Now as the central government seemed stable, party spirit ran high. After the initial popularity of Hancock and Samuel Adams, whose elections to the governorship were almost unanimous, competition for office became more keen. In the voting, partisans would divide, forming in line on one side or the other of the town square, depending on which side they favored. In 1802, a tie between Gerry and Strong for governor was broken by bringing a sick man from his bed to carry the town for Strong 192 to 191. Twenty years before, only seventy-eight votes had been cast in all. By 1835, the population was 2,000.

Political feeling amounting almost to mass hysteria marked the anti-Masonic campaign in 1834, the Log Cabin campaign in 1840, and the Know Nothing campaign in 1854. The differences of opinion which had been constant in Concord from its founding, involving religion, then independence from Britain, now continued as party loyalty, until the parties themselves were split on the question of slavery.

*The natural increase of her population has been drained by the
constant emigration of her youth. Her sons have settled the
region around us and far from us. Their wagons have
rattled down the remote Western hills.*
        *Emerson:* Century Discourse

Even before the Revolution, many Concord boys had gone off to new towns and now hundreds went off to fertile-looking places which they had seen while on the march. The Brown family will illustrate this scattering. Bridget Brown (an aunt of Major Abishai Brown) had married Benjamin Harwood in 1733 and moved to Hardwick and then to Amherst where her husband died in 1758. She then took her nine children to Bennington, Vermont, in June, 1761, where she is said to have been the first settler, arriving first in a race from Hoosac Fort. Her son, Zachariah, married Lavinia Rice, whose ancestors were first settlers of Sudbury. His grandson married Eunice Farrar whose ancestors had lived close to the Browns in the North Quarter of Concord, and their children moved to St. Joseph County, Michigan, from Rupert, Vermont.

Captain David Brown's oldest son, Purchase Brown, who had been in his father's company at the north bridge, moved to Clarendon, then to St. Albans, and then to Swanton, Vermont. He had been named Purchase after his great-great-grandfather, Oliver Purchase, part owner of the ironworks, whose daughter, Hannah, wife of James Blood, Jr., had lived in the old house on the Old Manse site and was the grandmother of Purchase Brown's grandmother who inherited that property in 1741.

Purchase's sisters, Molly and Abigail, had married Nathan and Thomas Flint, near neighbors in Concord, and moved to Winchendon. Their brother-in-law, John Cuming Flint, had been interested in the settlement of a new town near Lake Sebago in Maine called at first Flintstown (now Baldwin). David Brown, Jr., and Ephraim Brown, his brother, both moved there. In October, 1794, Captain David Brown wrote to tell his sons in Maine that he could not visit them because his son Reuben had taken his horse to Vermont to bring back David's sister Hannah. Hannah had been visiting her nephew, Purchase. A month later he writes that Purchase's wife had died after childbirth.

The older child, David, was brought down to stay with his grandfather. The next year Purchase had married again, the widow Mason, and came to visit Captain David with a baby six weeks old. This second wife had been born in Concord, "a Starns, her mother was a Farrar." A letter in February, 1800, tells more about Purchase.

Purchase and his wife was here in January. He has been sorely visited with sickness since he moved up to St. Albans near the lake and after he had spent $500. in his sickness and recovered his health again, some time about September last he had the misfortune to have a ladleful of scalding hot potash fall onto his foot in the instep, which had been like to be fatal to him. His doctors gave over all hope and concluded to cut off his leg. His leg turned all black up to his hip. Though mortified, he would not consent to have it cut off without the advice of another doctor which lived a great distance from him and in the time that they sent for him, he being gone from home and could not come, they was still in the use of medicine and applied bitter herbs in hot baths, and in a short time brought it to the right color again and his doctors took courage and cured it so that he can go without limping. To be perceived he has let out his house in St. Albans and gone up further about 8 miles to a town called Swanton where he tells me he left Reuben to fix up an old log house which they intend to live in til they get able to build a better. Purchase owns 100 acres of excellent land with it, he tells me, and is to carry Reuben's wife and child up with him when he goes up.

The brothers in Maine prospered, but what became of Purchase and Reuben, the record is not certain. After one generation they had all gone west from Vermont. Left at home in Concord was William, who was deranged, and the youngest son, Joseph, who inherited the farm but was deep in debt when he died in 1821. Last to live on the farm was Captain David's widow, Abigail Munroe Brown, who lived to be ninety-nine and died in 1832. Her father had been Thomas Munroe of Lexington, the tavern keeper, who had bought the Wright tavern in 1751. William Brown died at the poorhouse in 1849. He had been a familiar figure on the milldam, asking for pennies. Henry Thoreau wrote of his death to little Ellen Emerson who knew all the characters in the house across the brook from her own. The old Stratton farm on the Walden road had been bought by the town for the poor, using a legacy left by Hugh Cargill who had come from Ballyshannon, Ireland, to Boston with the British troops and later prospered there as a merchant.

*In unploughed Maine he sought the lumberer's gang*
*Where from a hundred lakes young rivers sprang*
*He trod the unplanted forest floor whereon*
*The all-seeing sun for ages had not shone.*
        *Emerson:* Woodnotes

There is a happier ending to the story of Nathan Barrett, Jr., who was born in 1763 on the farm on the top of Punkatasset Hill, the eldest of fifteen children. His grandfather, Colonel James Barrett, had bought the farm from the Hunt family for his son, Captain Nathan, Sr., who served as a militia captain on April 19th. In 1785, young Nathan went with a group of Concord boys to Maine to found the town of Hope, called Barrettstown at first. They went by ship, a seasick twenty-four hour journey as far up the coast as possible, then walked the remaining miles from Camden through the forest, young Barrett carrying on his back the heaviest item, the grindstone. Now he writes that he wants the logging chain borrowed from his uncle, James Barrett, Jr., and sent down to him, since he has a contract to supply logs to a new mill. "The country settles fast. I piloted twenty all at once to a town right back of ours. Our wheat, corn and oats look very well. Reuben thinks I am from hum too much"—thus hinting at the attractions of a neighbor's daughter.

After this promising start, he had to give up the whole project and come home to help his mother after his father's death in 1791. Here he prospered on the farm and as a cooper. In 1795, he married Mary Jones from the Bullet-hole House.

He was a large, handsome man with a hearty manner somewhat hampered with a terrible stammer which made him hard to understand. His biographer says of him:

A little given to drink, he could always get the mare safely home of the darkest nights and he never got so much of a load on that anyone could get the better of him in a bargain.

He assessed the town taxes for many years and was Selectman for ten years after 1811.

He was a staunch Democrat and carried on a running feud with his minister, Ezra Ripley, a Federalist, who felt it incumbent on himself to correct the political as well as the doctrinal errors of his parishioners. A letter written by Ezra Ripley to Mr. Barrett has survived.

Mary Jones, wife of Nathan Barrett, Jr. (Courtesy of the Concord Antiquarian Society.)

August 24, 1812

Sir:

The freedom with which you have expressed your political sentiments, the warm desire I feel for your highest interests, the hope I still entertain that you may be convinced of those errors which are leading you and many other people into extreme difficulties which you and they now little apprehend, induce me to send you the pamphlet entitled Mr. Madison's War. It contains a statement of facts clearly proved and a force of reasoning that must, it seems to me, convince every impartial mind. It will show you why my political creed is different from yours.

If you will give it a calm and candid perusal, it will at least induce you to be mild and charitable toward those who differ from you in opinion respecting the leading men and measures of the present day.

I am

Your friend and humble servant<br>Ezra Ripley.

One Sunday after a night of drifting snow, Nathan Barrett came down to town from his hilltop to break out the road to church, and started to turn in the narrow drifted road between the gateposts of the Manse, with loud swearing and stuttering. Instead of being grateful for this chance to get downtown to his pulpit, the doctor came to the door and rebuked him for breaking the Sabbath while breaking the road, suggesting that he did it only to save time for the weekday's work. Without another word, Barrett turned his team and left the drifts in the long driveway, continued to town, and stopped short of the meetinghouse to wait until the doctor had made his way on foot, keeping warm in the tavern meanwhile until after the minister had struggled home through the drifts. Roads were not plowed in those days. The snow was broken down by driving a pung over it, the oxen (several yoke in heavy going) struggling through the drifts but in the end packing the snow so that sleighing lasted for weeks at a time.

Ezra Ripley had worked on a farm until he was twenty-one in order to support himself while he prepared for admission to college. After his senior Harvard year in Concord, he studied for the ministry, was ordained in November, 1778, called to Concord, and two years later married his predecessor's widow, Phebe Bliss Emerson, then thirty-nine, and already the mother of five children. They had three more children: Samuel who became minister in Waltham; Daniel Bliss Ripley, a lawyer; and Sarah. William, oldest of the Emerson stepsons, was to be the father of Ralph Waldo Emerson, who wrote a just biography of his stepgrandfather for the Social Circle. Ripley never forgot his church and parish, said Emerson:

He looked at every person and every thing from the parochial point of view. I remember when a boy driving about Concord with him, and in passing each house he told the story of the family that lived in it; and especially he gave me anecdotes of the nine church members who had made a division in the church and showed me how every one of the nine had come to bad fortune or to a bad end. So firm was his faith in a personal Providence that at a time of severe drought, he did not trust his assistant to make the prayers for rain but took over that prayer personally. He seemed in fact the embodiment of practical simple old-time faith, in that post-war era of inflation and ferment

when every farm family was losing its boys to the frontier and tradesmen were losing their apprentices to the city and often their own bodies to debtor's prison.

Dr. Ripley's influence on the town was practical and direct. He organized a school committee in 1799, taking the supervision of the schools away from the Selectmen and the local groups, so that the same standards would apply in each of the districts. Each district got its new building. On the first committee with him were Dr. Joseph Hunt, Abiel Heywood, Esq., Deacon John White, and Deacon George

Reverend Ezra Ripley, from a portrait. (Courtesy of the First Parish in Concord.)

Minott. The two-hour sermon preached to the children when these schools were dedicated emphasized the duty and obedience owed by each child to his parents and the gratitude they owed to the generous town. Soon the church had a singing school and a Sunday school. Ripley's stern appearance did not hide from the children the essential kindness of his nature. Little Jerry and Willy Robinson were sent up to the Manse one November day with a turkey. They knocked and when the minister opened the door, they thrust the turkey at him and started to run away. The minister stopped them and scolded them for their lack of courtesy.

"Let me show you the proper way to deliver a gift," he said, stepping outside where he could hand the turkey to the boys in the doorway.

"My mother sends her compliments," he said, pitching his voice high, "and wishes you a happy Thanksgiving."

Quick as a wink Willy took the turkey and said solemnly "Thank you, boys, and now if you will go to the kitchen, Madam Ripley will give you some cookies." In later years Willy became an editor and author of *Pen Portraits*, using the pen name Warrington. Jerry became a dentist and author of the *Evolution of Dentistry*.

Academy building, Middle Street, where Thoreau taught. This building was made over into a double house for Ellery Channing.

In 1822, as Ripley's energy failed, conditions in the center school under two out-of-town teachers became so bad that pupils came home black and blue from the unrestrained bullying of older boys as well as from punishment inflicted by the master. Five men living near the center decided to set up a private school. They were Samuel Hoar, Abiel Heywood, Josiah Davis, Nathan Brooks, and William Whiting. They built a two-story building on Academy Lane, about where Middle Street was later cut through. The teacher with the longest term was Phineas Allen of Medfield (Harvard 1825) who taught until 1836 when his anti-Masonic political activities had alienated the proprietors of the school. Allen ran against Abiel Heywood for Town Clerk—and won. Henry Thoreau and his brother, John, were enrolled in this school in 1828, and Henry was prepared there to enter Harvard in 1833. The town continued to elect its best to the school committee and they tried to improve the public schools, stimulated by the competition of Concord Academy. They began to make an annual report to the town to explain their plans and methods, but their outspoken evaluation of each teacher must have been hard for the teachers to bear. For in-

Henry Thoreau as a young man, from a crayon by Rowse. (Photograph by Keith Martin.)

stance, the printed report of 1849 says: "In the teacher for the winter school in district 2 we were disappointed. He failed entirely in his government and was not felicitous in his mode of imparting knowledge. At our suggestion he left." "The winter school in #6 was kept by Mr. G. D. Robinson of Lexington, a young man of good promise, but being young and inexperienced, he was unfortunate in his first impressions on the school, and after three weeks, the committee thought best to close it." Fortunately, this latter young man's life was not blighted. He was elected governor of the State in 1883 and was the town's honored guest in 1885. He was a grandson of the Revolutionary adjutant, Joseph Hosmer. The committee had appointed their young fellow-townsman, Henry Thoreau, to teach as soon as he finished Harvard in 1837.

The brick school had been built on the old site (on the square where it still stands) after the wooden schoolhouse burned in 1820. It occupied one small room downstairs while the Masons had the second floor. Nearby on Lowell Road lived Deacon Nehemiah Ball, a committee member who was glad to tell the new teacher that he could never succeed unless he used the rod liberally. Thoreau called out several of the pupils and strapped them, then wrote out his resignation. This, in 1837, was the first of several occasions in his life when Thoreau used a dramatic act to illustrate his beliefs. He said of this: "I have ever been disposed to regard the cow-hide as a non-conductor." After several vain attempts to get another position, since the panic in 1837 had started, Henry and his brother John started a private school for both girls and boys which moved into the Academy building when that became vacant a couple of months later. This school was highly successful and its experimental methods were ahead of their time. All who attended remembered it with affection. In 1841, the sudden death of John Thoreau closed the school.

*I have never got over my surprise that I should have been born into the most estimable place in all the world, and in the nick of time, too.*

    *Thoreau:* Journal IX 160

Henry Thoreau was born on Virginia Road in a house still standing on Deacon Jonas Minot's farm. This had been his mother's girlhood home after his grandmother Mary (Jones) Dunbar married the deacon as her second husband. Thoreau was of mixed racial strains, Yankee, Scottish, and French and the more American on that account. He grew up in an atmosphere that was seething with new ideas. Concord gave him its best schooling, sent him to Harvard, and gave him a livelihood. He improved his father's pencil-making, perfected the process of preparing plumbago for electrotyping, and had the congenial task of surveying many woodlots and laying out roads for the town, so that he could easily afford the time he spent writing. He was fortunate in having the stimulus of such minds as Emerson's, Alcott's, and Channing's. Too much has been said about the disapproval of Thoreau by some of his fellow-citizens. That was true, but he had the approval of all children; Edward Emerson called him a beloved older brother. The common laborers liked him, the farmers told him stories and brought him unusual birds and animals, and he had a respectful hearing at the Lyceum. An account of his last days shows the genuine affection felt by many. Few men indeed could bring forth such a chorus of praise as is found in the local papers and in the Harvard Alumni bulletin after his death in May, 1862.

Thoreau birthplace on Virginia Road.

It was his unique service to look at every familiar object and common belief with a fresh and critical eye so that down to the present day he is the delight of the anthologist. Whatever one's specialty, one can compile a booklet of Thoreau's observations on it, whether the subject be flowers, birds, weather, fish or turtles, bees, civil disobedience, Latin authors, ecology, conservation, puns or style in writing. His observations on old Concord houses and inhabitants would run to many pages. His Journals are especially wide-ranging. Though physically bound to Concord for most of his life, and glad to be so, Thoreau was what William Wood in 1633 had called a "mind-traveling" reader. He made use of the Harvard College library and of Emerson's fine library and read Greek, Latin, and German and translations from Persian and Hindu. Thoreau tells in *Walden* that the ingenious Yankee operator Frederic Tudor shipped ice to India from Walden Pond. This was in the winter of 1846–47 when a business quarrel shut off the Cambridge and Woburn ponds to him. Surely this infusion was a slight return to India for the books of Hindu literature which inspired both

Thoreau's *Journal* in the box he made for it. (Courtesy of the Pierpont Morgan Library.)

Emerson and Thoreau. However, Thoreau's books returned the debt manyfold, for Gandhi read them and learned about the tactic of civil disobedience which at last brought independence to India.

Perhaps another factor in the cross-fertilization of ideas was the boardinghouse. Mrs. Joseph Ward, widow of a Revolutionary Colonel, and her daughter Prudence boarded with Mrs. John Thoreau for long periods of time and took an interest in her children, referred to them in their letters, and recommended them as teachers. Lucy Jackson Brown inspired Henry's poetry and arranged his meeting with her brother-in-law, Ralph Waldo Emerson. Behind the scorn for some of the reformers at his mother's table, which Henry Thoreau confided to his Journal, remains the fact that they kept him in touch with the ferment of ideas which was seething all over New England.

Emerson's father had been in the center of Boston society. His guests

The cairn. (Photograph by Norman Foerster.)

and the topics they discussed must have had an effect on his children. In those days, children had no conversation of their own at table. They perforce were seen and though not heard, could hear. After her husband's death, Mrs. Emerson took boarders. They were interesting and important people, their conversation was of large affairs. Mary Moody Emerson, who came to help her sister-in-law, and of course had her place at the table, would have kept it so. The interest that some of this *Stammtisch* took in the Emerson children was useful to them in later life. The mother of the family did not merely supply the table, she chose its guests and presided over it.

Walden Pond, June, 1901. (Photograph by Herbert W. Gleason.)

# Chapter VII   The American Renaissance

*Each honest man shall have his vote*
  *Each child shall have his school*
*Equal on Sunday in the pew*
  *On Monday in the mall.*
*For what avail the plough or sail*
*Or land or life, if Freedom fail.*
    *Emerson:* Boston

An ambitious attempt to improve the public schools was made here in March, 1847, following the passage by the 1846 Legislature of an enabling act at the instigation of Horace Mann, then Secretary of the State Board of Education. A Teachers Institute was held in Concord for ten days. The institute committee—Samuel Hoar, Nehemiah Ball, Calvin C. Damon, Addison G. Fay, and John S. Keyes—found lodgings for seventy teachers with board not to exceed two dollars per week. Tuition was free but the teachers from out of town paid their own board and travel expenses. The circular read:

The duty of preparing one's self for whatever business he may undertake, the rapidly advancing standard of qualifications for teachers in our common schools, the danger of exposure and condemnation which impends over incompetent teachers, the increased vigilance of the school committees in seeking out teachers of high talents and attainments and the readiness of the public to give good teachers a more adequate remuneration for their services: all these considerations call upon every person who has entered this noble field of labor to avail himself of every opportunity for improvement.

Concord was then paying $147.00 a year to teachers in the district schools and $395.45 to the master in the center school, with a total appropriation of $2,500.00. Despite this liberality Concord was still behind Brookline, spending only three-fifths as much for each scholar as did their wealthy neighbor.

Dr. Josiah Bartlett, who was by this time an outspoken abolitionist, was a Concord character in the best sense of the word. His practice in Concord extended from 1819 to 1878. Only once in fifty years had he failed to get to a patient and then his sleigh upset every two rods and when he changed to horseback, his horse floundered in a drift and slipped him off his tail. He took a lively interest in the temperance cause and suffered for it. He lived in a brick-end house on Lowell Road only a hundred yards from the tavern and gangs under the influence of alcohol found this a convenient target. One night all his apple trees were girdled; on another night a bottle of acid was thrown through the parlor window and ruined his carpet. Another time his chaise top was cut to ribbons and the tail of his horse shaved, but he rode with the streamers flying to the shame of his persecutors. He always drove at breakneck speed and always bought the fastest horses he could find. Once, at a temperance meeting, Timothy Prescott said, "It is easy to cry out against drinking in which he did not wish to indulge, while he still clung to the filthy habit of chewing." Bartlett rose and said that if his use of tobacco induced anyone to hold to the use of rum, so help him God, he would never touch it again. He walked over to the stove, threw in his quid, and never touched tobacco again. His controversial opinions made a second doctor necessary for those who disagreed with him. Dr. Isaac Hurd had settled here after Dr. Cuming's death and he was succeeded by Dr. Henry A. Barrett. They lived on Main Street next to the south burying-place in the old Jones-Wheeler-Prescott-Bliss house, later called the Block House and moved to Lowell Road to make way for the modern Savings Bank.

*What a debt is ours to that old religion which in the childhood of most of us, dwelt like a Sabbath morning in the country of New England.*
    *Emerson:* Century Discourse

By 1830, Mr. Ripley's church no longer enjoyed a monopoly. Although the parish tax was still collected with the town taxes, the church could no longer force people to attend. Soon anyone who wished could "sign off" from paying the parish tax. On the surface the institution seemed at its most prosperous when, in 1792, the meetinghouse was enlarged and a tall pointed spire added. At long last the church bell could be

Dr. Josiah Bartlett's office and house on Lowell Road.

hung. Inside, family pews filled the body of the meetinghouse. Favoritism was avoided by auctioning each pew to the highest bidder. The singers were seated in the gallery; a bass viol or a pipe set the pitch.

Mr. Ripley being a practical man, his sermons were likely to deal with practical matters which he observed in his daily parish calls, and the services drifted into a pragmatic state which was close to Unitarianism. In 1828, the conservatives, led by Deacon White, caused a final split through the establishment of the Trinitarian Society with its church across the brook on Walden Street. Massachusetts law completed the disestablishment.

In 1842, a new Universalist Church was organized in a small building on the newly opened Bedford Street, paying a salary of $450.00 to Addison G. Fay, its minister. Two liquor-sellers in his tiny congregation remonstrated with him for preaching on temperance. He declared: "If my salary were $2,000.00 I should be tempted to hold my tongue, but on $450.00 I can afford to keep a conscience." He gave up the salary four years later. The church was soon abandoned and was then sold to the Roman Catholics who enlarged it in 1865 and turned it around to face the square.

Mr. Fay went into pencil-making, then began the manufacture of powder in Barre, soon moving the business to the extreme southwest corner of Concord and adjacent Acton. In 1873, in one of the frequent explosions, he was blown into the canal and was killed.

Mr. Ripley lived until 1840 but in his last years he had an assistant. The first, Hersy B. Goodwin, died young. The second, Barzillai Frost, saw the church moved around in 1840 to face Lexington Road and beautified outside with a Greek porch and inside with a carpet and pew cushions. Mr. Ripley's sermon of dedication was read after his death by Mr. Frost who became his successor. The Ripley funeral had to be held in the church across the brook. Everyone said it was the end of an era, and indeed it was, but the beginning of another.

*I sing New England as she lights her fire*
  *In every prairie's midst, and where the bright*
  *Enchanting stars shine pure through Southern night;*
*Oh, feel how faithfully New England's will*
  *Beats in each artery and each small part*
  *Of this great Continent, their blood would start*
*In Georgia, or where Spain once sat in state,*
  *Or Texas neath her lone star desolate.*
    *Ellery Channing:* New England

Before the Revolution, Concord's legal business had been handled for the most part by the local magistrates. Holding commissions under the Crown, each held court to settle small causes and could also perform marriages or draw up deeds and wills.

After the Revolution one lawyer settled in Concord and opened an office. He was Jonathan Fay of Westboro. While still a Harvard student, he had married Lucy Prescott but had been obliged to keep it secret because it was against the college rules. He studied law with Mr. Hichborn in Boston, then opened an office in the Asa Heywood house on Walden Street, moving over to Lexington Road when his father-in-law gave him the Beatton house in 1790. Here in a little green office he trained several students. Soon there were eight or ten lawyers to handle the enormous increase in business caused by the archaic laws about debts, by the increase in crime, and by the complications of land titles as heirs dispersed to new settlements. The legal profession had been generally held in contempt unless one were a magistrate, but now in Concord it increased in glamor. Of the sessions of the superior court, every third one was held in Concord. The leading lawyers of the State moved in with their clerks, took over the best rooms in hotels and boardinghouses, and tried their cases before a crowded audience of townspeople who enjoyed hearing an Adams, a Webster, or their own Samuel Hoar orate in the grandiloquent manner of the day. Even the children could not be kept in school on court day. Food, rum, and cider were sold from booths set up on the common and it was an exciting day although it had its inevitable morning after. The young lawyers who emigrated from town found their talents in demand on the frontier. General (of the militia) William Jones, whose father was a blacksmith on Main Street, became a judge in Portland, Maine. Thomas Heald, a Carlisle farmer's son, left Concord to practice in Montpelier, Vermont, and Albany, New York, before moving to the new State of Alabama where he became judge of the State Supreme Court. He was one of the first sons of Concord to go to Dartmouth instead of to THE College. Daniel Bliss Ripley, son of the minister, also moved South to Charleston where prejudice against Yankees was not then general. Many "first families" of Alabama, Mississippi, and Texas were of Yankee origin. Charleston, South Carolina, had an active New England club before the Civil War.

Concord's first postmaster had been William Parkman whose house and shop were on the Library corner behind the Black Horse tavern. This itself became the post office when Parkman was succeeded by John L. Tuttle who had moved down from Littleton to practice law here. Tuttle enlisted in the War of 1812 and was sent to Sackett's Harbor as a paymaster to the troops invading Canada. There he was murdered for the money he was carrying. John Keyes, his pupil and successor, was also a Dartmouth man. Born in Westford, one of twenty children, he was not robust enough for farming, so he taught in a district school until he got through college. He continued as postmaster until 1837 when he lost his position in the anti-Masonic furor. He bought a house between the new courthouse and the corner which had been built by Joseph Mulliken for his clockmaking. Under the spoils system the postmastership changed hands whenever the political party in Washington changed and the office moved accordingly. John Stacy had the post office from 1841–1845 and his son Albert from 1849–1853 and from 1861–1868 in his bookstore. Charles B. Davis of the White Block was a Democratic postmaster from 1838–1839, 1845–1849, and 1853–1861. John Gourgas held the office briefly in 1839–1840.

John Keyes took an active part in all parish and town affairs and was chairman of the bi-centennial celebration of the founding of the town in 1835. His son, John Shepard Keyes, presided at the celebration in 1885 and his grandson, Prescott Keyes, at the tercentenary "literary exercises" in 1935. Concord regularly celebrated anniversaries of the founding and the fight with parades and orations.

With the increase in the number of educated men in Concord came the start of several organizations destined to play a large part in forming the character of the town. The first of these was the Social Circle which dates its founding to 1782. It originated with the wartime meetings of the Committee of Safety and included most of the men of substance who lived near enough to the center to make meetings feasible on Tuesday evenings from October to March, to enjoy together cider or grog and in later years, a dinner. Limited to twenty-five members, there was no program except conversation, but it performed a priceless service to the historian—it kept a book of biographies of every member. These were read and corrected at meetings, the convivial character of which made it possible to describe the late member as he was, without the formal eulogy customary in describing the dead.

Every improvement made in the town in the next hundred years was first talked over in the Circle. Doubtless, too, many nominations for town offices were first suggested there; certainly every worthwhile institution got its initial backing there.

Corinthian Lodge of Masons was founded in 1797 with the blessing of Ezra Ripley who did not forget that his idol, George Washington, was a Mason. The first meetings were held in Joshua Jones's hall, in a handsome new brick building on the corner of Main and Walden Streets, but at a rent of thirty dollars per annum.

The next year brother John Richardson offered to open his hall in the Middlesex Hotel free of charge and supply refreshments at tavern prices. The Masons' desire to do good outside their own membership is reflected in their vote in 1800

to purchase 100 copies of the sermon delivered by Brother Ezra Ripley on the day of the execution of Samuel Smith for burglary, with a view of distributing numbers of them gratis to jail-keepers for the particular use of criminals in their custody, for whose benefit principally the sermon is published.

This is the only execution recorded as taking place in Concord although there must have been others. It was held in the field east of the new burying-ground, which is now Sleepy Hollow, used at that time for a training field and cattle show grounds, and the spectators and prisoner walked there directly from the church just after Christmas in 1799.

Only fifty years later, four hundred Concord citizens signed a protest against the hanging of Washington Goode, a Negro convicted in Boston of murder on circumstantial evidence given by persons of low character. Henry D. Thoreau's name is near the head of the petition. Perhaps he carried it around. Goode was hanged but not publicly. However, citizens of Boston crowded the roof-tops nearby in an attempt to look over the walls of the jail yard where the execution took place.

*I mean no reproach to our Concord train-bands, who
certainly make a handsome appearance—and dance well.*
    *Thoreau:* Journal I 497

The founding of the Concord Light Infantry company and the Concord Artillery had more a social than a military purpose. The Light Infantry wore buff and blue uniforms with bell-topped leather shakos; they made their headquarters in Shepard's tavern on Main Street. The Artillery used the Middlesex Hotel and paraded in blue coats faced with red, with white vests, black pantaloons, and black hats with red cockades. Each tried to outdo the other in the elegance of its annual ball, the excellence of the orchestra, and the lavishness of the supper. The rivalry culminated in a grand training in October, 1838, when each company hired a band from the city. As they paraded on opposite sides of the square, each tried to drown out and crowd out the other. Charles Bowers was captain of the Artillery that year. Both companies looked down on the militia which had lost all its military bearing and now elected its officers for their generosity in treating after the training was over. There was no enemy in sight and the possibility of another war was undreamt of.

In 1839, Cornwallis Day was celebrated with the uniformed companies under General Joshua Buttrick representing the British under Cornwallis. The militia, dressed in any old costume to be found in the attic, represented the American forces under General Washington. They were commanded by Colonel Sherman Barrett. After much firing of blank cartridges in a sham battle, the "British" retreated to the taverns where they fraternized for the last time with the militia. Under a State re-organization the militia was disbanded the following year. James

Russell Lowell attended this last fracas and celebrated it in the *Biglow Papers*, changing the town's name.

> This kind 'o' sogerin' aint a mite like our October trainin',
> A chap could clear right out from there ef't only looked like rainin'.
> An the Cunnles, tu, could kiver up their shappoes with bandanners
> An' send the insines skootin' to the bar-room with their banners,
> (Fear o' gittin' on 'em spotted) an' a feller could cry quarter
> Ef he fired away his ramrod arter tu much rum an' water.
> Recollect wut fun we hed, you'n I an' Ezry Hollis,
> Up there to Waltham plain last fall, a-havin' the Cornwallis?

The Light Infantry gave up its charter in 1848. When the Concord Artillery was chartered in 1804 the Quartermaster General was directed to give the new company two brass field pieces inscribed in honor of Major John Buttrick and Captain Isaac Davis and the Nineteenth of April. These were retired in 1846 to a place of honor in Doric Hall in the State House and two new identical pieces substituted, still fired on all ceremonial occasions.

The re-organized militia was made up of volunteers but it took in the old Concord Artillery company without its cannon. The men became an infantry company in 1855 which filled its ranks as Company A Fifth Massachusetts before the Civil War.

Governor Banks assembled the whole militia in 1859 for a five-day encampment in Concord. Seven thousand soldiers were reviewed by State officers, the Legislature, and thousands of spectators, an impressive array which became the subject of a huge engraving. The encampment provided very little preparation for war but it was the only field training the militia had experienced before the battle of Bull Run. They considered themselves equipped and ready to answer Lincoln's first call for troops.

*A river of thought is always running out of the invisible world into the mind of man . . . but there is no end to the praise of books, to the value of the library.*

> *Emerson:* Address at the Dedication of the Concord Free
> Public Library in 1873

After the mention of lending town books in 1672, which lets Concord claim to have had the first public library, the next mention of a library was in 1795 when a Charitable Library was founded which kept a few books in one of the stores. This was succeeded in 1821 by a Social Library which in turn gave its books in 1851 to a Town Library. The Town Library was located in the new Town House. A new building to house ten thousand books came in 1873. At least there was some mental stimulus here for those who wanted to take advantage of it.

Another popular mental stimulus came from the Concord Lyceum, a series of lectures given each year during the winter season.

In 1822, as an outgrowth of the Academy's Friday declamations, a debating society was started where such topics were discussed as "Does it require more talent to make a good writer than a good extemporaneous speaker?" or "Is a good memory preferable to a good understanding in order to be a distinguished scholar at school?" One of the bright young disputants on these topics was the young pupil named David Henry Thoreau, who also debated at Harvard.

The debating society soon merged with the Concord Lyceum. Weekly during the winter, all the townspeople were able to hear all sorts of stimulating topics which gave food for thought and an interesting dinner-table topic for succeeding weeks. Beginning in 1829, the Lyceum also gave local men a chance to be heard and to test their ideas before a jury of their peers. Reverend Ezra Ripley was an active member. The Lyceum began with fifty-seven members paying dues of one dollar, and admitted schoolboys free to its meetings. Debates and concerts were a part of its programs. In its first fifty years it presented 784 lectures, 105 debates, and fourteen concerts. Three hundred and one of the lectures were by residents of Concord, ninety-eight of these by Mr. Emerson, nineteen by Henry Thoreau, and seventeen by Deacon Nehemiah Ball who used a magic lantern to illustrate his lectures on science. Other speakers were Holmes and Lowell, Dana, Whipple, Fields, Dr. Palfrey and Agassiz; two Harvard presidents, Felton and Hill; Horace Greeley, Jones Very, Theodore Parker, John Weiss, Orestes Brownson, Dr. Hedge, Henry Ward Beecher, Starr King, Edward Everett Hale, and James Freeman Clark. In the early days, before their untimely deaths, Ralph Waldo Emerson's talented brothers, Edward Bliss Emerson and Charles Chauncy Emerson, were heard. This was stimulating fare. Henry Thoreau took the affirmative in a debate with Bronson Alcott on the question "Is War ever Justified?" There was no decision but Henry Thoreau was obviously not a pacifist.

One hundred years ago on the milldam; at left, the first bank building.

*Who sings the praise of Woman in our clime?*
  *I do not boast her beauty or her grace;*
*Some humble duties render her sublime*
  *She, the sweet nurse of the New England race,*
  *The flower upon the country's sterile face—*
*The mother of New England's sons, the pride*
*Of every house where those good sons abide.*
    *Ellery Channing:* New England

Up to this point there has been almost nothing in the records about Concord women. Five of them had signed the non-importation agreement in 1774 and a number contributed supplies to the military hospital in Cambridge. A few joined together to give Ezra Ripley a new gown and cassock in 1791. But in 1814, nearly a hundred Concord women banded together to form the Concord Female Charitable Society and began the first systematic organized charity. They were particularly

The milldam 100 years ago. Stacy and Whitcomb kept the post office in the left half of the building between the present Howe-Kennedy building and the old building on Richardson's Corner. The Jones brick house may be seen and, to the extreme right, Black Horse Tavern (Brook's house).

interested ". . . in relieving distress, encouraging industry and promoting virtue and happiness among the female part of the community." They would also ". . . inquire into the situations and wants of the poor children and . . . see that they were provided with decent clothing so that they could go regularly to church and school." To avoid dissension between the churches, the society paid two dollars to hire the hall in the Middlesex Hotel for their first meeting. The first president, Mrs. Jonas Heywood, was a farmer's wife, a second wife with many stepchildren and a big household to manage. Before the railroad came, the Heywood farm ran from Sudbury Road to the river (its house still stands on what is now Cottage Lane). Mrs. Stephen Wood, the vice-president, was thirty-five and also a second wife. She was a granddaughter of Colonel James Barrett and her husband was a tanner with his tanyard on the north side of the milldam and his house nearby on Lowell Road.

Mrs. Tilly Merrick, the first treasurer, was forty-four. She was Sally

Minot, daughter of Dr. Timothy Minot, who had taken care of the wounded on April 19th at his house on the square. After that time, Tilly Merrick, Jr., had been an attaché to John Adams in France and Holland and later had an interest in Sigourney and Ingraham's wholesale house in Amsterdam. Following this, he had a wholesale business in Charleston, but this failed and he returned to Concord in 1798 to marry Sally Minot and start a small retail business next to his house on Sudbury Road opposite the Library corner. Their daughter, Mary, married Judge Nathan Brooks and lived on that corner in the old Black Horse Tavern. Mrs. Merrick died in 1816.

Abby Brigham Fay, the first secretary, was one of the six children of Judge Fay, the post-Revolutionary lawyer. On the first board of managers were Mrs. Jonathan Hildreth whose husband ran a store next to his brick house at Hildreth's corner, Mrs. Nathan Barrett from the top of Punkatasset Hill, and Mrs. Josiah Davis who became the second president.

Mrs. Davis was Betsy Waters, daughter of the minister in Ashby. Her husband's family (he was one of fourteen children) had emigrated from Concord to New Ipswich, New Hampshire, just over the State line from Ashby. He came back to Concord in 1805 with his brother to run a store in the old block on the church green but had dissolved the partnership in 1813 and built a house and store on Main Street which he thought would soon be the business center. The house is now the main Academy building but did not have the big pillars in those days. The large store was later moved to Belknap Street and made over into a double house. Mrs. Davis was in her new house when the society was formed and her husband (said to be worth $15,000.00) was among the wealthiest in the village. She was said to be a very nice housekeeper, her house the newest and best in the village. She used to board the leading lawyers and judges during the court sessions. Her husband was a born organizer. He got up a planting bee to set out the elms on Main Street and on Academy Lane. He built several houses near him on Main Street and helped start the Academy, the bank, the insurance company, and the milldam company. Disastrous land speculation in the new factory village of Lowell was to contribute to his failure in the panic year of 1837 and the last years of Mrs. Davis's life were spent running a boardinghouse in Boston.

Mrs. Samuel Hoar, an early treasurer, was Sarah, daughter of Roger Sherman of New Haven. She had married the promising young lawyer in 1812 and the first of her six children was born in 1814. At first they had boarded with the widow of Asa Heywood on Walden Street, but they were soon installed in the brick-end house on Main Street which

Josiah Davis's store was moved to Belknap Street and was made into a double house. Here John Brown spent the night.

had been used in an unfinished state as a recruiting center in the War of 1812. Samuel Hoar always had a high respect for the character and capacity of women and carried out his belief by giving as thorough an education to his daughters as to his sons. His wife, Sarah Sherman, had, as a young girl, demonstrated that she inherited the character of a signer of the Declaration of Independence by starting a school for Negro children in New Haven at a time when it was still illegal there to teach a black to read and write.

Miss Phebe Wheeler, secretary for many years of the Charitable Society, was daughter of Peter Wheeler, the local butcher and tanner, who lived in what is now the First Parish parsonage. She had a private dame school in her house. Her grandfather, Timothy Wheeler, was the miller whose storehouse had been searched on April 19th.

These were some of the women who had the courage and initiative to start a society to fill a real need, to keep books and minutes, and to deal in a sensible practical manner with problems as they came up.

Among those who were aided was Betty Tower who was given tea and sugar in February, 1814 and then in March the society used muslin for a cap in which to lay her out. Hannah Hunt was given six yards of factory gingham to make up for herself. Mrs. Josiah Holden was aided until her death at ninety-five. Her husband had served in Major John Minot's company in 1740. Her son, Tilly Holden, died in the army in 1777. The ladies gave clothing, caps, and kerchiefs to Theodore Bliss's widow when she came back to the parsonage to live. Small cash sums were sent sometimes and other help was given to Rose Robbins, wife of Caesar, a former slave, and to Zilpah White who lived alone in a cabin near Walden "at the very corner of my bean field," said Henry Thoreau. The ladies sent her yarn to be woven, but also gifts of snuff, rice, tea, brandy, and spirits. Mrs. John Thoreau joined the Society in 1825 and Emerson's mother, wife, and daughter were members in turn.

The men, in contrast, whose Social Circle had no other purpose but talk, made fun of the Female Charitable Society. They called these monthly sewing meetings, at which fifteen or more devoted women made quilts, knitted stockings, or cut and made clothes, the "chattable society." The men did not always jest. Dr. Abiel Heywood, the town's most eligible bachelor, gave them two dollars toward the making of gingham for children's dresses. Two dollars added from the treasury bought the material for sixteen yards of gingham and paid for getting it woven. Mr. Samuel Cordis Lee invited the ladies to meet at his house and sew on material that he would give them. So in March, 1815, they gathered in what is now the Art Centre on Lexington Road. "Nine members were present. Mr. Lee gave a surtout, 2 straight-bodied coats, one pair pantaloons but little worn, of good broadcloth, calico for three gowns and fine gingham for four infants frocks, a large gown, vandykes and bonnets, nearly two yards of fine white cambric, three pieces of ribbon, and three boxes cotton sewings. The ladies were very grateful and industrious and the afternoon passed in a most cheerful and pleasant manner." A calico frock went to Hitty Hollowell and one to Sally Trumbull. The board agreed to give the surtout to Mr. Joshua Stone. He was the blacksmith whose son, John A. Stone, did so well in the school declamations he was encouraged to go to New York to go on the stage. In 1829, he wrote *Metamora* which won a prize offered by Edwin Forrest for a play with a native Indian as hero. It was a great success. Throughout Forrest's life the play remained in his repertory but Stone died by drowning at the age of thirty-three.

The success of the Charitable Society doubtless encouraged the formation of a Bible Society, a Temperance Society, a Missionary Society, and the Women's Anti-Slavery Society.[1] The ladies were quick

---

[1] Concord was on the Underground Railroad, but there are no records of its stations or of the extent of its use.

The mill at West Concord. "Damondale," old "1775" house of Roger Brown.

to make use of a new mill, started in the west part of town by John Brown of Framingham, where cotton could be woven.

The growth of manufacturing almost passed Concord by, except for one business at the west end of town. Brown's mill had been started before 1715 as a fulling mill on the site of the old ironworks. It had been run for nearly a century by Lot Conant, Jr. (formerly of Beverly), and his descendants. In 1808, the Conants had sold out to Brown and to Ephraim Hartwell of New Ipswich, New Hampshire. As the mill prospered it grew into a wooden building five stories high and one hundred feet long, which was sold in turn in 1834 to Calvin C. Damon. Around it grew up a factory village which came to be called Damondale. The wooden building burned in 1862 and was replaced with brick. Beyond it on the Acton border were the small separate sheds of the powder mills, with a ghastly record of accidents.

One of the first to change to the factory system from the old one-man trade carried on in one's own home was Elijah Wood, who built a large ell onto his house on Wood Street in 1821 and employed ten to twenty apprentices to make shoes for the Southern and Western trade. The apprentices worked until nine at night by lamplight, a surprising sight when seen across the river in the village. Although he employed some women, he carried bundles of uppers to them to be stitched at home.

Ephraim Wood house and ell used as a shoe factory, Wood Street.

The business was not incorporated and was gradually relinquished in favor of farming during Wood's own lifetime. The Whiting family had a carriage manufactory on Main Street, but the famous Concord coaches were made in Concord, New Hampshire, by others, not here.

In 1819, David Loring started the manufacture of lead pipe and sheet lead at another millsite where Nashoba Brook fell into the Assabet River, forming a pond above his dam. This pond is now called Warner's Pond after the owner of a wooden pail factory which succeeded the lead factory in 1850.

Daniel Shattuck came to Concord from Ashby as a boy working for, and then succeeding, John White who kept a store in the central part of the present Colonial Inn. Shattuck was a member of the Social Circle and a prime mover in starting the Middlesex Mutual Fire Insurance Company in 1826, the Concord Bank in 1832, and the Middlesex Institution for Savings in 1835. A new building for all three, plus a lawyer's office for Nathan Brooks, was built with a Greek pediment and pillars opposite Walden Street on Main Street. This became one end of a development called the Milldam Company, incorporated in 1828 with a capital stock of $20,000.00 by Daniel Shattuck, Cyrus Stow, Ephraim Merriam, Abel Moore, John Keyes, and Nehemiah Ball. This proved a happy combination of public spirit and personal profit. They bought the property on both sides of the milldam, drained off

The Colonial Inn as it looked when it was D. Shattuck's store. On the right is the house owned by Thoreau's aunts. From an old drawing.

the pond, widened the road by twenty feet, and then sold lots for business buildings several of which are still in use. The tanyard on the north side was succeeded by a general store. Stone's blacksmith shop on the corner of Walden Street, a favorite place to warm one's hands and feet after skating on the millpond, disappeared along with the pond and was succeeded by another general store which later became a drugstore with a wooden canopy over the sidewalk.

Daniel Shattuck's brother, Lemuel, followed him to Concord and wrote his *History of Concord* before moving to Boston where he made a name for himself in the fields of statistics and public health, subjects in which he became interested while writing the mortality tables for his history.

Reverend Peter Bulkeley's old house on the corner had been made over after Dr. Timothy Minot's death for a county house and sheriff's residence. The County had built a new courthouse in 1794 opposite the school and the old combination town and county house. The town gave the land for the new courthouse and in exchange had the right to hold town meetings in its lower story. Here the fruits and vegetables of the cattle shows were exhibited. A county agricultural association held such shows annually using what is now the central part of Sleepy Hollow for the cattle and horses. In front of the courthouse was a large elm tree (said to have been planted on April 19, 1776) which was used as a whipping post. In this courthouse took place the trials, and acquittals, of the rioters who burned the Ursuline Convent in 1836 as well as many another important trial, including Professor Webster's trial for the murder of his colleague on the Harvard faculty, Professor Parkman. This courthouse was burned in 1849 in an incendiary fire which also destroyed the Mulliken-Keyes house beside it. Judge Keyes always liked to tell the story of the fireman, intent on salvage, who had gone into the house cellar, picked up a pitcher, thinking it was full of cider, and taken a deep draught only to come up quickly, sputtering and choking and wiping his mouth to cry out, "Soft soap, by God!" The town decided in 1851 to build its own town house and sold to Keyes the little store built by Elnathan Jones and used by John Thoreau and Daniel Smith, buying the lot from him while he moved the store over to Monument Street to form the rear of a house for his family. The ancient town house meanwhile became Deacon White's barn and was moved behind his store. The courthouse was rebuilt, but in 1867 the upper courts were removed to Lowell and this new courthouse was given to the town which thriftily sold it to the Middlesex Mutual Insurance Company. One room was set aside for the district court later presided over by Judge Keyes who was also an officer of the insurance company.

John Richardson was a trader who moved here from Newton starting with a store at 9 Lexington Road and then opening a tavern in a house which is now the Catholic Rectory. After 1794, the County needed only a sheriff's house and now Richardson traded this tavern to the County and made the old county house into a hotel which he called the Middlesex House. One of its proprietors was Thomas Wesson. This burned in 1845 but was rebuilt and for a time continued to be the center for meetings and balls as well as the hotel for court attendants and lawyers. Its capacious bar was also a favorite port-of-call, until the coming of the railroad, the consequent decline of the stage business, and the loss of the courts brought about its final demise. The sheriff had to supply food to the prisoners either from the hotel or from his own kitchen. One Thanksgiving Day a visitor at the sheriff's found Abel Moore's daughter, Harriet, making sixty-nine apple, squash, and mince pies, one of each for each of twenty-three prisoners.

Samuel Staples, one of ten children of a blacksmith in Mendon, left home with little schooling and worked as a carpenter and hostler before being made barkeeper at the hotel, by Wesson. He married the proprietor's daughter in 1839. Temperance agitation had made old

The Charles Miles house, corner of Williams Road and old road to Nine Acre Corner, sold at auction to John Keefe.

Wesson dislike the two settled ministers so his daughter was married by Ralph Waldo Emerson with Bronson Alcott and John Dwight (who happened to be Mr. Emerson's guests that night) coming along as witnesses. In 1843, Staples succeeded Moore as jailer and moved to the county house with the Wesson family, making his brother-in-law, Johnny, the turnkey. Johnny was the town fiddler and helped the prisoners while away their days with his fiddling. Staples was also constable, auctioneer, and tax collector and his popularity was such that he was elected to the Legislature in 1847 on the Democratic ticket defeating the Whig, John S. Keyes, who bore him no ill will, however, and in fact saw to it that he kept his position as sheriff as long as he wanted. Staples was always hospitable. In after years Judge Keyes often crossed the square from his office in the insurance building "to look at the potatoes in Staples' cellar," potable potatoes to be sure.

Both Sheriff Moore and Sheriff Staples were noted for their practical jokes, and for the gusto with which they told of them. Moore sometimes resented the free and easy way with which fellow-townsmen, instead of taking the stage, invited themselves to ride with him on his business trips to and from Boston. One such climbed into his carriage in Boston uninvited and Moore started back, remarking as they approached Lexington that his rider would of course pay for their dinners and for oats for baiting the horse when they stopped. After dinner, Moore thought of an errand in Waltham, from there detoured on an errand to Wayland, where it was late and they must spend the night. Next morning he remembered an errand in Framingham requiring a stop-over for dinner, so that the free rider was considerably out of pocket before reaching Concord at the end of the second day.

Staples was unable to prevent his wife from bidding at his auctions. One day after he learned that hers was the last bid on a set of commode crockery, he said: "Knocked down to Mrs. Samuel Staples," and proceeded to knock it down to the ground where it smashed to pieces. When he had to sell the Charles Miles house on the Old Road to Nine Acre Corner, he hated to see it go for a pittance to Ebenezer Conant, the shrewd and wealthy farmer who held the mortgage and had already foreclosed on the land. Conant's $250.00 was the only bid, because everyone thought it was a foregone conclusion that he would bid it in. Staples paused and looked around until he saw John Keefe hoeing potatoes in a field across the road.

"Come over here, John," he shouted.

When John had laid down his hoe and walked over, Staples said "Don't you think this house is worth $500.00?"

"I do that," said Keefe.

"Sold," said Staples, and Keefe found himself the owner of a house.

Captain Moore was one of the most progressive farmers of his day. He bought Dr. Abel Prescott's farm, then largely grown up to bushes, and enlarged the house for his son, John B. Moore. When the mill-pond was drained, he improved the meadows by ditching and by hauling in sand over the frozen ground in winter to be plowed in, until they were productive of high quality hay. The envious objected to his use of prison labor, but in fact he used volunteers and paid them for their work. His hillside above the road was terraced for grapes. He was one of the first to build a large barn for milking cows which became profitable after the railroad made the Boston market available. He encouraged his neighbor, Ephraim Bull, to go on with the experiments that led to the selection of the Concord Grape which was introduced in 1854 and Moore himself introduced new varieties of grapes, corn, fruit, and flowers.

The Concord is still the most widely cultivated grape in the United States. At least seventy-five per cent of all grapes grown in this country are either Concord or a hybrid based on the Concord. Disease-infested

Grape-vine cottage as it looked in 1855.

Ephraim Bull and his Concord grape. (Photograph by Alfred Hosmer.)

vines in France were rescued by using disease-free Concord stock for roots on which the old varieties could be grafted, an early example of the new world coming to the rescue of the old.[1]

Emerson observed Moore's methods with great interest and although he was temperamentally unfitted for farming himself, used Captain Moore as an inspiration and example in an essay on farming and a poem:

> To these men
> The landscape is an armory of powers,
> Which one by one, they know to draw and use
> They set the wind to winnow pulse and grain
> And thank the spring-flood for its fertile slime
> And on cheap summit-levels of the snow
> Slide with the sledge to inaccessible woods
> O'er meadows bottomless. So year by year,
> They fight the elements with elements
> And by the order in their fields disclose
> The order regnant in the yeoman's brain.

The farmers were not separated from the intellectuals. Farmers belonged to the various clubs and the military companies. Emerson liked to talk with Edmund Hosmer on Sandy Pond Road on philosophical topics, not simply on the weather. "I have never seen a man who could not teach me something," he confided to his notebook. John Barrett and his wife from October Farm attended all the balls and the School of Philosophy as well. During one month in 1849 Daniel Clark of Estabrook Road helped his brother, James, move Thoreau's cabin from Walden woods to the farm where James thought he would enjoy a qualified solitude. In addition to his farm work Daniel noted:

September 9, went to meeting. September 10, went to town meeting to elect a representative; September 16, attended church, went to singing meeting; September 23, went to the lyceum, Mr. Thoro lectured upon Cape Cod; September 30, to lyceum, Mr. Thoro lectured; September 26, went to the other side of the hill and helped lift up two sides of the frame of Miss Ripley's house. Heard a political lecture from R. H. Dana. October 5, attended an abolition meeting, went to school meeting in District No. 5.[2]

The revolution in farming was one of the most interesting changes which began before the Civil War. A farmers' club led by Simon

---

[1] Other American grapes, resistant to Phylloxera, were exported as well as the Concord, in what proportion we do not know.

[2] Manuscript in possession of Miss Gladys Clark.

South Margin Farm, Sandy Pond Road, former Edmund Hosmer house. Here George William Curtis and his brother lived. The house at right was owned by Captain John Prescott. (Photograph courtesy of Mrs. George F. Root.)

Brown, editor of the *New England Farmer,* encouraged the changes until milk, asparagus, sweet corn, and strawberries became the main crops and Boston was the market rather than the farmer's own family. These new crops demanded much more hand labor. Simon Brown and his wife, Ann (French), had come here from New Hampshire to buy the old Bateman and David Brown farms above the north bridge. He became Lieutenant Governor. His wife's nephew was the sculptor of the Minuteman Statue.

*Oh! transient gleams yon hurrying noisy train,*
*Its yellow carriages rumbling with might*
*Of volleyed thunder on the iron rail*
*Pieced by the humble toil of Erin's hand*
*Wood and lake the whistle shrill awakening.*
    Ellery Channing: The Wanderer

The family farm was beginning to fail when a new population came
to supply the man power which had been drained off by settlements
on the frontiers and by the growth of cities.

Famine was hanging over the little farms in Ireland; the Cunard
steamship company was finding steerage passengers profitable; and
the great age of railroad building was asking for manual labor. All
combined to encourage emigration. Thousands of Irishmen came here
to get a start and, if possible, send for their families.

The Fitchburg railroad began buying up land for a right of way
through Concord before 1842. The rails reached Waltham in 1843 and
the first train reached Concord on June 17, 1844. The Irish workers
came out from Boston in work trains or camped in shanties along the
right of way and several stayed behind when the railroad went on.

Meanwhile there was a sudden demand for chestnut wood for ties
and for oak and maple for firewood or lumber.

Every family in Concord was affected in one way or another by the
railroad. The stage and wagon traffic declined and business fell off at
the taverns, smithies, harness makers, and general stores. Business increased for the surveyor when the demand for wood made it important
to learn the exact boundaries of the wood lots. Now the lecturer could
widen his field as far as the rails ran, so it became the golden age of
the Lyceum. A few businessmen and lawyers began to live in Concord
but work in Boston.

On the farms, sheds were raised a story to provide summer quarters
for the hired men and now the neighbor's daughter was supplanted
by the Irish servant as help. The new servant was willing to make do
with a primitive room under the eaves as she learned to cook on an
iron stove and use a pump at the kitchen sink, palatial luxury compared to her old home. It is not fair to say that the Irish were exploited.
Clothes, food, and shelter were provided and cash wages, small as
they were, could be saved. Many a man saved enough to buy his own

Railroad near Belknap Street, about 1880.

farm or start his own business, and three generations were enough for the leap from the primitive civilization of rural Ireland to the lace curtains of the successful family here.

Faith in the virtues of universal education brought every child into school where at least one superintendent appreciated them. Bronson Alcott wrote:

The Centre District includes the best part of our Irish population, which mingles its children with ours, and perhaps to the advantage of both. . . . It is a sprightly element, and a spur to the classes, wheresoever it enters. Yankee blood first deliberates, then aims carefully, sure to be mortified at missing the mark. But this foreigner shoots at the venture, hitting or not hitting, it matters not to him; so there is fire and the stroke.[3]

Many a Concordian stood in a sort of feudal relationship with his handyman, helping him with money and advice, getting him out of trouble or started on the road to independence. His wedding brought new clothes, a party or a cash gift, and if one farmer was so miserly as to deprive his hired man of the cash premium he won by his skillful spading at the "cattle show," there were a hundred to make it up to him when Henry Thoreau carried around the subscription paper. In the next generation the town moderator saw to it that the minority

[3] Bronson Alcott, *Concord School Report,* 1860.

was represented on every committee. The Irishman indeed had a genius for politics. His outgoing, genial personality, his interest in people, his dogged patience, and his ability to talk, all helped him. Meanwhile his children were educated and the Female Charitable Society saw to it that they were properly dressed for school. When one member complained that they were helping the Irish to the exclusion of others, the president said, "Where want and distress is found to exist, we must extend all the aid in our power without respect to persons or nationalities."

The doctor seldom charged poor people for calls. Even fifty years later when Dr. Titcomb was arrested for exceeding the ten mile per hour speed limit and fined five dollars, he was able to turn in open court and say, "All right, chief, you pay me five dollars for that last baby." It was undoubtedly the first time payment had ever been suggested.

Growing throughout these years was the conviction that slaveholding, although a moral question, would have to have a political solution, but here the conservatives, North and South, had the majority. The period from 1840 to 1860 was a turbulent one in Massachusetts politics; friends of anti-slavery had no party to join. The Free-Soil people were an offshoot of the Whig party, but that party had a conservative wing called the Cotton Whigs, and it had the eloquent Daniel Webster, who was the idol of the people. As late as 1834, Emerson wrote

> It seemed
> When at last his clarion accents broke
> As if the conscience of the country spoke.

But Webster lost the support of the Free-Soil wing after his compromising Seventh of March speech in 1850. It now was a struggle to keep the new territories as free states. Franklin Sanborn, now teaching in Concord, was secretary of the Boston people who were raising money for the Emigrant Aid Society and so he came to know John Brown.

The Fugitive Slave Law brought the question close home to Massachusetts with the arrest of Shadrach and the later surrender of Anthony Burns and Sims. Shadrach was freed by a mob who swept through the hearing room from one door and out through another, taking Shadrach with them. He was put in a carriage, driven out to Concord and kept overnight in the house of Francis Bigelow, the blacksmith, at 3 Sudbury Road. When Elizur Wright, a well-known Abolitionist, was arrested and tried for aiding in the rescue, Richard H. Dana, his counsel, was pleased to find Bigelow seated on the jury. Wright was acquitted. The attempt to free Burns in the same way failed, in spite of Higginson's and Alcott's efforts, and he was sent back to slavery.

In 1850, the Free-Soilers in Massachusetts voted with the Democrats in exchange for the latter's promise to send Charles Sumner to the Senate. This sort of compromise was unsatisfactory at best but now a new question arose. Between 1852 and 1856 a violently anti-Catholic furor swept the State. Popularly called the Know-Nothing Party, it took all the State offices in 1854 and put the Whig Party out of business. Simon Brown of Concord was elected Lieutenant-Governor. Charles Sumner never compromised with it. Though it was never heard from again after 1857, some of its ideas survived underground, but Lieutenant-Governor Brown was not himself a bigot and soon joined the Abolitionists.

With the end of the Whig Party, its anti-slavery wing organized the Republican Party. The aged Samuel Hoar of Concord presided at the meeting in Boston on August 16, 1855, which called for a State convention. This was held in Worcester on September 20, and here Squire Samuel Hoar's son, Ebenezer Rockwood Hoar, was made a candidate although he proved to be a losing one. He was then sent as a delegate to a Republican convention in Pittsburgh in February, 1856, as well as to the Philadelphia Convention in June and was on the platform committee. Fremont was defeated nationally but Massachusetts elected Governor Banks who appointed Hoar to the State Supreme Judicial Court. He succeeded his father as Concord's leading citizen and with his brother, George, a Senator, they were called Concord's Royal Family. E. R. Hoar was later named Attorney General in Grant's cabinet.

Concord's concern with slavery had first been aroused in 1844 when the elder Samuel Hoar was sent by the Governor of Massachusetts to South Carolina to protest against the practice of locking up every colored seaman who came into Charleston harbor on a Massachusetts ship. If his ship sailed without paying substantial charges, the Negro was sold into slavery. It seemed like a simple errand. The Squire took his daughter, Elizabeth, along, but in Charleston it became a question of States Rights and "southern honor." A mob surrounded his hotel, threatening to tear it apart. The southern governor did not make himself available for a conference. The agitation increased and seventy leading citizens requested Hoar to leave to prevent bloodshed. On his second refusal they forced him and his daughter to go out a back door and be driven to the boat in a carriage. This experience convinced

Samuel Hoar house on Main Street; built in 1812.

many of the anti-slavery party that sweet reason was not likely to be
enough. Elizabeth Hoar had been engaged to marry Charles Emerson,
who had died in 1836. Ralph Waldo Emerson always regarded her as
a sister and this experience of hers touched him nearly, although he
had been hesitant about actively working against slavery. When the
anti-slavery society was started in 1837, it had seventy members in
Concord, but after William Lloyd Garrison burned a copy of the
American Constitution and attacked the church as a bulwark of slavery,
many members withdrew. After this the variety of good causes weakened each. When violent advocates of woman suffrage, pacifism, and
total abstinence appeared on the anti-slavery platforms, many men
were alienated.

*So from a stubborn boulder-rock*
  *Beside the bridge in Concord road*
*Bred of that Freedom-sinewed stock*
  *Which wrenched away a tyrant's goad*
*Flowered in dream and artistry*
*Our village prophets of Democracy.*

*Here mused the sweet sequestered sage*
  *Who guessed Rhodora's secret being*
*And one who filled the mirrored page*
  *Of Walden Pond with high foreseeing,*
*And one who wrought of fecund fancy*
*A scarlet letter with his necromancy.*

*Such sought and found the flowering goal*
  *Where grandeur springs from simple duty.*
*Where, healed by balsams of the soul*
  *The battle-scar is turned to beauty,*
*And where, outwintering old wrong—*
*Young April whistles in the robin's song.*
  *Percy MacKaye:* April Fire (1925)

Ralph Waldo Emerson, although born in Boston in 1803, was a child of Concord in many ways. His father had been brought up in the Old Manse and it was still a second home to young Waldo after his father's death in 1811 when Waldo was scarcely eight years old. His widowed mother brought her family there in 1814 as William, the oldest of five brothers, entered Harvard. Waldo attended the little wooden schoolhouse in the square that winter and made progress in writing and drawing and Greek and even had practice in the writing of verse, but he excelled in declaiming, for he recited from memory not only in school but from the top of a sugar barrel in Deacon White's store across the way. After that term, while he was at Boston Latin School and at Harvard, Concord was associated in his mind with happy vacation visits, although most vacations had to be used for earning money by teaching.

Even the teaching was close to Concord for it was in his half-uncle's school at Piety Corner in Waltham. Later, after his Boston pastorate

Ralph Waldo Emerson, painted by David Scott in Edinburgh in 1848. The artist put a rainbow in the corner to show the promise he felt in the young writer. (Courtesy of the Concord Free Public Library.)

and his wife Ellen's death, when he began receiving a steady income from the estate of this first wife, Emerson could afford to re-marry and buy for $3,500.00 the house on Lexington Road that was ever after his home. The house was in a way symbolic—it was in the village but slightly withdrawn and separated by the road, the mill brook, and a row of pine trees from near neighbors.

In the old meetinghouse, the day before his wedding in 1835, he delivered a bi-centennial address for which he had studied, for two months past, the old records and other original sources, as well as the proof sheets of Lemuel Shattuck's forthcoming history. The address lasted an hour and three quarters and was Emerson's permanent passport to the affection of his fellow-townsmen. He had even worked out his ancestry which proved his relationship with almost all of the succession of ministers of the First Parish. Thereafter Concord called a public meeting to observe every important event and usually called on Emerson to make a suitable address: as a welcome to Kossuth or to celebrate West Indian Emancipation, to deplore the attack in the Senate on Charles Sumner, and so forth.

The Orchard house made famous by Louisa Alcott's *Little Women*. The front part was the seventeenth-century house of John Hoar.

Emerson depended on the stimulus of other minds, both in books and in conversation. He enjoyed the conservative ideas of his Aunt Mary and his stepgrandfather as well as the speculative ideas of his brothers, Edward and Charles. The death of these brothers was a severe blow, but frequent trips to Boston and to ever-widening fields on his lecture circuits kept him in touch with everything new. His wife, Lydian, was able to make his home a hospitable haven. There were always guests. His mother was a permanent resident. There were two Irish maids and a resident mother's helper when needed, who was likely to be a young cousin and sometimes a contributor to the *Atlantic Monthly*, as was Mary Russell of Plymouth. The hospitality sometimes overflowed to extra rooms in the Reuben Brown house nearby.

Bronson Alcott was the most stimulating of his friends; no idea was too elusive for him to pursue and push to its furthest reach. In his company Emerson must have felt himself to be practical and well-balanced, however radical his own ideas might seem to other people. Emerson could test himself against practical people like Edmund Hosmer and John Moore, the farmers, or Sam Staples and Daniel Shattuck and the rest of the Social Circle, and he had a steady stream of visitors in his hospitable study. From Brook Farm the Minot Pratts came to settle in the old Thomas Flint house on Punkatasset Hill. The charming Mrs. Barlow, still attracting J. S. Dwight, the musician, came

The Emerson house, east side.

to live on Court Lane while her sons were educated here. Her son Francis followed his teacher Frank Sanborn in refusing membership in Phi Beta Kappa at Harvard, considering it too aristocratic. Barlow was later to be a Civil War General and Attorney General of New York State and the natural choice to lead the parade in 1875 at the centennial celebration of Concord Fight. The young Ellery Channing married Margaret Fuller's sister, Ellen, and lived at first in a cottage beyond Emerson's orchard on the Cambridge Turnpike. He had an artist's eye for beauty. He was a frequent guest at Emerson's table and a walking companion. Margaret Fuller herself was often a visitor before she went to Italy. And then there was Henry Thoreau, both a protégé and a reproach as he lived out—in Emerson's wood lot—some of Ralph Waldo's own theories. He was often invited to Emerson's to meet Agassiz or some other distinguished guest.

Nathaniel Hawthorne and Sophia Peabody, his young bride, spent three years in Concord after their marriage in 1842 and were immediately part of the circle. He, too, enjoyed walking. When they arrived in Concord they found that Elizabeth Hoar and Mrs. Emerson had cleaned the Old Manse, and brought in food and flowers, and Henry Thoreau had spaded the garden. Then in 1852, remembering their

Nathaniel Hawthorne in 1840; oil by Charles Osgood. (Courtesy of the Essex Institute, Salem, Mass.)

happiness here, the Hawthornes bought Wayside. Here Hawthorne wrote a campaign biography of his college friend, Franklin Pierce, and invited the Concord Democrats to meet him. "Don't worry none, we'll put him over," said one of the convivial guests as he slapped his shy host on the back. Hawthorne was obsessed with his ancestral Puritanism, haunted by its strengths and its weaknesses, inspired by its moral fervor, and repelled by its inhumanity. During the Hawthornes' absence abroad, another Peabody sister, Mrs. Horace Mann, lived at Wayside. Her son, Horace, Jr., was soon to be a promising botanist.

When Mrs. Alcott's family had bought the old house now called The Wayside, the Mays kept it in their own names so that Bronson Alcott's creditors could not attach it. Emerson bought eight acres opposite so that Mr. Alcott could raise his own potatoes, cabbages, and carrots and contribute directly to his family's support.

With the same characteristic generosity Emerson left his wood lot to Thoreau in an early will. When Mrs. Emerson's sister, Mrs. Brown, needed a home after her husband deserted her, Emerson bought a house for her opposite his own.

This house was built by Emerson for his wife's sister. The stone wall at the left is an original 1635 house-lot boundary.

As canals and railroads pushed westward, Emerson's lecture tours followed all the way to San Francisco so that in fact Emerson was the first American writer to have a national experience, as Mark Twain and Walt Whitman later had.

That Concord wanted the best schools for her children was made evident in 1859 with the appointment of Bronson Alcott as Superintendent at a salary of one hundred dollars a year. He walked regularly to the six outlying district schools and the three center schools and sat down, a benign and approving presence, until he had noticed something to praise, for he believed that every teacher should be encouraged in what she did well. Then would follow a reading from some good book, usually *Pilgrim's Progress*, and a conversation with the children suggested by the reading. "Next to thinking for themselves," he wrote in 1860, "the best service a teacher can render his scholars is to show them how to use books." For a half day each month each teacher took her pupils to visit school in another district and once a month took them for a walk in the woods. Alcott believed in exercises for physical fitness, he believed in beautifying the schoolroom, and he discarded numbers in referring to the districts, giving each a name.

The validity of his ideas is proved by the fact that, one by one, they have slowly come to be accepted over the last hundred years.

Through his daughter Louisa May's descriptions in *Little Women* of her own family life, Bronson Alcott left his mark on the American family. The Puritan and Victorian ideal of the wife and children as obedient slaves of the master of the house had no place in his home. Here love was the rule, and mutual consideration, and though doctors had not yet come to prescribe them, exercise, fresh air, and frequent bathing were part of the regimen. His children were encouraged to develop what skills appealed to them, writing or painting or music; their girls' minds were respected and their faults were gently corrected. Louisa's descriptions of her home life went far toward revolutionizing home life in many distant places. In far-off India, *Little Women* was often an English textbook. Bronson Alcott also taught pride in the home town. Geography for him began with a map of the schoolyard. History began with the story of Concord, and literature with readings from Concord authors.

Another who came from Brook Farm in Roxbury to Concord was George W. Curtis, afterwards the editor of *Harper's Magazine*, who lived here for a year with his brother, working mornings for his board. He and his brother lived with Nathan Barrett, Jr.'s family and marveled that the farmer's wife had a piano though she did the cooking and washing for ten hired men with only one Irish girl to help her. The Curtises sometimes went to Boston to hear a symphony concert and walked home.

Harvard used to rusticate unsatisfactory students, sending them to Reverend Barzillai Frost to be tutored. One of these was James Russell Lowell. In later years Curtis and Lowell were both anniversary speakers.

The visits of John Brown had a great impact on the Concord conscience. His first visit was in March, 1857, when Sanborn was living in Channing's house across Main Street from the Thoreau's where they took their meals. Next day Thoreau took him down to Emerson's and Emerson put him up the next night in the Reuben Brown house. During his talk at the town hall, Brown showed the bowie knife he had taken from a Missouri border ruffian, and the trace chain with which his son had been bound and half dragged to keep up with mounted men who were taking him prisoner to Lecompton, Kansas. Emerson wrote: "One of his good points was the folly of the Peace Party who believed that their strength lay in the greatness of their wrongs, and so discountenanced resistance. Well, was their wrong greater than the Negro Slave's? and what kind of strength has that given to the Negro?"

In May, 1859, when Brown made his second visit and spoke again in the town house he stayed in the double house on Belknap Street that had been made over from Davis's store. He had now decided that some violent act would be necessary to rouse the North and rally the slaves, who would, if properly led, he thought, throw off their chains. Probably Sanborn knew of his plans, but no one else in Concord was told, and they were shocked when five months later the news came that he had seized the arsenal at Harper's Ferry. This dramatic gesture appealed to Thoreau who had dramatized his own beliefs, and he spoke in defense of Brown on October 30 and organized a memorial service on December 2, the day of the hanging. Concord was still not wholly decided on the question of slavery, but besides Alcott, Emerson, and Thoreau, such townsmen as Dr. Josiah Bartlett, John S. Keyes, Samuel Staples, and former Lieutenant-Governor Simon Brown attended the meeting.

It was now only a year and four months before the fall of Sumter, and eleven months before the election of Lincoln. Undoubtedly, the discussion aroused by John Brown's death made people realize that there was no quick and easy solution. At the memorial service, the Wayland minister, Edmund H. Sears, author of the Christmas Carol "It Came Upon A Midnight Clear," read his poem:

> Not any spot six feet by two
> Will hold a man like thee
> John Brown will tramp the shaking earth
> From Blue Ridge to the sea.

Here was the suggestion for the Union Marching Song, "John Brown's body lies a-mouldering in the grave,/His soul is marching on."

Emerson read John Brown's own last words which had been telegraphed throughout the world, although in Harper's Ferry Robert E. Lee's troops had drowned them with a drum roll. Emerson later said that they stood with Lincoln's Gettysburg Address as the most eloquent words ever written.

After Brown's arrest, Concord had an exciting day April 3, 1860, when a Senate investigating committee ordered its sergeant-at-arms to arrest Sanborn as a witness. Two deputies seized him outside the house at 5 Sudbury Road where he was living with his sister. She snatched the whip and applied it vigorously to the horses and the deputies while Sanborn kicked at the doors of the carriage with his

long legs. A sympathetic crowd gathered while John S. Keyes ran over
to Judge Hoar's and got a writ of *habeas corpus*. Next day in court the
Judge ruled that the deputies were improperly authorized and Sanborn
was never brought to trial. After the War, Sanborn was editor of the
*Springfield Republican* for three years. He returned to Concord in
1872 and for the rest of his life was a regular contributor of a literary
letter, and a Boston letter, to the Springfield newspaper. Written often
on the train and depending on a faulty memory, the literary letters
were not always accurate and even when collected into books about
Emerson, Thoreau, Samuel G. Howe or others, they were not checked
for dates, so that they present problems to students. Sanborn made a
lifework of prison and institutional reform and made valuable contributions to this aspect of government. An incidental result came one
day when he was visiting the Tewksbury almshouse. A little girl
named Ellen Sullivan spoke to him and begged to be sent to school.
He had her transferred to the Perkins Institution for the Blind and she
grew up to become the miracle worker who taught Helen Keller and,
with her success, brought hope and courage to the blind and deaf
everywhere.

Among Sanborn's pupils in the school he was running in 1860 were
Wilkinson and Robertson James, brothers of William and Henry.
Robertson enlisted later in a colored regiment.

Daniel Foster, minister of the Trinitarian Church in 1850 and 1851,
also enlisted with the Negro troops and was killed in action. He had
been present when Sims was returned to slavery. Sims was led down
State Street to his ship between a double file of soldiers because a riot
was feared. The dock had been cleared of spectators and speeches
were forbidden but Daniel Foster got through as Sims's clergyman
and, in defiance of the edict against speeches, knelt and prayed aloud,
the only voice that could be heard that day on the side of Freedom.
Henry Thoreau at this time (April, 1851) expressed himself at length
and bitterly in his Journal. He was proud to read that the man who
made the prayer on the wharf was Daniel Foster of CONCORD but
when he thought what a short time Foster had lived in Concord, he
was ashamed that the Buttricks and Davises and Hosmers, descendants of the men who had fought at the bridge for their own liberty,
should be celebrating that fight on April 19th while themselves unwilling to do anything to help three million slaves attain their freedom.

"But I would have done with comparing ourselves with our ancestors,
for I believe that even they, if somewhat braver and less corrupt than
we, were not men of so much principle and generosity as to go to war

in behalf of another race in their midst. I do not believe that the North will soon come to blows with the South on this question. It would be too bright a page to be written in the history of the race at present."

History in 1861 was to show how wrong Thoreau was in this estimate. Books on the Civil War may say that the war was fought to preserve the Union, but slavery was the issue as seen from the North Bridge, and the descendants of the Buttricks and Davises and Hosmers all enlisted.

Mary Rice, a little spinster who lived behind the town house, was a single-minded Abolitionist, constantly active in the Women's Anti-Slavery Society. She tended John Jack's grave and planted lilies on it. She contributed to the anti-slavery papers the story of Martha Prescott, most popular girl in her school, who saw the little colored girl left alone when the procession formed and left her white friend to march with Jack Garrison's daughter. She kept a private infant school above Jarvis's bakery in an ell of the Wright tavern where the warmth from the ovens and the smell of fresh bread and ginger cookies made learning delightful.

In 1862, when the Abolitionists were still critical of Lincoln for not freeing the slaves, she walked from district to district to collect 350 signatures of Concord school children on a petition to free all slave children. Lincoln took the time to write to her that the petition had been handed to him by Senator Sumner.

. . . Please tell these little people I am very glad their young hearts are so full of just and generous sympathy and that while I have not the power to grant all they ask, I trust that they will remember that God has, and that, as it seems, He will do it.

It was just at this time that the Boston branch of the Women's Anti-Slavery Society was sending Concord girls to Summerville, South Carolina, to open schools for Negro children in the coastal lands occupied early by the Northern armies. The society's directive said "no school shall recognize any distinction of caste or color," but the Northern correspondents watched with interest when Jane Hosmer wrote that she had taken in several white pupils in her school because it seemed unfair to leave them in ignorance when the black children were learning to read. They directed her: "You must not allow the blacks, from their vantage ground of loyalty, to insult the whites."

A high point in school experience came with the annual exhibition held in the new town hall on March 18, 1861. Ephraim Bull had given out the picture cards to the best scholars and Reverend Mr. Reynolds

John S. Keyes, a founder of the Concord Antiquarian Society and author of many historical articles.

of the First Parish made the prayer. John Shepard Keyes, as chairman of the school committee, greeted three hundred children, almost as many parents. (Keyes was soon named by Lincoln United States Marshal and guarded the President at Gettysburg and at the second inaugural.) Frank Sanborn made a brief address. Each school took the platform in turn for a song, a recitation or a demonstration of arithmetic. Mr. Thoreau, it was announced, was kept away by illness but was still working, it was hoped, on his promised natural history of Concord for school use. Then the principal speaker was Ralph Waldo Emerson, who rarely missed such an occasion. He first read the song

> Come now from Barrett's mill, Bateman's blue water
>> Nine Acre Corner, the Centre and all;
> Come from the Factory, the North and East Quarter,
>> For here is a Union that never need fall.
>>> Here every blossom grows
>>> Shamrock, thistle and rose
> And fresh from our hillsides the Pilgrim's mayflowers.

It had been written for the occasion by Louisa Alcott and was then sung by three high school girls. The patriotic and Union pieces were much applauded, we are told. Master Harlow presented the Superintendent with a beautifully illustrated copy of *Pilgrim's Progress* and Mr. Alcott, in thanking the children, said "I did almost covet it as it lay

Miss Jane Hosmer and the old Deacon Hunt house bought by Edmund Hosmer in 1853. (Photograph by Alfred Hosmer.)

at Mr. Stacy's bookstore, borrowed it to look at and kept it I believe three weeks before I could return it; for I felt I was not rich enough to buy it. It is a sacred classic and I shall thank you for it every time I look into it." There was some confusion as the little folk became restless after three and a half hours. Then the children were served with cake and apples and all went home in the dusk over the snowy roads. Where else could such an array of talent have been found?

The high school exhibition was postponed by another severe snowstorm into April and, when the day came, most of the older boys had enlisted in the Concord company that went off to war on April 19th. The high school teacher said "Dark as is the present hour we will not despair." Then he quoted Lowell:

> Gray Plymouth rock hath yet a tongue and Concord is not dumb;
> And voices from our fathers' graves and from the future come;
> They call on us to stand our ground, they charge us still to be
> Not only free from chains ourselves, but foremost to make free.

On that nineteenth of April in the morning Asa Melvin left the Hiram Jones farm on Westford Road where he had been working since his father's death, and walked down to town to see the Concord com-

Samuel Melvin.

John Heald Melvin.

Asa Heald Melvin.

Louisa May Alcott in 1875.

pany off for the war. He heard that the roster was not full, so he enlisted and left a few hours later under Captain George L. Prescott. He was in the battle of Bull Run and then, when his hundred days were up, he re-enlisted. He fell in the charge at Petersburg June 16, 1864, where Colonel Prescott, still his commanding officer, also was killed. Two of his brothers died in service, one in 1863 at Fort Albany, Virginia, and one at Andersonville prison in September, 1864. One of their ancestors had been Simon Davis who fought at Brookfield in King Philip's War. One commanded a company at Crown Point, and one was the sentinel who rang the bell on the morning of April 19, 1775. On his mother's side were four militia officers named John Heald in four succeeding generations, leaders of Concord militia companies.

Emerson seemed to be the voice of Concord. His was the poignant recollection of Concord in *Lines Written in Naples*, in 1833:

> Not many men see beauty in the fogs
> Of close low pine-woods in a river town.
> But unto me not morn's magnificence,
> Nor Rome, nor joyful Paris, no nor even the song
> Of any woman that is now alive,
> Hath such a soul, such divine influence
> Such resurrection of a happy past.

His had been the unforgettable description of Concord Fight:

> Here once the embattled farmers stood
> And fired the shot heard round the world.

Now, moved by the death of Robert Gould Shaw at the head of his Negro troops, he wrote:

> So nigh is grandeur to our dust
> So near is God to Man
> When Duty whispers low "Thou must"
> the youth replies "I can."

These simple lines seem to express the spirit in which Concord lived and acted. With its background of adventurous pioneers, never ceasing to call every religious and political idea into question, reinforcing general debate with general education; with a population small enough so that there could be no stratification, and the meanest as well as the most generous could be heard; with every chance to hear new ideas from books and lectures and travel; with half a dozen fine minds spurring each other on, Concord became a center of world culture. It was by chance that Thoreau was born here, by the pull of family tradition that Emerson was drawn here, by the attraction of like minds that Alcott, Channing, and Sanborn came, for this Concord can claim little credit, but that Concord supplied a climate for Freedom, in which this American Renaissance flourished, for this Concord can always remain proud.

"Not many men see beauty in the fogs." (Photograph by Eliot Porter, Sierra Club.)

# *Appendix A*

The large number of families who came and went in the early years can be realized if one goes through the records (incomplete as they are) of births, marriages, and deaths. We find the following surnames: Atkinson, Bennett, Browne, Brooks, Blood, Bulkeley, Buss, Chandler, Coslin, Dane, Doggett, Draper, Edmunds, Edwards, Evarts, Fowle, Farwell, Fasset, Flint, Fox, Fuller, Gamlin, Griffin, Halsted, Hartwell, Harvey, Heaward, Hosmer, Jones, Lettin, Hunt, Martin, Meriam, Miles, Odell, Potter, Prentice, Rice, Rogers, Squiers, Symons, Thwing, Tompkins, Turney, Underwood, Wheat, Wheeler, Willard, and Wood.

Other names mentioned in deeds are: Adams, Alline, Baker, Ball, Barrett, Bateman, Beardsley, Bellows, Billings, Burgess, Buttrick, Dakin, Davis, Doubty, Fletcher, Gove, Hall, Heald, Heywood, Howines, Jeffrey, Judson, Mason, Richardson, Rigby, Smith, Scotchford, Stow, Smedley, Taylor, Thwaites, Tomline, West, Wylie, Willcox, Woodis, and Wooley. Two Concord planters of Fairfield, Connecticut, not mentioned above, must be added: Middlebrook and Johnson.

The complete list of Concord men who moved in 1644 to found Fairfield, Connecticut follows: Reverend John Jones, Thomas Bulkeley, who had married Jones's daughter, Thomas Jones, John Tompkins, Daniel Bulkeley, Joseph Middlebrook, Ephraim Wheeler, Thomas Wheeler, Jr., William Odell, James Bennett, William Bateman, Richard Lettin, John Evarts, Peter Johnson, George Squire, and Benjamin Turney.

*Names on the 1664 Petition Pledging to Assist "with persons and estates" in Maintaining the Charter (our earliest list of inhabitants, but incomplete)*

| | | |
|---|---|---|
| William Baker | Thomas Brooks | Joseph Dane |
| Nathaniel Ball | Boaz Browne | Thomas Dane |
| John Barker | Jabez Browne | Dolor Davis |
| Humphrey Barrett | Thomas Browne | Samuel Davis |
| Thomas Bateman | William Burton | Simon Davis |
| Nathaniel Billings | Joseph Buss | William Doule |
| James Blood | Nathaniel Buss | Roger Draper |
| James Blood | William Buss | Francis Dudley |
| Caleb Brooks | William Buttrick | Patrick Farre |
| Gershom Brooks | Thomas Chesman | John Farwell |
| Joshua Brooks | Thomas Dakin | Francis Fletcher |

| | | |
|---|---|---|
| Luke Fletcher | William Hunt | Samuel Stratton |
| Robert Fletcher | Joseph Jenks | William Taylor |
| Ephraim Flint | John Jones | Samuel Wheat |
| John Flint | Samuel Marble | Moses Wheat |
| William Frizell | George Meriam | George Wheeler |
| John Graves | John Meriam | John Wheeler |
| William Hall | Samuel Meriam | John Wheeler |
| John Hartwell | John Miles | Joseph Wheeler |
| Samuel Hartwell | William Osborn | Joshua Wheeler |
| John Harwood | Richard Rice | Obadiah Wheeler |
| George Hayward | John Scotchford | Samuel Wheeler |
| Joseph Hayward | John Slater | Thomas Wheeler |
| Gershom Heald | Baptist Smedley | Thomas Wheeler |
| John Heald | John Smedley | William Wheeler |
| John Heywood | John Smedley | Edmund Wylie |
| Daniel Hoar | Samuel Smedley | Michael Wood |
| James Hosmer | Cyprian Stevens | Joseph Woodard |
| Stephen Hosmer | Samuel Stow | Henry Woodis |
| William How | Samuel Stow | Christopher Wooley |
| Nehemiah Hunt | Thomas Stow | Edward Wright |

*Proprietors in 1666*

In 1723, John Flint made a list of the Concord men who had rights in Acton (Concord Village). Each of the inhabitants of 1666 or 1684 had a five-acre right which belonged to his heirs or assigns. In a few cases, the name of the original owner was not known in 1723 and the right was listed under the name of the contemporary owner of the lot. This list was found in an attic in Temple, New Hampshire, in 1933 and is now in the Public Library by gift of the heirs of Allen French. It is more complete than the 1664 list. It is not arranged alphabetically because the clerk, John Flint, seems to have thought of names more or less according to the neighborhood in which they lived just as later assessors' lists were made:

John Shepard, John Law, Edward Wright (2), Roger Chandler, John Heald II, Richard Temple, Stephen Hall (for where James Davis dwelt), Lieutenant Simon Davis, Baptist Smedley (for where John Hunt dwells), Thomas Bateman, William Hunt, Thomas Browne, John Heald, William Buttrick, Captain John Flint, Nehemiah Hunt, Robert Blood, James Blood I and II (2), John Smedley, John Jones (for where Samuel Jones lives), Humphrey Barrett (2), the living where Captain James Minott, Esq., now dwells, Thomas Dean, Roger Draper, John Farwell, Deacon Luke Potter, Thomas Wheeler (of Virginia Rd.), Moses Wheat (2), William Baker, Nathaniel Stow, Francis Fletcher (2), Eliphalet Fox (the living where Mr. John Hoar, deceased last dwelt), Nathaniel Ball, William Heartwell, James Taylor, Christopher Wooley, William Stow, Captain Timothy Wheeler (for where MaK dwelt), Gershom Brooks, Caleb Brooks, Joshua Brooks, Richard Rice.

Captain Ephraim Flint (2), Thomas Goble, Lieutenant Daniel Dean, the farm that was Mr. Prout's (2), Nathaniel Billings, John Billings, Samuel Stratton I, the living that was Mr. Joseph Estabrook's, William Wood, Samuel Meriam, Lieutenant Joseph Wheeler for where Captain Bulkeley dwells, Mr. John Wheeler for where he last dwelt by the millpond. Joshua Wheeler, George Wheeler, Oliver Barrett, Lieutenant William Buss, John Heywood I, Mr. Edward Bulkeley, James Hosmer I, John Scotchford, John Miles I, Thomas Stow, Edmond Wigley, Mr. Henry Woodis, Thomas Dakin, Michael Wood, Obadiah Wheeler I, William Wheeler I, James Hosmer I, Stephen Hosmer, Thomas Wheeler I, John Hayward, George Hayward I (for his living at town), the livings at the old iron works (2), where Thomas Pellet dwelt by the burying ground, Boaz Browne, Francis Dudley, John Heartwell, Daniel Goble, John Blood I, William Taylor, the living where Sergeant Joseph Fletcher now dwells, Samuel Marble for the living where Samuel Chandler now dwells.

*A list of the second order of proprietors (1694):*

Peter Wright, Joseph Lamson, Abraham Temple, John Jones I (2), Samuel Davis for Parlin's place, James Adams for the place where Lieutenant Heald last dwelt, Isaac Temple, Thomas Estabrook, Dr. Simon Davis, John Green, Isaac Hunt, Eleazer Flagg, Captain Jonathan Prescott, Deacon John Heywood, Samuel Wheeler by Dakin's place, Nathaniel Buss, Isaac Wood, the living where John Hosmer now dwells, Joseph Hayward, Obadiah Wheeler, Abraham Wood, Sr., Eliazer Ball, John Ball, Noah Brooks, Peter Rice, Deacon John Wheeler, Sergeant Thomas Wheeler of Virginy, Lieutenant Joseph French, Thomas Pellett, Joseph Dean, Samuel Stratton, Samuel Heartwell, Ensign Thomas Browne, Samuel Buttrick, Richard Parks I, John Smedley II, Judah Potter, John Taylor, Daniel Hoar, Sr., Mason, James Adams, Samuel Taylor, David Comee, the living where Benjamin Graves lived in the year 1684, Captain Timothy Wheeler by the schoolhouse, the living at the old iron works place, Ensign John Jones (for where Holdin lives), Walter Powers, Nathaniel Harwood, Ensign Thomas Wheeler, Joseph Buss, Simeon Hayward I, Abraham Taylor, Cornet Samuel Fletcher, Paul Rice, Timothy Rice, Dr. Philip Read, Deacon Humphrey Barrett, John Flint, Captain Ephraim Flint, Walter Hastings, Samuel How, Samuel Stratton, by Gobles.

# Appendix B

*The Founding of Concord as told by Edward Johnson of Woburn in his Wonder-working Providence of Sion's Saviour in New England (1653)*

The Twelfth Church of Christ gathered at Concord.

Yet further at this time entered the field two more valiant leaders of Christ's soldiers, holy men of God, Mr. Bulkeley and Mr. Jones, penetrating further into this wilderness than any formerly hath done, with divers other servants of Christ: they build an inland town which they call Concord, named from the occasion of the present time as you shall after hear: this town is seated upon a fair fresh river, whose rivulets are filled with fresh marsh, and her streams with fish, it being a branch of that large river of Merrimack. Alewives and shad come up to this town, but salmon and dace cannot come up by reason of the rocky falls, which cause their meadows to lie much covered with water, the which these people, together with their neighbor town have several times assayed to cut through but cannot, yet it may be turned another way with an hundred pound charge, as it appeared. This town was more populated once than now it is. Some faint-hearted soldiers among them, fearing the land would prove barren, sold their possessions for little and removed to a new plantation (which have most commonly a great prize set on them). The number of families at present are about 50, their buildings are conveniently placed in one straight street under a sunny bank in a low level, their herd of great cattle are about 300. The church of Christ here consists of about seventy souls, their teaching elders were Mr. Bulkeley and Mr. Jones, who removed from them with that part of the people who went away, so that only the reverend grave and godly Mr. Bulkeley remains.

> Riches and honors, Bulkeley lays aside
>     To please his Christ, for whom he now doth war,
> Why Bulkeley thou hast riches that will bide
>     And honors that exceed earth's honor far.
> Thy body's worn and days in desert spent
>     To feed a few of Christ's poor scattered sheep;
> Like Christ's bright body, thy poor body, rent,
>     With saints and angels company shall keep.
> Thy tongue and pen doth to the world declare
>     Christ's covenant with his flock shall firmly stand,
> When heavens and earth by Him dissolved are;
>     Then who can hold from this His work at hand?
> Two Bulkeleys more Christ by His grace hath taken,

And sent abroad to manage His great wars.
It's Bulkeley's joy that Christ his sons new making,
Hath placed in's churches for to shine as stars.

This holy and sincere servant of Christ was put upon the greater trial, by reason he and his were tenderly brought up, and now by the provident hand of Christ were carried far into this desert land where they met with some hardships for a long time; till the place was well peopled, they lived barely.

Now because it is one of the admirable acts of Christ's providence in leading His people forth into these western fields, in His providing of huts for them to defend them from the bitter storms this place is subject unto, therefore here is a short epitome of the manner how they placed down their dwellings in this desert wilderness, the Lord being pleased to hide from the eyes of His people the difficulties they are to encounter withal in a new plantation, that they might not thereby be hindered from taking the work in hand; upon some inquiry of the Indians who lived to the north-west of the Bay, one Captain Simon Willard being acquainted with them, by reason of his trade, became a chief instrument in erecting this town, the land they purchase of the Indians, and with much difficulty traveling through unknown woods and through watery swamps, they discover the fitness of the place, sometimes passing through the thickets, where their hands are forced to make way for their body's passage, and their feet clambering over the crossed trees, which when they missed, they sunk into an uncertain bottom in water, and wade up to the knees, tumbling sometimes higher and sometimes lower, wearied with this toil, they at the end of this meet with a scorching plain, yet not so plain, but that the ragged bushes scratch their legs foully, even to wearing their stockings to their bare skin in two or three hours; if they be not otherwise well defended with boots or buskins, their flesh will be torn; (that some being forced to pass on without further provision) have had the blood trickle down at every step, and in the time of summer the sun casts such a reflecting heat from the sweet-fern, whose scent is very strong so that some herewith hath been very near fainting, although very able bodies to undergo much travel, and this not to be endured for one day but for many, and verily did not the Lord encourage their natural parts with hopes of a new and strange discovery, expecting every hour to see some rare sight never seen before, they were never able to hold out and break through: but above all, the thirsting desires these servants of Christ have had to plant His churches, among whom the forenamed Mr. Jones shall not be forgotten.

In desert's depth where wolves and bears abide,
There Jones sits down a wary watch to keep,
O'er Christ's dear flock, who now are wandered wide;
But not from Him whose eyes ne'er close with sleep.

Surely it suits thy melancholy mind,
  Thus solitary for to spend thy days,
Much more thy soul in Christ content doth find,
  To work for Him, Who thee to joy will raise
Leading Thy son to land yet more remote,
  To feed His flock upon this western waste:
Exhort him then Christ's kingdom to promote;
  That he with Thee of lasting joys may taste.

Yet farther to tell of the hard labors this people found in planting this wilderness, after some days spent in search, toiling in the day time as formerly is said; like true Jacobites they rest them on the rocks where the night takes them, their short repast is some small pittance of bread, if it hold out, but as for drink, they have plenty, the country being well-watered in all places that yet are found out. Their farther hardship is to travel, sometimes they know not whither, bewildered indeed without sight of sun, their compass miscarrying in crowding through bushes, they sadly search up and down for a known way, the Indian paths being not above one foot broad, so that a man may travel many days and not find one. But to be sure the directing Providence of Christ hath been better unto them than many paths, as might here be inserted, did not haste call my pen away to more weighty matters; yet by the way, a touch thus, it befell with a serving maid, who was traveling about three or four miles from one town to another losing herself in the woods, had very diligent search made after her for the space of three days, and could not possibly be found, then being given over as quite lost, after three days and nights, the Lord was pleased to bring her feeble body to her own home in safety to the great admiration of all that heard of it. This intricate work no whit daunted these resolved servants of Christ to go on with the work at hand, but lying in the open air, while the watery clouds pour down all the night season, and sometimes the driving snow dissolving on their backs, they keep their wet clothes warm with a continued fire, till the renewed morning give fresh opportunity of further travel; after they have thus found out a place of abode, they burrow themselves in the earth for their first shelter under some hillside, casting the earth aloft upon a timber; they make a smoky fire against the earth at the highest side and thus these poor servants of Christ provide shelter for themselves, their wives and little ones, keeping off the short showers from their lodgings, but the long rains penetrate through to their great disturbance in the night season: yet in these poor wigwams they sing psalms, pray and praise their God, till they can provide them houses, which ordinarily was not wont to be with many till the earth, by the Lord's blessing, brought forth bread to feed them, their wives and little ones, which with sore labors they attain, every one that can lift a hoe to strike it into the earth, standing stoutly to their labors, and tear up the roots and bushes, which the first year bears them a very thin crop, till the sward of the earth be rotten and therefore they have been forced to cut their bread very thin for a long season. But the Lord is pleased to provide for them a great store of fish in the spring-time and especially alewives about the bigness of a herring, many thousands of these, they used to put under their Indian corn, which they plant in hills five foot asunder, and assuredly, when the Lord created this corn, He had a special eye to supply these His people's wants with it, for ordinarily five or six grains doth produce six hundred.

As for flesh, they looked not for any in those times (although now they have plenty) unless they could barter with the Indians for venison or raccoons whose flesh is not much inferior unto lamb, the toil of a new plantation being like the labors of Hercules never at an end, yet are none so barbarously bent (under the Massachusetts especially) but with a new plantation they ordinarily gather into church fellowship, so that pastors and people suffer the inconveniences together, which is a great means to season the sore labors they undergo, and verily the edge of their appetite was greater to spiritual duties at their first coming in time of wants, than afterward: many in new plantations have been forced to go barefoot, and bareleg, till these latter days, and some in time of frost and snow: yet were they then very healthy, more then than now they are: in this wilderness-work men of estates speed no better than others, and some much worse for want of being inured to such hard labor, having laid out their estate upon cattle at five and twenty pound a cow, when they came to winter them with inland hay, and feed upon such wild fodder as was never cut before, they could not hold out the winter, but ordinarily the first or second year after coming up to a new plantation, many of their cattle died, especially if they wanted salt marshes: and also those who supposed they should feed upon swine's flesh were cut short, the wolves commonly feasting themselves before them, who never leave neither flesh nor bones, if they be not scared away before they have made an end of their meal. As for those who laid out their estate upon sheep, they speed the worst of any at the beginning (although some have sped the best of any now) for until the land be often fed with other cattle, sheep cannot live; and therefore they never thrived till these latter days; horse had then no better success, which made many an honest gentleman travel afoot for a long time, and some have even perished with extreme heat in their travels: as also the want of English grain, wheat, barley and rye proved a sore affliction to some stomachs, who could not live upon Indian bread and water, yet were they compelled to it till cattle increased and the plows could but go: instead of apples and pears they had pumpkins and squashes of divers kinds. Their lonesome condition was very grievous to some, which was much aggravated by continual fear of the Indians' approach, whose cruelties were much spoken of, and more especially during the time of the Pequot wars.

Thus this poor people populate this howling desert, marching manfully on (the Lord assisting) through the greatest difficulties and forest labors that ever any with such weak means have done.

In the meantime here is to be remembered Mr. Thomas Flint, a sincere servant of Christ, who had a fair yearly revenue in England, but having improved it for Christ by casting it in the common treasury, he waits on the Lord for doubling his talent, if it shall seem good unto Him so to do, and the mean time spending his person for the good of his people in the office of magistrate.

At Christ's commands thou leav'st thy lands and native habitation:
His folk to aid, in desert strayed, for gospel's exaltation,
FLINT, hardy thou, wilt not allow, the undermining fox,
With subtile skill, Christ's vines to spill, thy sword shall give them knocks
Yet thou, base dust, and all thou hast, is Christ's, and by Him, thou
Art made to be, such as we see; hold fast forever now.

# *Appendix C*

### Date of the Act of the General Court Incorporating Concord

A careful reading at the State House of the manuscript record of the meeting of the General Court which passed the order for the incorporation of Concord shows that although boldly headed September 2, the eighth manuscript line reads: "The Court adjourned to 8 o'clock in the morning." It was, then, September 3 before the vote incorporating Concord was passed. When the Julian calendar was changed to the Gregorian calendar in 1752, many historians added ten days to all dates in the seventeenth century and eleven days to dates from 1700 to 1752. The Concord Town Clerk wrote in 1852 for a transcript of the old record and got back a certified copy with the date of September 2 which with ten days added became September 12 and that has been the official birthday ever since. Shattuck used the September 2 date but Ezra Ripley correctly says September 3 in his *Sermon at the Dedication of the Meeting-house* in 1792. It makes but little difference if we acknowledge that Hingham and Weymouth were voted upon on September 2, before the adjournment, making Concord's founding after theirs rather than on the same day.

*How firmly based the peaceful State.*

# Appendix D

## The Franchise in 1635 was Not Confined to Freemen

*The Body of Liberties* was the first body of laws ever printed in an English-speaking country. Proposed at a meeting of freemen in 1635, a committee of four including Nathaniel Ward of Ipswich was appointed to draw it up; it was established to stand in force in 1641 and was printed in 1648. It is very specific in giving the vote to non-freemen in town affairs:

This court, taking into consideration the useful parts and abilities of divers inhabitants which are not freemen, who have taken the oath of fidelity [do order] the freemen of every township with such other inhabitants as have taken the oath of fidelity shall have full power to choose town officers and may choose non-freemen. They may vote in ordering schools, herding cattle, laying out highways and distributing land.

Provided no non-freeman shall have his vote until he have attained the age of twenty-one years.

Evidently Major Willard administered the oath of fidelity to every male inhabitant, for we find just one, John Blood, cited to appear in court for refusing to take the oath. There is no record of any fine for non-attendance at town meetings but a fine was levied on the town by the colony if it was not represented in the General Court.

Further proof that the franchise in town affairs included non-freemen is shown in the fact that in 1689 when the province charter took up the matter only 17 of the Concord citizens were Church members or "freemen" against 35 men of voting age who were not.

It should be emphasized that in the things that were important to the Concord farmer, everyone voted: in dividing land and laying out roads, in school matters, and in the care of the poor.

When one thinks of Massachusetts as the sum of its individual towns, it becomes evident that the citizens had been schooled in democracy at their town meetings and were ready for the great experiment in government which the Constitution of 1787 provided.

The idea of representatives chosen by the towns and often instructed by them had also been successfully used in Massachusetts for 150 years.

It is hard to find a general historian who makes the point that every householder voted in town meetings. The fact that only freemen (or Church members in full communion) could vote in Colony affairs has led them to emphasize this restriction. Walcott in Concord in the Colonial Period notes that when a count was made in Concord the town meeting non-freemen voters were 35 and the freemen 17, and that most of the town officers were not freemen.

# *Appendix E*

## Concord in 1717

In 1932, Mrs. Bertha Wright, Secretary to the Concord Assessors, permitted me to have the oldest extant Assessors list copied in the Town House. Since in the intervening years the original list has disappeared, it seems worthwhile to print my copy. The original consisted of a few sheets of paper sewn together to make a little booklet. On the outside was this notation: "The sum of the Town's estate in the year 1717 is 4853 £ 14s and the number of polls 293 the real estate being 2268 £ and the personal estate 2585 £ 14s. The province treasurer's warrant was in the sum of 155 £ 2s." The constables were Daniel Davis for the East Quarter, Samuel Heywood for the South, and William Wilson for the North Quarter. Cows were valued uniformly at one pound, ten shillings, horses at two pounds and oxen at two pounds, sheep at four shillings, and the two Negroes were each valued at fifteen pounds. A faculty tax of a pound or two was levied on the tradesmen or blacksmiths.

A figure at the left of the name indicates more than one poll or males above twenty-one years. The figure after the letter "R" indicates the value of the real estate in English pounds.

John Barker, Sr.   R15, 1 horse, 4 oxen, 5 cows, 5 sheep
John Barker, Jr.   no R, 1 horse, 2 oxen, 1 cow, 4 sheep
2   Samuel Prescott   R14, 2 horses, 2 oxen, 7 cows, 10 sheep
Joseph Fletcher   R7, 1 horse, 2 oxen, 5 cows
Abraham Wood, Sr.   R6, 1 horse, 2 oxen, 3 cows, 5 sheep
Henry Sparks   R2, 2 oxen, 1 cow
George Robbins   R6
Samuel Davis   R6, 1 horse, 2 cows
Daniel Shepard   1 horse, 2 cows
Jonathan Hartwell   R7, 1 horse, 2 oxen, 3 cows, 5 sheep
Stephen Law   R9, 2 oxen, 2 cows
Thomas Law   R6, 1 horse, 2 cows, 2 sheep
2   Jonathan Herrick   R8, 2 horses, 2 oxen, 4 cows
2   Lot Conant   R8, 2 horses, 4 oxen, 4 cows, 16 sheep
2   Edward Wright   R27, 2 horses, 2 oxen, 4 cows, 8 sheep
Josiah Hayward   1 horse, 2 oxen, 3 cows, 2 sheep
John Britton   1 horse, faculty 1 £ 10 sh.
Samuel Wright   R10, 1 horse, 4 cows
Joseph Wright   R10, 2 oxen, 2 cows
Joseph Harris   1 horse

Peter Wright   R17, 1 horse, 2 oxen, 4 cows, 10 sheep, Fac. 1 £
2  Joseph Lamson   R5, 2 horses, 2 oxen, 4 cows
Ebenezer Townsend   R4, 2 cows
Thomas Estabrook   R3, 1 horse, 2 oxen, 2 cows
John Barker, Sr.   R9, 1 horse, 2 oxen, 5 cows, 10 sheep
John Temple   R6, 1 horse, 3 cows
Abraham Temple   R13, 1 horse, 5 cows
Benjamin Temple   R8, 1 horse, 2 oxen, 3 cows, 3 sheep
Mary Chandler, widow   R7, 4 cows
2  Samuel Chandler   R12, 1 horse, 4 oxen, 3 cows
Benjamin Barrett   R14, 1 horse, 4 oxen, 8 cows
Dr. Simon Davis   R12, 1 horse, 2 oxen, 2 cows, 8 sheep
Simon Davis   1 cow, faculty 1 £
Isaac Temple   R4, 1 horse, 3 cows
Ebenezer Allin   R1, 1 horse, 2 cows
2  Eliazer Brown   R8, 1 horse, 2 oxen, 6 cows
2  Abraham Estabrook   R5, 3 cows, faculty 1 £
John Melvel   R5, 1 horse, 2 oxen, 4 cows
Jonathan Melvel   R3, 1 horse, 1 cow
Benjamin Melvel
David Melvel   R3, 1 horse, 2 cows, faculty 1 £
Thomas Brown, Tertis   R6, 2 oxen, 6 cows, 8 sheep
Ebenezer Hartwell   R6, 3 horses, 3 cows
John Hartwell   R2, 1 horse, 1 cow
2  Jacob Farrar   R20, 4 horses, 4 oxen, 7 cows, 20 sheep
Jacob Farrar, Jr.   R0, 1 horse, 2 cows
Joseph Brabrook   R0, 1 horse, 3 cows
Joseph Temple   R8, 1 horse, 3 oxen, 1 cow
John Davis   R4, 1 horse, 2 oxen, 3 cows
Eleazer Heald   R4, 1 horse, 3 cows
Gersham Heald
William Russell, Jr.   R2, 1 horse, 1 cow
Jonathan Wheeler   R4, 1 horse, 2 oxen, 2 cows
Samuel Wheeler   R1, 1 horse, 2 oxen, 2 cows
John Heald, Jr.   R1, 1 horse, 2 cows
2  John Parling   R8, 1 horse, 4 oxen, 5 cows
Joseph Parling   1 horse, faculty 1 £
2  Sgt. John Heald   R20, 1 horse, 6 oxen, 7 cows
William Russell   R11, 2 horses, 2 oxen, 5 cows
James Russell
Nathaniel Ball   R3, 1 horse, 2 oxen, 4 cows
2  Jonathan Blood   R14, 3 horses, 4 oxen, 5 cows
2  Josiah Blood   R34, 3 horses, 4 oxen, 12 cows
John Blood   1 horse, 2 cows

Hugh Cargill's old house on Lowell Road.

Birthplace of the four Melvins off Lowell Road. (Photograph by Ralph Holden.)

The house bought by the Brook farmer, Minot Pratt, built by Thomas Flint.

Samuel Blood   R25, 2 horses, 4 oxen, 12 cows
James Blood   R21, 1 horse, 2 oxen, 8 cows
David Whitaker   R8, 1 horse, 3 cows, 6 sheep
Samuel Hunt   R5, 3 cows, 5 sheep
William Hunt   R14, 1 horse, 2 oxen, 4 cows, 8 sheep
Nehemiah Hunt   R9, 1 horse, 8 cows
Nehemiah Hunt, Jr.   R8, 2 horses, 4 oxen, 6 cows, 11 sheep
Lt. John Flint   R14, 2 horses, 2 oxen, 5 cows, 1 sheep
Thomas Flint   R5, 1 horse, 2 oxen, 3 cows
Samuel Buttrick   R11, 1 horse, 2 oxen, 4 cows, 4 sheep
Samuel Buttrick, Jr.   1 horse, 1 cow, faculty 1 £

John Hunt house. The original painting from which this was photographed is now in the possession of the Concord Free Public Library, gift of Mrs. Stedman Buttrick.

Jonathan Buttrick   R6, 1 horse, 4 oxen, 1 cow
2   Thomas Brown, Smith   R8, 2 oxen, 3 cows
James Davis   R7, 1 horse, 2 oxen, 4 cows, 4 sheep
2   Ebenezer Davis   R15, 2 horses, 2 oxen, 6 cows, 10 sheep, faculty 1 £
2   John Hunt   R21, 1 horse, 2 oxen, 7 cows, 12 sheep
Sgt. Bateman   R5, 1 horse, 1 ox, 2 cows
John Bateman   R12, 1 horse, 2 oxen, 4 cows
Ens. Brown   R10, 1 horse, 2 oxen, 3 cows
2   Lt. Wilson   R22, 2 horses, 4 oxen, 8 cows
John Smedly   R9, 2 oxen, 2 cows
Samuel Jones   R12, 1 horse, 2 oxen, 4 cows, faculty 1 £
2   Joseph Barratt   R24, 1 horse, 4 oxen, 8 cows, 14 sheep
Capt. James Minott   R22, 1 horse, 2 oxen, 5 cows, 9 sheep, faculty 3 £
James Minott   R10, 1 horse, 2 oxen, 2 cows
Sgt. Eliazer Flag   R3, 1 horse, 2 oxen, 1 cow
Joseph Flag   R3, 2 cows, 2 sheep
2   William Wood   R2, 1 cow, faculty 1 £
Jonathan Ball   R4, 1 cow, 1 horse, faculty 10 s
2   Capt. Jonathan Prescott, Jr.   R17, 2 horses, 2 oxen, 4 cows, 20 sheep, faculty 5 £

James Smedly   R11, 2 oxen, 2 cows
Ellias Barron
Mr. William Keen   R2
2   Nathaniel Jones   R15, 1 horse, 2 oxen, 3 cows, 8 sheep
Benjamin Barron   R5, 2 horses, 2 oxen, 2 cows, faculty 1 £
3   Deacon Edward Wheeler   R13, 2 horses, 4 cows, faculty 2 £
Joseph Hubbard   R9, 1 horse, 3 cows
Judah Potter   R15, 2 horses, 2 oxen, 5 cows
Capt. Jonathan Prescott   R16, 2 horses, 2 oxen, 2 cows
John Miles   R17, 1 horse, 2 oxen, 5 cows
Samuel Hubbard   R8, 4 cows, faculty 1 £
2   Samuel Heywood   R7, 1 horse, 4 oxen, 3 cows, faculty 1 £
Deacon John Heywood   R10, 1 horse, 2 oxen, 4 cows
John Buss   R13, 1 horse, 4 oxen, 4 cows, 7 sheep
Nathaniel Buss   R4, 2 cows
Deacon Joseph Lee   R13, 1 horse, 2 oxen, 3 cows
Woodis Lee   R11, 1 horse, 2 oxen, 2 cows, 5 sheep
Jonathan Hubbard, Jun.   R13, 1 horse, 2 oxen, 4 cows
3   Joseph Dakin   R13, 2 horses, 2 oxen, 3 cows, faculty 1 £
3   Nicolas Shavally   R14, 3 horses, 2 oxen, 3 cows
John Shavally for Thos. Stow and faculty 1 £
Abraham Wood Cloth^e   R11, 3 horses, 3 oxen, 3 cows
2   Jacob Wood   R6, 2 oxen, 3 cows
2   Isaac Wood   R12, 1 horse, 4 oxen, 3 cows
Isaac Wood, jun.   R2, 2 oxen, 1 cow
Mr. Richard Kates   R5, 1 horse, 2 cows, 1 Negro
John Hosmer   R15, 1 horse, 2 oxen, 6 cows
John Holdin   R11, 1 horse, 2 oxen, 4 cows
Sgt. John Wood   R3, 2 cows
John Wood, jun.   R11, 1 horse, 2 oxen, 6 cows
Samuel Miles   R10, 1 horse, 2 oxen, 6 cows, 9 sheep
John Griffin   2 cows
Isaac Patch   R1, 1 horse, 2 oxen, 1 cow
George Wheeler   R6, 2 horses, 4 oxen, 4 cows, 2 sheep
Obadiah Wheeler   R7, 3 cows
4   Sgt. William Wheeler   R16, 2 horses, 6 cows, 14 sheep
Jn^o Wheeler, sr.   R10, 1 horse, 2 oxen, 3 cows
2   William Wheeler, jun.   1 horse, 2 oxen
Ens. Wheeler   R13, 3 horses, 2 oxen, 6 cows
Samuel Wheeler, sr.   1 horse, 1 cow
Stephen Hosmer   R20, 2 horses, 2 oxen, 5 cows
Samuel Wood   R10, 1 horse, 2 oxen, 3 cows
Thomas Hosmer   R15, 1 horse, 4 oxen, 8 cows
2   John Willard   R12, 1 horse, 2 oxen, 4 cows

An early William and Joseph Wheeler house, corner of Powder Mill and Sudbury roads, owned in 1967 by Harding U. Greene.

Mostman   R8
2   Simeon Hayward   R16, 2 horses, 4 oxen, 10 cows, 9 sheep
Ebenezer Olds   1 horse
2   Walter Power   R15, 2 horses, 2 oxen, 6 cows, 7 sheep
2   David Russel   R6, 1 horse, 1 ox, 3 cows
John Power   R6, 1 horse, 2 cows
John Meriam   R2, 1 horse, 2 oxen, 1 cow
Daniel Hubbard   R3, 1 horse
William Clark   R10, 1 horse, 1 cow, faculty 1 £
John Brown   R1, 2 cows, faculty 1 £
2   Ens. John Jones   R11, 2 cows
Peter Harwood   R8, 1 horse, 2 oxen, 3 cows, 10 sheep
Boaz Brown   R10, 1 horse, 2 oxen, 2 cows
Eleiazer Flagg   R7, 1 horse, 2 oxen, 3 cows, 12 sheep
Joseph Baker   R5, 1 horse, 1 cow
2   Joseph Fletcher   R15, 2 horses, 4 oxen, 4 cows, 12 sheep
Benjamin Fletcher
Benjamin Hoar   2 horses, 2 cows, 7 sheep
Daniel Hoar   R15, 1 horse, 4 oxen, 3 cows
Samuel Fletcher   R2, 1 horse
2   Nathaniel Ball   R10, 2 horses, 2 oxen, 5 cows, 3 sheep
Thomas Ball   1 horse, 1 faculty

Samuel Hartwell   R8, 1 horse, 1 ox, 4 cows
Jonathan Hartwell   R7, 1 horse, 1 ox, 1 cow
2   Joseph Wooley   R10, 2 horses, 2 oxen, 3 cows
Samuel Wooley   R2, 1 cow
Jnº Wooley   R5, 1 horse, 2 oxen, 2 cows
Benjamin Clark   R2, faculty 1 £
2   Abraham Taylor   R9, 1 horse, 2 oxen, 4 cows
2   Jacob Taylor   R12, 1 horse, 4 oxen, 4 cows
Jacob Taylor, Ju.   1 horse, 2 oxen
Ebenezer Meiriam   R6, 1 horse, 2 oxen, 4 cows
Joseph Meiriam   R7, 1 horse, 6 cows
John Meiriam   R9, 1 horse, 2 oxen, 4 cows
Samuel Fox   R2, 1 horse, 2 oxen, 3 cows
2   Samuel Fletcher   R12, 1 horse, 2 oxen, 3 cows, 8 sheep
John Fletcher   1 cow, 8 sheep
John Jones   R5, 1 horse, 2 cows
2   Nathaniel Stow   R25, 2 horses, 4 oxen, 6 cows, 12 sheep
John Stow   1 horse, 2 oxen
Daniel Brooks, ju.   R12, 1 horse, 4 cows, 2 oxen, 8 sheep
3   Daniel Brooks, sr.   R18, 2 horses, 4 oxen, 8 cows, 14 sheep
Joseph Brooks   R11, 1 horse, 2 oxen, 4 cows, 10 sheep
2   Noah Brooks   R13, 2 horses, 2 oxen, 7 cows, 10 sheep, faculty 1 £
Hugh Brooks   R11, 1 horse, 2 oxen, 6 cows, 7 sheep
Joshua Brooks   R6, 1 horse, 2 oxen, 4 cows, 5 sheep, 1 faculty
Joseph Wheat   R8, 1 horse, 2 oxen, 3 cows, 4 sheep
2   Ebenezer Brooks   R6, 1 horse, 2 oxen, 3 cows, 1 sheep
2   Samuel Hartwell   R14, 2 horses, 2 oxen, 4 cows, 15 sheep
3   Benjamin Whittemore   R13, 2 horses, 2 oxen, 5 cows, 10 sheep
2   Ebenezer Lamson   R8, 2 horses, 2 oxen, 2 cows, 9 sheep
2   Lt. Joseph French   R17, 1 horse, 4 oxen, 4 cows, 18 sheep
Samuel French   R8, 2 cows
Jonathan French   R8, 1 horse, 1 cow
Eliezer Davis   R10, 1 horse, 1 ox, 4 cows, 5 sheep
2   Daniel Davis   R11, 2 horses, 2 oxen, 5 cows, 4 sheep
Simon Davis   R11, 1 horse, 2 oxen, 4 cows, 6 sheep
Benjamin Colburn   R6, 1 horse, 2 oxen, 4 cows, 6 sheep
William Colburn   1 horse, 2 cows
Thomas Pellet   R8, 1 horse, 2 oxen, 3 cows
Daniel Dean   2 horses, 2 cows
2   Joseph Dean, Ju.   R11, 1 horse, 2 oxen, 5 cows, 7 sheep
Joseph Wheeler   R18, 1 horse, 4 oxen, 5 cows, 7 sheep
John Wheler   R12, 2 horses, 2 oxen, 3 cows, 10 sheep
Jonathan Wheeler   R4, 1 horse, 3 cows
2   Timothy Wheeler   R18, 3 horses, 3 oxen, 8 cows, 10 sheep

Ed Garfield at old Garfield house, Garfield Road. (Original Esther Anderson.)

2  John Sterns   R6, 1 horse, 2 oxen, 3 cows
William Hartwell   R19, 1 horse, 5 oxen, 8 cows, 10 sheep
Stephen Davis   R5, 1 horse, 2 oxen, 3 cows, 3 sheep
Joseph Fasset   R3
John Fasset   R11, 2 horses, 2 oxen, 9 cows, 9 sheep
Nathaniel Meiriam   R12, 2 horses, 2 oxen, 8 cows
John Taylor   R10, 1 horse, 2 oxen, 3 cows
Samuel Meiriam   R4, 1 horse, 2 oxen, 3 cows
Rebekah Wooly, widow   R10, 1 horse, 2 oxen, 5 cows, 10 sheep
Ruth Meed, widow   R4, 2/4 of a horse, 4 cows
Caleb Ball   R8, 1 horse, 4 oxen, 2 cows
Nathaniel Whitteker   R5, 1 horse, 2 oxen, 2 cows
Thomas Wheeler   2 oxen, 1 cow
Capt. Ephraim Flint   R24, 2 horses, 4 oxen, 5 cows, 10 sheep
Edward Flint   R4, 2 horses, 2 oxen
2  Simon Dakin   R14, 2 horses, 4 oxen, 8 cows
Simon Dakin, ju.

Cambridge Turnpike house bought from Hezekiah Fletcher by Robert Cuming.

2   Jonathan Whitney   R27, 2 horses, 2 oxen, 9 cows
2   Richard Parks   R20, 2 horses, 4 oxen, 7 cows, 14 sheep
Joseph Parks   R3, 1 horse, 2 oxen
Ebenezer Hunt   R4, stock
John Pilsbury   R9, 1 horse, 2 oxen, 2 cows
Lt. Daniel Deen   R24, 2 horses, 2 oxen, 5 cows, 6 sheep, 1 Negro
Daniel Addams   R4, 1 horse, 3 cows, 7 sheep, faculty 1 £
Joshua Hutchinson   R10, 2 cows
Thomas Gobl   R7, 2 horses, 2 oxen, 2 cows
2   George Farrar   R20, 2 horses, 4 oxen, 7 cows, 16 sheep
Joseph Farrar   R0, 1 horse, 1 cow
Samuel Straton at gobls   R3, 2 horses, 2 oxen, 3 cows
Jonathan Pike   1 cow
2   Daniel Billing   R20, 1 horse, 2 oxen, 2 cows, 4 sheep
2   Samuel Billing   R22, 1 horse, 2 oxen, 7 cows, 20 sheep
Nathaniel Billing   R8, 1 horse, 2 oxen, 4 cows
Samuel Allin
Samuel Straton, jur   R7, 1 horse, 2 oxen, 2 cows, 5 sheep
Samuel Straton, Sr.   R15, 1 horse, 2 oxen, 3 cows
Joseph Straton   1 horse, 2 oxen, 2 cows
2   Samuel Meriam, jur   R14, 1 horse, 2 oxen, 7 cows

Capt. Joseph Bulkley   R16, 1 horse, 2 oxen, 2 cows
Ebenezer Wheler   R18, 2 horses, 2 oxen, 4 cows
2   Jonathan Hubbard, Sr.   R15, 1 horse, 2 oxen, 5 cows
2   Samuel Wheler at mill   R17, 1 horse, 4 oxen, 5 cows, 5 sheep
Hezekiah Fletcher   R15, 1 horse, 6 oxen, 3 cows
John Fletcher, Sr.   R10, 1 horse, 2 oxen, 4 cows, 8 sheep
John Fox   R8, 1 horse, 2 oxen, 4 cows, 6 sheep
Joseph Fletcher, jur   1 pair of oxen
Widow Brower of Weston   R4

*Old Roads*

As early as 1719 the Minots who owned the mill began taking gravel from the ridge to widen the dam until by 1740 the town ordered Ephraim Minot to build a bridge over his flume and the milldam became a road. The loop around the south burying-ground was abandoned and the land given to Jonathan Prescott in 1693, and in 1747 Daniel Bliss, then owner of this place, was allowed to take in part of the burying-place provided he put up a fence on the new line. After Holden's Black Horse tavern was built on our Library lot, the road to Sudbury was laid out to the south of the tavern on its present course, going over swamp bridge along the Wheeler land on one side, and passing the southeast ends of the Jonas Heywood and the Hubbard farms. It continued over our Fairhaven Road past the Potter farm into the woods to the rocks (Fairhaven Hill) where John Miles had a pasture. The road then turned more to the south to bypass Well Meadow and pass the Samuel Billings house, on a road that can still be traced on Pleasant Meadow (Baker Farm in Thoreau's day), and the Nathaniel and John Billings houses, still standing on the Old Concord Road in Lincoln. It crossed Halfway Brook where John Billings had a mill (near St. Anne's Church), went by the Daniel Dean and the Farrar farms (formerly Goble's), and so to the Sudbury line, for present-day Wayland was the first Sudbury town center. Off this the north road to Watertown passed the Jonathan Whitney and the Parks farms.

An alternate road to Lincoln went north of Walden Pond from the Stratton farms west of the Town Forest to Ephraim Minot's farm, which later became Jacob Baker's, joining the other road near the Nathaniel Billings place. Off this a road to Lincoln meetinghouse passed the Ebenezer Prout place on the south corner of Flint's Pond, meeting here a very ancient way west of the pond to the Bay Road, passing Dr. John Prescott's house, a Fox house, Hezekiah Fletcher's and crossing the millbrook at Foxes' bridge over what we now call Hawthorne Lane. Two other roads toward Lincoln went from the Bay Road toward Thomas Wheeler's and Edward Flint's on the north and east sides of Lincoln hill.

Among Peter Bulkeley's possessions in the early days was a nine-acre meadow in the southwest part of town as well as a seven-acre piece in the northwest corner. The way to the former was called the way to the Nine Acres and from this the picturesque name Nine Acre Corner developed. The name appears in the town records in 1667 when George Wheeler, who had bought this land, was ordered by a town meeting to lay out a road to Mr. Bulkeley's "nine acres of meadow above Fairhaven," and from the three "went" ways on the top of the pine hill. "Went" is an old English word meaning "lane" from the same Saxon root as the English "wend" or the German "winden." This was the old Road to Nine Acre Corner which left the Lancaster road by John Hosmer's house, near our Emerson Hospital, with Michael Wood's big holdings on the east side and the Samuel and Ezekiel Miles houses on the corner of a branch of the Marlborough Road (now called Williams Road). Also living near was Woodis Lee who had married Elizabeth Wood. Lee's mother was Mary Woodis, whose father had bought the Simon Willard farm between the rivers which was left to her and her husband, Joseph Lee, formerly of Ipswich, who inherited the Willard farm from his first wife. His second wife was Mary, widow of Edmund Wylie (spelled Wigley), whose second division land was here at three went ways. One of these ways led over toward the river where Stephen Hosmer had built a house on land bought from John Wood, his brother-in-law. The main road led on by Joseph Wheeler's house and by Nathaniel Hosmer's where Betsy Hosmer, granddaughter of Nathaniel Hosmer, married Ebenezer Conant in 1812; so that the farm came to be known as the Conant farm and was dubbed Conantum by Henry Thoreau. Betsy Hosmer Conant's sister, Sarah, married Silas Holden and lived on Garfield Road. The Garfields, who had originally lived east of Beaver Pond near Watertown Corner, came to the corner of this road, now named for the Garfields, when Polly Binney, the cousin of Sarah and Betsy Hosmer, married Daniel Garfield, descended from the same ancestor as President Garfield. A picturesque old house built by Woodis Lee, Jr., overlooks the river and Lee's Bridge near the end of Garfield Road. A house, blacksmith shop, and tavern were built after the Fitchburg turnpike was put through. The original settlers in the South Quarter were Samuel Stratton, Nathaniel Billings, Luke Potter, George Wheeler, Obadiah Wheeler, George Hayward, Jonathan Heywood, Ensign William Buss, James Hosmer, John Miles, Michael Wood, and Oliver Barrett, according to a list dated 1699. The present section of Sudbury Road between Fairhaven Road and the river began as a right of way through Hubbard's barnyard to give the Wheeler's access to a riverside pasture and became a road only when Hubbard's Bridge was built in 1802. Place names in the South Quarter are Mento, Scotland, Bear Garden, Green Pond, White Pond, Dunge Hole, and Barberry.

In present-day Lincoln the old Woburn road led from the Bay Road at the corner of Virginia Road where Joseph Wheat and Ebenezer Brooks lived, passed Widow Ruth Mead's and Caleb Ball's Rocky Meadow, in Bedford, on by Samuel and Nathaniel Meriam and John Taylor to John Fasset's house at Shawshine Corner. Most of this road is now swallowed by Hanscom Airfield.

The old road to Billerica was later called the Old Bedford Road. It led from Meriam's Corner with its three Meriam houses, passing first a lane into the ancient common fields which connected with a similar lane opposite the old Manse.

Old Bedford Road passed between two houses, still standing, built by sons of Eliphalet Fox and passed a third house, built by Enos Fox, his grandson; then beyond the Bedford town line to the French, Wooley and the Davis farms, to the Colburns on a road to the north, with a farm belonging to the Deans and Pellets on a side road to the south.

On the Bay Road itself beyond Meriam's Corner was the house of Deacon Samuel Minot who bought for his son, Jonas Minot, the farm across the fields on Virginia Road which had belonged originally to Sergeant Thomas Wheeler and to his son, Deacon John Wheeler. They had called the road after a manor Virginia in their English home town, Cranefield, near Odell. Beyond the deacon were four houses built by Wheeler descendants. Because Jonas Minot's second wife was Mary Jones Dunbar, this was the girlhood home of Cynthia Dunbar and the birthplace of her son, Henry David Thoreau.

A second son of Deacon Samuel Minot and heir to the Bay Road Minot house was Captain George Minot, owner in 1775. Another son was Samuel Minot, Jr., a goldsmith, who left Boston with many other patriots at the time of the Revolution. Examples of his communion silver are treasured in the Boston Museum of Fine Arts. Deacon Samuel Minot's father had been James Minot, a farmer cousin and contemporary of James Minot, Esq., who lived in the center of town in the oldest part of the Colonial Inn, but had also a house in Boston as befitted his position as Colonel, Justice, Representative, and member of the King's Council.

On Lexington Road, beyond the Minots, were the Fletcher farm; John Jones and Nathaniel Stow with Daniel Brooks, Junior and Senior, on the hillside; Joseph Brooks on the hilltop; and Noah, Hugh, and Joshua Brooks on the east side of the hill sloping down to the tanyard. Two Hartwell houses beyond the Woburn Road corner, one a tavern, were followed by a Whittemore place, and next to the old town line were Ebenezer Lamson, Dr. Philip Read and Richard Rice, who died in 1709, last survivor of the first settlers. The Rice house was burned to the ground in 1953 as it was considered not worth saving.

Connecting the East and North Quarters was a lane running from Meriam's Corner to the North Bridge, which had strategic importance on the 19th of April 1775.

In the North Quarter the main road to Groton over the North Bridge began at the meetinghouse, went through the training field, where Dr. Timothy

Minot, Jr., lived in Peter Bulkeley's old house, then by the town house, the schoolhouse, and the schoolmaster's (Timothy Minot, Sr.); then turning on a right angle by Captain James Minott's wound out of the training field over a muddy brook in Captain's Hollow. Across from Minott on the corner, after the war Joseph Mulliken built himself a house and clock-making shop. He was a younger brother to Lydia of Lexington. John Keyes of Westford came to Concord in 1812 and bought this house. Then the road went by the poorhouse, Humphrey Barrett's, John Jones's, and the Smedleys' (later Jones's house), to turn again toward the bridge past the house once owned by James Blood. The James Blood house had become William Wilson's by marriage and was later, in 1770, bought by William Emerson and enlarged or rebuilt for his parsonage.

Across the bridge, the road skirted Buttrick's four-acre meadow and turned up the hill with David Brown's farm on the west and the Buttrick land on the other side. Ephraim and Willard Buttrick had houses here in the corner made by a lane running over to John Flint's. On the north side of this lane on the first settler's, William Buttrick's, house lot lived his great-grandson, Major John Buttrick, brother of Ephraim and Willard. The lane led over to the original Flint house lot, owned after the pioneer, Thomas, by three generations named John Flint. Here it turned to go through the land inherited by Thomas Flint, Jr., and through a Jonas Bateman farm to the Nehemiah Hunt farm on the hilltop. Part of the Hunt farm was sold to Colonel James Barrett for his son, Nathan, who was captain of a company of militia on April 19, 1775. Beyond the hill were three farms inherited by Buttricks through Samuel Buttrick's marriage to Sarah Blood. On a lane behind the hill was a Whittaker farm acquired through a Buttrick marriage, and on the east side the John Barrett place, part of Humphrey Barrett's second division land. Near the river was a farm bought by Caleb Ball in 1750, and beyond Barrett's a Thomas Hodgeman place (he married a Buttrick) and the Lawrence farm.

In 1717, the land beyond, extending into present-day Carlisle, was owned by James Blood, Samuel Blood, John Blood, Josiah Blood, and Jonathan Blood.

Beyond the Buttricks on the Groton road was the house and blacksmith shop of John Brown and the Davis farm owned in turn by Dolor, Simon, and James Davis. The old road to the twenty score turned off beyond the blacksmith shop toward Benjamin Clark's, the Samuel and Thomas Estabrook houses, and John Green's toward Carlisle. It is now called Estabrook Road. As the Groton road approached the old Fifty-Acre Way, it made a triangle with the present Lowell Road. Next were several farms belonging to descendants of Eleazer Brown, one of whom, Abishai, had a tavern at the crossroads on land his wife had inherited from the Chandlers. The Browns had also bought land from the Batemans near the pond. The road took a deep turn to the west, nearly to Spencer Brook, where there was an old Melvin house, before coming to the fork where Westford Road turned from a road to Carlisle. On the latter were old Adams and Hartwell houses. On the Westford Road were Jones, Melvin, Farrar, and Heald farms.

The road to Barrett's mill was thickly settled. Opposite the tavern was Samuel Chandler, then William Wilson, Christopher Dodge, Joseph Dudley, Simon Davis, Samuel Chandler, Jr., Benjamin Temple, Thomas Barrett, the miller; then James Barrett and Richard Temple whose land became James Barrett, Jr.'s farm; then Jonathan Brooks and William Barker, and Joseph and David Lamson (later Dr. Cuming's), Lieutenant Joseph and Samuel Wright, and the Darby place with Lot and Andrew Conant at the Westvale mill on the Assabet.

Back near the north bridge on a lane above the Assabet River was the Sergeant Bateman farm and the John Hunt place with the land bought by the Hunts from Baptist Smedley providing an alternate way to Barrett's mill. This is now Lowell Road and was the main road after Hunt's bridge was built in 1792.

# *Appendix F*

We, his Majesty's most dutiful and loyal subjects, the Inhabitants of Concord, in Town Meeting assembled this 11th day of January 1773 after expressing our most firm attachment to and ardent love for, our most gracious sovereign, King George, in the support and defence of whose person and dignity we are always ready not only to spend our fortunes, but lives, (while we are in the enjoyment of our invaluable privileges granted us by Royal Charter) but can not in this time of general concern throughout the Province, do otherwise than express our sentiments that some of our invaluable privileges are infringed upon by those heavy burthens, unconstitutionally as we think, already laid upon us, and that by some late laws and innovations other of our liberties and privileges equally dear to us are in danger of being affected and curtailed, as a report has of late prevailed that the Justices of the Superior Court of this Province have a salary appointed them by the Crown, thereby rendering them more dependent on the Crown than we think any Judge ought to be on the Crown or People, whereby a foundation is laid for our Courts of Justice, which always should be uninfluenced by any force but that of Law, being immediately under the influence of the Crown.

And whereas an act was passed in the last session of the British Parliament entitled "An Act for the Preserving of His Majesty's Dockyards, Magazines, Ships, Ammunition and Stores" by which act, we in this Country are exposed to the rage of some malicious persons, who out of complaisance to some court sycophant may accuse any person and thereby cause him to be hurried out of his Country and carried to some distant place from all his friends and acquaintance, and thereby deprived of the advantages of his common character, to be judged by strangers and perhaps by foreigners, and whether innocent or guilty is in danger of being ruined in person and estate, which we look upon as a great infringement of our rights and privileges and contrary to the true sense of MAGNA CARTA and Spirit of Law: we therefore think proper to instruct you, our Representative in the General Assembly of this Province, that you in a Constitutional manner endeavor to prevent those innovations we too sensibly feel and those we fear, by using your influence in the present sessions of the General Assembly for an humble remonstrance to His Majesty that all those violations of our rights and privileges which we are entitled to by the British Constitution and made over to us and our successors by the Royal Charter may be redressed—and also we would further advise you to use your best endeavors that an honorable and an adequate support be granted to the judges of the Superior Court as a recompense for their important services in their exalted station, relying on your loyalty and respect for His Sacred Majesty, your love and affection for your Country, we trust that you will, in all matters that may come before you, conduct with that wisdom and prudence, that integrity and coolness, that circumspection and firmness which so well becomes the Senator and Patriot.

| | |
|---|---|
| Mr. Joseph Lee | Deacon Thomas Barrett |
| Charles Prescott, Esq. | Capt. Stephen Hosmer |
| John Cuming, Esq. | Mr. John Flint |
| | Ephraim Wood, Jr. |

# *Appendix G*

Taking into consideration the rights of the colonists and of this Province in particular, as men, as Christians and as subjects, as stated by the Town of Boston, we would say they are well stated and deserve the commendation of all, and will have of all who are friends of their Country—for as men we have the right to Life, Liberty and Property, and as Christians we in this land (Blessed be God for it) have a right to worship God according to the dictates of our consciences, which is granted to us and declared to be an original right, that there should be Liberty of Conscience to all Christians (Papists excepted) by the Royal Charter of this Province, and as subjects we have a right to personal security, personal Liberty and Private Property, these principal rights we have as subjects of Great Britain, and have a right to enjoy them and no Power on Earth can, agreeable to our constitution, take them from us or any part of them without our consent—let us therefore stand fast in the glorious liberty in which the King of Kings has made us free—also taking into serious consideration the list of infringements exhibited to us, we would say that we believe they are as truly stated, for by Acts of Parliament lately enacted wherein they assume the power of legislation for the Colonies without our consent, which we look upon as great infringements on our Charter rights, and by virtue of the above acts, have laid revenue taxes upon us in this Province, whereby our money is extorted from us by a number of officers unknown of in the Royal Charter, and the money so extorted from us employed to very destructive purposes, fleets and armies have been introduced to guard those unconstitutional officers and by instructions from home, our only place of defense in this Province, with the arms and ammunition in the hands of those troops over which our Commander-in-Chief declares he has no control, under these and the like instances of oppression, we have been groaning several years.

|                   |                   |
|-------------------|-------------------|
| Joseph Lee        | James Barrett     |
| Charles Prescott  | Stephen Hosmer    |
| John Cuming       | John Flint        |
| Thomas Barrett    | Ephraim Wood, Jr. |

# *Appendix H*

*Muster Roll of Concord Minutemen*

David Brown, Captain
David Wheeler, Lieutenant
Silas Man, Lieutenant
Abishai Brown, Sergeant
Emerson Cogswell, Sergeant
Amos Wood, Sergeant
Amos Barrett, Corporal
Stephen Barrett, Corporal
Reuben Hunt, Corporal
Stephen Jones, Corporal
John Buttrick, Jr., Fifer

Charles Miles, Captain
Jonathan Farrar, Lieutenant
Francis Wheeler, Lieutenant
David Hartwell, Sergeant
Amos Hosmer, Sergeant
Silas Walker, Sergeant
Edward Richardson, Sergeant
Simeon Hayward, Corporal
Nathan Pierce, Corporal
James Cogswell, Corporal
Daniel Brown, Drummer
Samuel Derby, Fifer

---

Phineas Allen
Humphrey Barrett, Jr.
Elias Barron
Jonas Bateman
John Brown, Jr.
Jonas Brown
Purchase Brown
Abiel Buttrick
Daniel Buttrick
Oliver Buttrick
Tilly Buttrick
Willard Buttrick
William Buttrick
Daniel Cray
Amos Davis
Abraham Davis
Joseph Davis, Jr.
Joseph Dudley
Charles Flint
Edward Flint
Edward Flint, Jr.
Nathan Flint
Ezekiel Hagar
Isaac Hoar
David Hubbard

Jacob Ames
Thaddeus Bancroft
Israel Barrett
Ephraim Brooks
Stephen Brooks
Simeon Burrage
William Burrage
William Brown
Jeremiah Clark
Joseph Cleasby
John Cole
Daniel Cole
John Corneall
Amos Darby
Barnabas Davis
Nathan Dudley
Samuel Emery
Daniel Farrar
John Flag
Oliver Harris
Daniel Hoar
Benjamin Hosmer
Joel Hosmer
Jesse Hosmer
Levi Hosmer

John Laughton
David Melvin, Jr.
William Mercer
John Minot, Jr.
Thomas Prescott
Bradbury Robinson
Ebenezer Stow
Nathan Stow
Thomas Thurston
Jotham Wheeler
Peter Wheeler
Zachary Wheeler
Ammi White
John White
Jonas Whitney
Aaron Wright

Samuel Jewell
Ebenezer Johnson
Amos Melvin
Samuel Melvin
Oliver Parlin
Major Raly
Solomon Rice
Stephen Stearns
Joseph Stratton
Daniel Wheat
Samuel Wheeler
Simon Wheeler
Oliver Wheeler
Warham Wheeler
Edward Wilkins

### The Atrocity Story

The very denial by the Americans that any scalping had taken place, and the concealment of the name of the man involved in the incident, gave rise to all sorts of stories. Lowell told Hawthorne. Hawthorne speculated that the perpetrator was a loutish boy, perhaps a servant to the minister, who had been chopping wood behind the manse during the battle, and that he suffered pangs of remorse for the rest of his life. Historians have handed down the name of Ammi White privately from one generation to the next, but surely no one can now be hurt by the disclosure. Ammi White moved to Concord as a young man and was in Captain David Brown's Minute company. In 1788, he married Mary Minot and lived in one end of the Minot family house which is now the Colonial Inn. They had five children before 1800 and then moved to Westmoreland, New Hampshire, where his gravestone, somewhat more pretentious than its neighbors, says he died in 1820, aged 66. This gives his age in 1775 as 21 or 22. It appears that the British soldier, left for dead by his comrades, was given the *coup de grâce* by a soldier in the heat of battle, a somewhat less horrible story than the whispered gossip or the loud accusations of 1775.

# Appendix I

*Extracts from Bronson Alcott's School Reports: (These have been reprinted in full by Scholars' Facsimiles, Gainesville, Florida, 1960.)*

During the years when Bronson Alcott was Superintendent of the Concord Public Schools he wrote annual reports which contain his ideas on education, many of which were years ahead of his time. A few paragraphs follow:

All studies should begin at home and geography particularly. The natural aspect, the occupations, products, customs, antiquities, and history of the town are the key to the general atlas and history of the planet on which we live. We have a good town history, a copy should be in every school as we have furnished each with a map of Concord.

Play is wholesome. A sound mind proves itself best by keeping its body sound. Conceive the quicksilver a child is and wonder by what skill he is held fast to his books.

We shall adopt dancing presently as a natural training for the manners and morals of the young.

Singing should prevail in all the schools. I think singing is a proper qualification in a teacher, indispensable in our primary and desirable in all our schools.

The new art of photography should be given to the service of education.

Grammar, taught under that name in our schools, is a waste study. Children dislike it, few find any use for it afterwards. For composition let the boy keep his diary, write his letters and find ways of expressing himself simply.

Some of the worst samples of language are to be found in the writings of our distinguished educators. Not Saxon but Latinized to an extent horrible to read.

The parent who seldom or never visits the school can not reasonably complain of what happens there. He should be slow of taking hearsay from any, least of all his own children when they are parties interested.

I have sought to inspire the teachers with confidence in their chosen ways rather than to interfere with counter-suggestions of my own. We require of each what she has to give, no more. Does the teacher awaken thought,

Bronson Alcott. (Courtesy of the Concord Free Public Library.)

strengthen the mind, kindle affections, call the conscience, so promoting habits that shall accompany the children outwards into life? The motive is the mainspring. A teacher entering her school for any reward other than the love of teaching shall not claim the praises due to devotion and genius. Teaching needs kindly sensibilities, simple feelings and sincere love abounding. No amount of learning avails without it. Mind refuses to be driven by mechanism. It moves by magnetism.

Let conversation displace repeating by rote unmeaning sounds from the memory. We want living minds to quicken and inform living minds. A boy's life is too precious to be wasted in committing words to the memory from books they never learn the use of.

Next to thinking for themselves, the best service any teacher can render her scholars is to show them how to use books. The young should have access to the wisdom and worth of genius. Reading-books should be simple and addressed to the ages and comprehension of the class.

# Bibliography

## Chapter I

Concord Town Records are non-existent for the early years and up to 1690 contain little except land transactions. Contemporary references in John Winthrop, *Journals,* ed. J. K. Hosmer, New York, 1908, and in Edward Johnson, *Wonder-working Providence,* New York, 1910, and in Cotton Mather, *Magnalia Christi,* Hartford, 1820, have been reprinted here. Modern historians are chiefly pre-occupied with colony affairs. The Middlesex County Court records in the Harvard Law School Library detail only the unusual. Family genealogies have been consulted but are not always dependable. I have found the following books useful:

Charles Andrews, *The Colonial Period of American History,* New Haven, 1931.
Charles E. Banks, *Planters of the Commonwealth,* Boston, 1930.
John Fiske, *The Beginnings of New England,* Boston, 1897.
Allen French, *Charles I and the Puritan Upheaval,* London, 1955.
Lemuel Shattuck, *History of Concord,* Concord, 1835.
Reverend Thomas Shepard, *Autobiography* in *Transactions,* Colonial Society, 1930.
Adams Tolman, *Indian Relics in Concord,* Concord Antiquarian Society Pamphlet.
Charles H. Walcott, *Concord in the Colonial Period,* Boston, 1885.
Albert E. Wood, *The Plantation of Musketaquid,* Concord Antiquarian Society Pamphlet.
William Wood, *New England Prospect,* London, 1634.
Alexander Young, *Chronicles of the First Planters,* Boston, 1834.

## Chapter II

Baker, *True Stories of New England Captives,* New Haven, 1934.
George M. Bodge, *Soldiers in King Philip's War,* Boston, 1906.
Mrs. Mary Rowlandson, *Captivity,* Lancaster Historical Society, 1966.
Samuel Sewell, *Diary,* New York, 1927.
Thomas Wheeler, *Narrative,* 1676.
Goble Papers in Concord Free Public Library.

## Chapter III

Charles Francis Adams, Jr., *The Town of Lincoln,* 1904.
Abram E. Brown, *Bedford* in Hurd's *History of Middlesex County,* Philadelphia, 1890.
Sidney A. Bull, *History of Carlisle,* Cambridge, 1920.
Joseph Estabrook, *Election Sermon,* 1705, in Massachusetts Historical Society Library.
Harriette M. Forbes, *Diary of Ebenezer Parkman,* Westboro, 1899.
Harold R. Phalen, *History of Acton,* 1954.
Townsend Scudder, *Concord, American Town,* Boston, 1947, though disappointingly brief about Concord's early years has a good account of Major Peter Bulkeley's life and a full and vivid account of Concord's relation to national affairs in the last two centuries. Like Shattuck's and Walcott's histories, it is now out of print.

## Chapter IV

The Town Records are valuable here.
Harriette M. Forbes, *Gravestones of Early New England,* Boston, 1927.
George Tolman, *Graves and Worms and Epitaphs,* Concord Antiquarian Society Pamphlet.
——, *John Jack the Slave and Daniel Bliss the Tory,* Concord Antiquarian Society Pamphlet.
The information about trade on the Bay Road comes from my own study of deeds which always include the occupation of the conveyor.

## Chapter V

Allen French, *The Day of Concord and Lexington,* Boston, 1925, was written before Mr. French discovered several contemporary British accounts. These he published in *A British Fusilier,* Cambridge, 1926, and in *General Gage's Informers,* Ann Arbor, 1932.
Shattuck's *History of Concord* is the basis of this account. He was a judicious historian and could still interview living actors in the events. I use his extracts from Colonel Barrett's list of stores.
Roger Sherman Hoar, *Constitutional Conventions,* Boston, 1917.
Hudson, *History of Lexington,* a full account of the day in Lexington.
Major John R. Galvin, *The Minute Men.*
Harold Murdock, *The Nineteenth of April 1775.*
George Tolman, *Preliminaries of the Concord Fight,* Concord Antiquarian Society Pamphlet.
——, *Events of April Nineteenth,* Concord Antiquarian Society Pamphlet.

## Chapter VI

Senator George F. Hoar, *Autobiography of Seventy Years,* New York, 1903.
John S. Keyes, *Concord* in Hurd's *History of Middlesex County,* Philadelphia, 1890. This is the best account of early manufactures and also has lists of schoolmasters and town officers to supplement Shattuck whose lists stop in 1835.
Reverend Grindall Reynolds, *Historical and Other Papers,* Concord, 1905.
Dr. Jeremiah Robinson, *The Evolution of Dentistry,* Jackson, Michigan.
William S. Robinson (Warrington), *Pen Portraits,* Boston, 1877.
R. R. Wheeler, *The Concord Friendly Aid Society,* Concord, 1950.
*Social Circle Memoirs,* Vols. I and II. These biographies by various authors are an invaluable source for the period after the Revolution. Cambridge, 1882.
The Brown family letters are in the collection of the Concord Antiquarian Society.


## Chapter VII

George Bartlett, *Concord,* Boston, 1885.
Van Wyck Brooks, *The Flowering of New England,* New York, 1936.
Walter Harding, *The Days of Henry Thoreau,* New York, 1965.
Margaret Lothrop, *Wayside, Home of Authors,* New York, 1940.
Lewis Mumford, *The Conduct of Life,* New York, 1938.
Ralph L. Rusk, *The Life of Ralph Waldo Emerson,* New York, 1949.
Odell Shepard, *Pedlar's Progress,* (Alcott) Boston, 1937.
Josephine L. Swayne, *The Story of Concord,* Boston, 1923.
*Exercises at the Dedication of the Melvin Memorial,* Cambridge, 1910, contains the diary kept at Andersonville prison by Samuel Melvin.

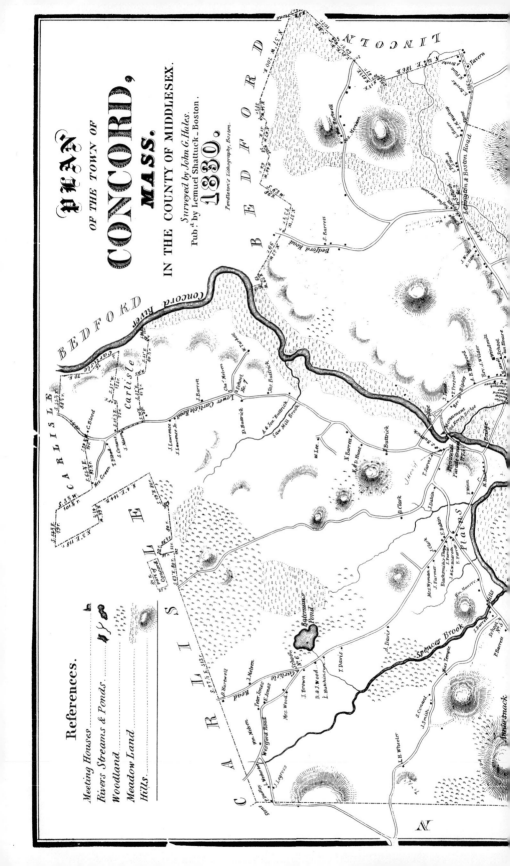

# PLAN
## OF THE TOWN OF
# CONCORD, MASS.

## IN THE COUNTY OF MIDDLESEX.

Surveyed by John G. Hales.
Pub.d by Lemuel Shattuck - Boston.

### 1830.

Pendleton's Lithography, Boston.

### References.

Meeting Houses
Rivers, Streams & Ponds.
Woodland
Meadow Land
Hills.

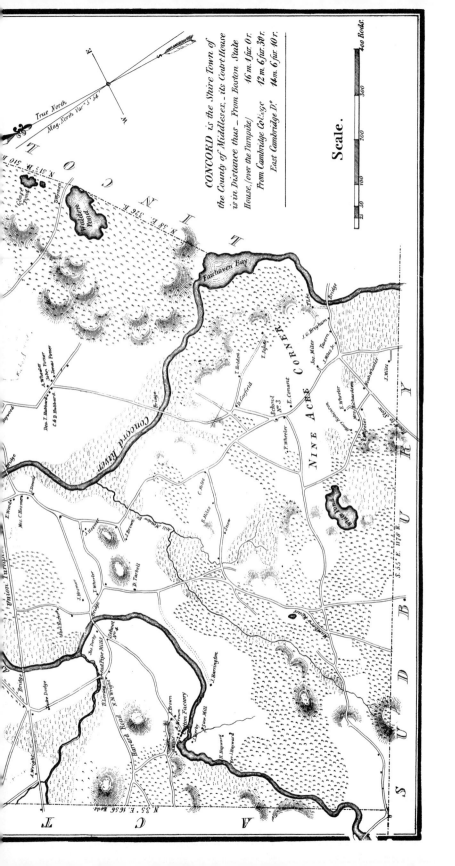

CONCORD is the Shire Town of
the County of Middlesex, — its Court House
is in Distance thus — From Boston State
House, (over the Turnpike)     16 m. 1 fur. 0 r.
From Cambridge College     12 m. 6 fur. 30 r.
East Cambridge D°     14 m. 6 fur. 40 r.

Scale.

True North
Mag. North Var. 5° 34′

# Index to Persons     General Index

# Index to Persons

# General Index